Transforming Schools with Technology

How Smart Use of Digital Tools Helps Achieve
Six Key Education Goals

Transforming Schools with Technology

How Smart Use of Digital Tools Helps Achieve Six Key Education Goals

ANDREW A. ZUCKER

HARVARD EDUCATION PRESS

CAMBRIDGE, MASSACHUSETTS

Library of Congress Control Number 2007941188

Paperback ISBN 978-1-891792-82-3
Library Edition ISBN 978-1-891792-83-0

Published by Harvard Education Press,
an imprint of the Harvard Education Publishing Group

Harvard Education Press
8 Story Street
Cambridge, MA 02138

Cover: YAY! Design

The typeface used in this book is Adobe Garamond Pro. Designed by Robert Slimbach, Adobe Garamond is a digital interpretation of the roman types of Claude Garamond and the italic types of Robert Granjon. With the introduction of OpenType font technology, Adobe Garamond has been reissued as a "Pro" type family that takes advantage of OpenType's advanced typographic capabilities.

Contents

Acknowledgments

My varied experiences in education mean there are many people to thank for their support. Although there are far more of them who helped me along the way than I can name in a short space, I would especially like to mention a few.

At SRI International, where I did education work for 17 years, I learned a great deal from dozens of first-class colleagues and mentors, including my friend Mike Knapp. Mike's expert approach to team-based research on challenging questions influenced many of us.

Staff members at the Concord Consortium, where I am a senior research scientist, were exceptionally supportive as I wrote the book. I appreciate their help, including a small grant that the organization provided to help me conceptualize and begin writing the book. Bob Tinker, Ray Rose, Allen Parker, Alvaro Galvis, Janice Gobert, Stephen Bannasch, and Ed Hazzard are among those who reviewed chapters and provided ideas and advice. Cynthia McIntyre's thoughtful editorial comments are much appreciated.

Others who provided generous help include David Rose, David Gordon, Liz Pape, Lynne Delise, and Jeremy Roschelle. Beth Hadas, a past director of the University of New Mexico Press, was a welcome cheerleader and provided valuable insights.

Doug Clayton, director of the Harvard Education Publishing Group, has been a pleasure to work with, as have others at Harvard Education Press.

Finally, I would like to thank my family, which has been supportive in innumerable ways, through good times and bad.

Of course, the opinions expressed here are mine, as are any errors in the book.

Preface

The nature of technology use in schools has changed dramatically in the past decade. By using computers, the Internet, and other digital technology in smart ways, schools are beginning to transform themselves into the more modern, effective, responsive institutions that our society needs. Although schools have arguably reached a tipping point in using technology to reform age-old ways of operating, the pace of change has been so fast that the modifications schools are making are not yet widely known or understood.

There has been phenomenally rapid growth in the number of government-sponsored online high schools across the country, as well as an increasing enrollment in state- and district-sponsored programs that provide students with personal computers to use as learning tools. Handheld digital devices of several types are widely used in tens of thousands of schools, including graphing calculators and so-called "probes" for collecting, graphing, and analyzing data in science and mathematics classes. Millions of students now use computers to take tests and quizzes, providing administrators, teachers, and students themselves with faster, sometimes instantaneous feedback that can improve teaching and learning and increase accountability.

This book provides readers with dozens of illustrations of constructive ways that schools are using computers, the Internet, and related digital tools. A large number of examples is needed to appreciate the range of uses and impacts of technology, but examples alone are not enough. It is essential to think more clearly than ever before about schools' uses of digital tools, identifying principles to guide decisions about using technology.

Although schools may seem to be aimed at a single goal—helping students learn—the nation's governors, Congress, school boards, other policymakers, and the public have established multiple goals for schools, not just one. More often than you might think, the goals are in tension with each other. For example, we want high school students' test scores to improve. But at the same time, enormous and appropriate pressure has grown in recent years to reduce the appallingly large dropout rates from high school, especially in inner cities where as many as half the students leave before graduation. Students who drop out typically have low test scores, so keeping them in school can actually *reduce* average test scores and result in tension between two political imperatives: raising test scores and reducing dropout rates.

Other important goals for schools create additional tensions, such as between educating to increase students' civic knowledge and promote their responsibility as citizens in a democracy, on the one hand, while simultaneously focusing time and resources almost exclusively on teaching and testing subjects required by the No Child Left Behind Act—notably reading, math, and science. The tension between these goals is evident in the many reports of school curricula being narrowed as a consequence of No Child Left Behind, with civics, current events, music, art, and other subjects minimized in favor of the courses and subjects that appear on high-stakes tests.

This book uses a framework of six key education goals as a way to better understand how schools use technology to meet the multiple aims policymakers have established for them. These goals enjoy widespread political support and are codified in national and state laws, such as Goals 2000. One of the important consequences of using these goals as a framework is to clarify thinking and conversations about the important roles technology is playing in schools. Notably, computers, the Internet, and other digital technologies should be, and are, used to do far more than raise students' test scores or "increase student achievement." A school system is *not* like a business that can express its profit or loss as a single number, the bottom line. Too often this fact is ignored in discussing the role of technology in schools, as well as in the national debate about strengths and weaknesses of the No Child Left Behind Act.

A broader perspective on using digital tools in schools is essential. An excellent example of a technology that can be used constructively by schools to help students learn is word processing. Word processors help students become better writers, and there are many other examples of using digital tools to raise achievement. But although increasing student achievement is a vital goal, it is not everything. Other important goals for education are:

- making schools more engaging and relevant (thereby reducing drop-out rates);
- providing a high-quality education for all students (including English language learners and students with disabilities);
- attracting, preparing, and retaining high-quality teachers;
- increasing parental and community support for children outside of school; and
- requiring accountability for results.

Separate chapters in the book focus on each of these key education goals and how digital tools are used to help achieve them. Transforming schools requires attention to all of these goals, not just one.

This perspective on technology in schools is based on a broad set of experiences in the field of education. I was a classroom teacher for seven years. In 1974, before popular personal computers were available, I became the director of a school computer center. Even 30 years ago, schools were beginning to use computers in ways that are by now familiar (although, of course, there was no Internet, and the technology was primitive compared to what is now available).

From 1978 to 1986, I worked for the U.S. Department of Education as a program manager, as well as a policy and budget analyst. My work there focused on education research and statistics, children's television, school improvement, science and mathematics education, and computers in schools.

Since leaving government, for more than 20 years I have been engaged in education evaluation, research, development, and strategic planning for a variety of clients, from federal departments and agencies, to state legislatures, individual schools, foundations, and the National Education Goals Panel. With colleagues, I developed award-winning video materials for classrooms, conducted a five-year study of online schools, evaluated federal education programs, and testified before a number of state and federal commissions and legislative committees. My work also focused on teachers' professional development, national education standards, and programs to reform science and mathematics education.

Throughout my career, I have not forgotten the teacher's perspective on important education issues. After all, if education policy does not promote good teaching, what is its purpose?

CHAPTER I

Educational Technology

A *New Yorker* cartoon shows a man in front of a microwave oven that has an imposing array of buttons. "No," he says to the microwave, "I don't want to play chess. I just want you to reheat the lasagna."

Most of us are ambivalent about technology, like the man in the cartoon. Can't these things simply work the way they are supposed to? Do I really have to answer five questions from the annoying computer voice on the phone before speaking to a live human being? Still, we're not ready to give up word processors, cell phones, the Internet—or microwaves with a myriad of buttons. You and I might live happily without a chess machine, but that doesn't change the fact that electronic games are becoming a bigger business than movies.

Are you a bit skeptical about technology? Good; that's healthy.

For years I have worked with a community of people who are passionate believers in the value of using computers, the Internet, and other digital technology in schools. While I believe many of their conclusions are right, much of their rhetoric is too often unpersuasive. You've heard these people, saying things like: "The Internet will change everything." "We are teaching a generation of digital natives, and they think differently than we do." "Schools *must* use the digital tools—iPods, e-mail, instant-messaging, and so on—that today's students use every day."

Their rhetoric is superficially appealing, but those are simply not compelling reasons to believe the United States should invest billions of dollars every year in computers, the Internet, and other educational technologies. Despite the lack of persuasive arguments by many proponents of educational technology, I believe that making these large expenditures is the right thing to do. In fact, school systems in the United States spend about $7 billion each year on technology—a figure that sounds large until one realizes it represents only $140 for each student.[1]

Aggravation with simplistic thinking should be aimed at the skeptics, as well. "Young people need to learn from people, not technology," they say. Or, "Which would you prefer—better teachers or more computers?" But it's unlikely those same skeptics would willingly give up their trusty word processors, calculators, and computers, or those their children use. And if good teachers don't need any technology, let's save money by taking out the schools' telephones and photocopiers. Teachers ought to handwrite all the assignments; no word processors allowed. To students, one might say, "We know the SAT allows you to use a calculator, but your parents tell us you can't. Sorry about that." And parents skeptical of technology: no e-mailing teachers for you, and no cell-phone calls, either. Writing letters was good enough for your great-grandparents; it should be good enough for you.

The simple fact is that digital technology has begun to transform schools. Online or "virtual" high schools are proliferating, offering a new vision of what constitutes a school; tutoring services are being provided to students over the Internet, from as far away as India; powerful software for learning writing, reading, mathematics, and other school subjects is used by millions of children; "clickers" (inexpensive handheld devices used to respond to teachers' questions in class) are becoming more common in schools and in postsecondary institutions; and, millions of required state tests have been administered online, saving money and providing faster feedback than paper tests. School systems are distributing laptop computers to students along with or sometimes instead of textbooks. There are thousands of educational websites, and some of them receive millions of "hits" every school day. Students in schools use graphing calculators, digital cameras, word processors, and many other computer-based products and services. Princeton Review SAT tutoring is being offered to students using cell-phone technology. And importantly, computers are becoming common in schools—there are more than 10 million of them—and, even more telling, a majority of teachers report on national surveys that computers are essential to their teaching.[2]

Today, after roughly two decades of significant computer use in schools, computers and other digital technologies are changing our assumptions about schooling, and the rate of change is accelerating. Nonetheless—and this is an important reason why you should care about what is happening—the positive impact of educational technology is not a foregone conclusion. Online schooling, for example, is being used to increase the number of students who are homeschooled (now estimated at about one million), contributing to a decades-long trend for Americans to become more isolated from one another, a trend that does not bode well for citizenship in a democracy. Yet online schooling is also strengthening public schools; for example, by making more widely available courses that are difficult for schools to provide face-to-face; by enlarging the learning community of which students feel they are a part; and by helping small schools expand their course catalogs.

Is there a middle ground between the excessive hype around digitization and the wish to keep schools firmly planted in the 19th or 20th century? It is abundantly clear that we're part of the 21st century and therefore part of a "flat earth."[3] It's also clear that there is widespread agreement schools need to be redesigned to become more effective. Technology will be an important part of that redesign, as our society moves from School 1.0, the school of the past, to School 2.0, the school of the future.[4] The United States faces important policy choices about how to use technology to transform schools that will be explored in the chapters that follow.

APPLICATIONS OF EDUCATIONAL TECHNOLOGY

For decades the benefits of computers and other educational technologies seemed like the jam that Lewis Carroll's White Queen offered to Alice in *Through the Looking Glass*, telling her that, "the rule is jam tomorrow and jam yesterday, but never jam today." The benefits of digital technologies for students and teachers were supposed to be just around the corner, waiting on tomorrow's next big technological advance, or else they were evident in yesterday's successful project, no longer up-to-date, that had once demonstrated what was going to be possible for everyone: talking typewriters for first graders; computer languages simple enough that all children would learn them; a multitude of courses stored on computers and accessed through telephone lines.

That is no longer the situation. For good teachers, educational technology is routinely providing capabilities that are not possible in any other way. Technology permits teachers to offer students courses not otherwise available to them, and it allows teachers to provide students with access to vast libraries of information, both in print and other media. Technology offers teachers unique tools to help students illustrate and understand difficult concepts through animations and other computer models, and it allows teachers and students to correspond with peers and experts anywhere on the globe. Students who use computers become better writers than those who don't.

The Web (which began to be widely used as recently as 1997) provides teachers and students with information in ways that are simply impossible with textbooks or other print media. For example, a website called The Valley of the Shadow (valley.vcdh.virginia.edu/) provides thousands of original documents from two communities, one in the North and the other in the South, during the period leading up to the American Civil War and extending through the era of Reconstruction. This site allows students the experience of conducting research in American history for themselves in ways never before possible—at least, not so easily and for so many students. For student writers, a classic reference, *The Columbia Encyclopedia*, is now available online (www.bartleby.com/65/), as are dictionaries, thesauruses, books of famous quotations, and countless other reference materials, all free. The NASA website (www.nasa.gov) provides video interviews with astronauts, a variety of science activities, and many other features especially designed for students of all ages, as well as Web pages for teachers. The National Science Digital Library (NSDL, at nsdl.org) provides teachers and students with organized sets of thousands of images, video and audio streams, animations, software, datasets, and text documents such as journal articles and lessons plans, all for science, technology, engineering, and mathematics education and research. NSDL also provides services such as search, browse, help, "Ask-An-Expert," news reports, and online community discussions.

There are thousands of education-related websites, and many experience substantial traffic. As an example, the National Library of Virtual Manipulatives (NLVM) is a website (nlvm.usu.edu/ en/nav/index.html) that provides teachers and students with small, free, interactive computer programs, known as applets, to illustrate, explain, and allow students to explore mathematics concepts, from fractions to algebra. Every school day NLVM receives more than two million hits. Similarly, Wikipedia, a group-edited encyclopedia on the Web (www.wikipedia.org/), reached an audience of more than 12 million users in the month of September 2005, many of whom were students. The use of educational reference sites on the Web is growing by more than 20 percent per year.[5]

Teachers appreciate what the Internet can provide. One high school teacher said that a student was able to locate a law about DNA databanks in the military and get an immediate answer to a question being discussed during a biology class. A middle school science teacher mentioned up-to-date information about new discoveries of moons around Jupiter. In the past, she said, questions raised by students often went unanswered. "Now," the teacher reported, "I can just say 'Look it up,' and students will immediately do so. The immediacy, the accuracy—it's just fantastic. I don't know if I could live without it now." Many schools subscribe to online video libraries. A California teacher in one of these schools typed earthquake into the search engine and was able to find a video about the 1989 earthquake that struck San Francisco. "It showed actual footage of it," she said, "and, of course, I used that right before the whole earthquake unit, and of course it gets the kids' big eyes and [they are] all excited and motivated, and we go from there. I love that tool."

In addition to the Internet, powerful stand-alone education software designed for schools allows teachers and students to explore mathematics and science concepts in ways that develop students' understanding of complex ideas and that are not feasible with paper and pencil. For example, Geometer's Sketchpad permits students to construct geometric figures and to interact with them by dragging the objects with a mouse. Because mathematical relationships are preserved, students can quickly examine many similar cases, leading to generalizations and conjectures. Sketchpad can be used for geometry, analytic geometry, algebra, precalculus, calculus, and other mathematics topics. Similarly, specialized software for data analysis and statistics, such as Fathom and Tinker Plots, permits dynamic interaction with large and complex data sets, simply by clicking and dragging. The ability of the computer to aid students' visualization of mathematics and science concepts and to link multiple representations, such as tables of data and graphs, makes them powerful tools for understanding complex ideas. These and many other useful software applications are used in thousands of schools.

Pittsburgh, for instance, has adopted Cognitive Tutor Algebra as its Algebra 1 curriculum.[6] Developed at Carnegie Mellon University, Cognitive Tutors are computer-based intelligent tutoring systems that do not replace teachers, but allow them to devote more time to individual students while others in the class use the computer. The computer software provides individualized instruction based on a student's strengths and weaknesses.

Technology is providing significant benefits to students served by special education classes, including both learning and physically disabled students. As an example, one website that provides mathematics activities for students also offers explanations for deaf students in short movies showing interpreters who use American Sign Language (www.shodor. org/succeedhi/interactivate/ToolsG.html). The website also provides suggested new sign language equivalents for more than 100 vocabulary words in Computational Science, thus offering deaf students a way of learning to use new language in this technical field (www.shodor.org/ succeed-hi/interpreters/index.html).

Standard computers can read text aloud, enlarge type fonts, translate to or from English, and provide many other accommodations for students. Computers also provide immediate feedback, which is important for special needs students. It is not surprising that special education teachers have been particularly enthusiastic about educational technology. As one such teacher said about an initiative that provides each student with a laptop computer, "It's like an instructional assistant in my class, because it helps me that much. . . . I don't know what I'd do without it."[7]

These examples provide a quick overview of what educational technology has to offer. Later chapters will explore a wide variety of technological innovations in depth, beginning in chapter 3, which includes an account of online schools and how they challenge our ideas of what is a school.

TECHNOLOGY SKEPTICS

In the face of examples like those just cited, isn't it obvious that using digital technology in schools is transformative? Unfortunately, it is not. For a decade most popular books about educational technology have been either skeptical or downright hostile. During the past decade, one might have read *Failure to Connect: How Computers Affect Our Children's Minds—and What We Can Do About It*, by Jane Healey,[8] *High-Tech Heretic: Why Computers Don't Belong in the Classroom and Other Reflections by a Computer Contrarian*, by Clifford Stoll,[9] *Oversold and Underused: Computers in the Classroom*, by Larry Cuban,[10] or *The Flickering Mind: The False Promise of Technology in the Classroom and How Learning Can Be Saved*, by Todd Oppenheimer.[11] Still more recently, a newspaper column by an MIT researcher published in March 2006 declares:

> Yes, the Internet is wonderful. Yes, state-run school systems require fundamental reform. Nevertheless, the shrewdest policy to improve public education while saving billions in government spending demands abstinence. Keep computers out of the classroom.[12]

This is an extreme view stated with a zealot's conviction, as if it were a well-reasoned policy. Unfortunately, it is not an isolated example.

It is true that there are appropriate concerns and criticisms expressed in these books and articles, notably that:

- trivial or inappropriate uses of digital technologies should be avoided;
- good teaching is still the key to effective schools; and
- computers alone won't cure the ills of public education.

Some of the skeptics' concerns are explored in this chapter. Still, apart from *The Flickering Mind*, their books don't even mention important developments of the past decade, such as the online schools being operated in half the states, some of which serve dozens of other states. Simply stated, the skeptics have the story wrong. On the other hand, the "utopians," who are as positive as the skeptics are negative, don't have the story right either; technology is not some type of magic wand one can wave to get the schools society wants. It is no wonder, then, that there is confusion about educational technology, confusion that makes it more difficult than it needs to be for the people who influence school policies to think and act clearly, whether at the local, state, or federal levels.

Leaders in economics, business, and industry now understand that information technologies have transformed their world, and ours, in fundamental ways. Thomas Friedman's book, *The World Is Flat: A Brief History of the 21st Century*, describes the transformation well. It is worth recalling that not long ago it was *not* obvious how important information technologies were to the economy, or that productivity gains would result. Indeed, it was considered newsworthy in 1999 when Alan Greenspan, then chairman of the Federal Reserve, articulated what many people had come to believe: that digital technology was an essential component of economic growth.[13] Although by now this fact has been accepted for years, where are the popular books that reflect a comparable and realistic understanding of the transformative force of technology in schools? It is far easier to find one written by a skeptic.

Although Clifford Stoll's book was written in 1999, some of his arguments can still be heard today. Stoll writes that "bad teachers ought to be replaced with good teachers." One certainly hopes Stoll and others with similar views will let the nation's governors, the Congress, and the president know. Wait, wait; I suddenly realize that there have been dozens if not hundreds of laws and programs aimed at accomplishing this goal. He writes, "[T]he effect of using computers in math education" is that "over the past fifteen years, colleges have seen an astounding growth in remedial math classes," and so clearly, "computers don't belong in math class." Hmmm; don't let facts get in the way of opinions! According to the National Center for Education Statistics, in both 1999 and 2004, only about half of 13-year-olds did *any* study of mathematics through computer instruction, while the comparable figure for 17-year-olds was just 36 percent. And given the difficulty of scheduling time in school computer labs, few students spent more than a very limited time studying math with computers. Nonetheless:

- At both ages 13 and 17, the mathematics test scores of students who studied math with computers were *the same* as the scores of those who did not.[14]

- If computers were used in ways that allowed students to explore mathematics, rather than simply to drill math facts, then "computer use is positively associated with student performance," meaning the students using computers for exploring did better on tests than students who did not use computers, or who did not use them in an open-ended way.[15]
- If one looks at the study of mathematics using calculators rather than computers (because calculators are used more often), the data show a mostly positive correlation between calculator use and eighth graders' mathematics achievement, with the *highest* scores being reported by students whose teachers said that calculators were used almost every day.[16]

None of these or many other data support Stoll's claim that computer use has led to a growth in remedial math classes. Indeed, Stoll seems to have little use for data, apart from anecdotes.

Jane Healy, Larry Cuban, and Todd Oppenheimer, on the other hand, are far more responsible writers whose books show some degree of balance, although their conclusions are weighted far to the skeptical side of the scale. Significantly, all three include positive examples of the use of educational technology and suggest, sometimes clearly and sometimes indirectly, that they believe technology has potential to help students and teachers. The first chapter in Cuban's *Oversold and Underused* that focuses on classrooms, chapter 2, begins with accounts of two teachers, Esperanza Rodrigues and Mark Hunter, who are very skilled at using computers creatively to change their usual instructional routines in a manner that helps students learn. Todd Oppenheimer begins the introduction to his book with a remarkable story about a group of tenth graders who were featured in the *Washington Post* because, with the aid of computers, they analyzed the pending midterm congressional elections in 1998 and proceeded to outguess thirteen "pundits" who had been asked by the *Post* to provide their predictions. (The story reminds me that in the mid-1970s—more than twenty years earlier—one of my students, then a high school senior, conducted a major research project on civil rights voting patterns in Congress using far more primitive software and without benefit of the Internet. He went on one summer soon after to help Andrew Young purchase computers for the United Nations.) *Failure to Connect* enthusiastically describes a groundbreaking TV- and computer-based science curriculum for schools called *The Voyage of the*

Mimi, developed with federal support during the 1980s—a project on which I am proud to say that several staff of The Concord Consortium, where I work, were key contributors. In other words, to their credit, these skeptics can appreciate examples of the value of educational technology. Oppenheimer, for one, writes, "Computers can, in select cases, be wonderfully useful in school."[17]

However, in the end the skeptics are far more deeply concerned about the mixed record of technology use in schools, including many trivial or inappropriate uses, than they are about positive examples. These skeptics suggest that technology introduces more difficulties than benefits. Healy believes that "Most educational computer use, however, misses the real point—getting children to take initiative and think deeply."[18] Cuban goes further, claiming, "without a broader vision of the social and civic role that schools perform in a democratic society, our current excessive focus on technology use in schools runs the danger of trivializing our nation's core ideals."[19] And Oppenheimer is still more negative, writing that "in the realm of education, technology is like a vine—it's gorgeous at first bloom but quickly overgrows, gradually altering and choking its surroundings."[20] Finally, the message in Stoll's book is clear: "As much as I love computers, I can't imagine getting an excellent education from any multimedia system. . . . [T]he dirty secret of educational technology is that computers waste teachers' time, both in and out of the classroom."[21]

In addition to common themes, each of the skeptics brings his or her particular point of view to the subject. Jane Healy is especially concerned about overuse of computers by younger students. "I have recently come to believe that computers—at least as they are currently being used—are not necessary or even desirable in the lives of most children under age seven (with the exception, of course, of children suffering from certain handicaps),"[22] she writes. Healy is worried that the focus on technology will displace emphasis by teachers and parents on core values. "Respect, responsibility, compassion, faith, commitment, love, and wisdom" are vital to raising children. " 'Information,' I note, didn't make the list."[23] Like other skeptics, she would be willing to give up educational technology, noting, "The brutal truth, despite all the hype to the contrary, is that children without computers and with a good education are far more likely to succeed than children walled in by technological fads."[24]

Aren't these reasonable concerns? No, not really. Consider:

- For those concerned about the use of computers with young children, a more realistic recommendation is to limit the amount of "screen time" young children spend with any medium, most importantly television and video games. Parents and teachers should be sure that children of all ages have plenty of experiences that don't involve media. Cuban observed computer use in 11 preschool and kindergarten classrooms and found no evidence that the teachers had abandoned their usual belief in the importance of "emotional, social, and intellectual ties that [reach] well beyond proficiency with machines."[25] The likelihood is that if computers are being overused with a young child, the problem is occurring at home, not at school.

- Healy's objection that "information didn't make the list" of core values is completely at odds with what a great many people are trying to change in schools. Providing information, and the skills and knowledge to use it well, is near the top of the list of tasks that schools exist to accomplish. In that context, as Oppenheimer writes, "the World Wide Web—the über-program of the modern age—is a useful if not invaluable research source for all of us."[26] Digital technology has already transformed how, where, and when people obtain many types of information. Among the other skills students should be taught in school is how to use the World Wide Web intelligently, just as generations of students have been taught to use library card catalogs.

Todd Oppenheimer is weary of what he sees as education's repeated infatuation with one fad or another, including technological "fixes." He sees hope in a variety of school programs unrelated to technology, including Waldorf schools, Expeditionary Learning Schools, and others. Like Healy, Oppenheimer is concerned that students are not being taught to think. He would like to see public schools funded more generously, and that includes doubling the average teacher salary, because "at its core, education is a people process."[27]

In response to Oppenheimer, I note that:

- Teaching *all* students to think more deeply, to solve problems, and to leave school with the skills and knowledge that allow them, say, to go on to higher education is a new and difficult challenge, which will be explored further in chapter 2 of this book. Our entire society, not just its schools and teachers, is still learning how to reach this goal, with or without technology. The solution is likely to include changes in health care, child care, popular media, afterschool programs, and other social institutions, not just schools. To blame the problem on educational technology is a patently ridiculous diagnosis. Technology used well provides enormous help solving the problem.

• The concern expressed by Healy and Oppenheimer that educational technology dehumanizes teaching is wrong, and we must work to make sure that it stays that way. In everyday life, e-mail is perceived by most people as *adding* to the "social glue" that binds us together as a community, allowing more people than before, including distant family members, to communicate and stay in touch. Cuban found that one of the most common uses of computers by teachers was to communicate "much more with colleagues, parents, and students than they had previously"[28]—*more* interpersonal communication, not less. In education, most online courses have a real teacher at the other end of the Internet; and, often, teachers and students find that they have unusually *close* communication in the online environment.[29] It is true that in both online and face-to-face classrooms, good teachers are a key to quality. According to well-respected research, however, good teachers are *more* likely to want to use technology tools than other teachers, not less.[30]

Larry Cuban finds that "computers are ubiquitous in schools."[31] Unlike the other skeptics, he does not report that they are overused; instead, he finds that despite all the money spent to buy computers and wire schools to the Internet, and promises of significant changes as a result, "less than 10 percent of teachers who used computers in their classrooms were serious users (defined as using computers in class at least once a week); between 20 and 30 percent were occasional to rare users (once a month); well over half of the teachers were nonusers."[32] A corollary is that "we found no clear and substantial evidence of students increasing their academic achievement as a result of using information technologies." Cuban is also very concerned that teachers primarily use computers to "sustain existing patterns of teaching," not for "fundamental change," and only a few "used the new technologies to accelerate student-centered and project-based teaching practices," especially at the high school level. He is not satisfied with routine use of the computer, noting that most students reported "typing up assignments, working on reports, and searching the Internet."[33]

How does one respond to Cuban's concerns?

- Cuban is wrong to claim that computers are "ubiquitous" in schools. According to his own data, the great majority of computers in the high schools he observed were in computer labs, not in classrooms. If digital technology is to become a common part of teaching, it is the technology in classrooms that matters most. The digital technology that is probably used most routinely of all in schools is the graphing calculator, which is personal and portable, and which is used widely in many mathematics and science classrooms. Students currently use computers predominantly outside of school, for the simple reason that access to the devices is easier there. Studies of programs where every student has a laptop computer show that computer usage increases dramatically.[34]

- What is wrong with such routine uses of the computer by students as "typing up assignments, working on reports, and searching the Internet"? In fact, one of the clearest areas in which computers measurably improve student achievement is writing. A meta-analysis (i.e., reexamination) of 26 studies of writing with computers found that "instructional uses of computers for writing are having a positive impact on student writing, both in terms of quantity and quality."[35] The authors added that, "In general, research over the past two decades consistently finds that when students write on computers, writing becomes a more social process in which students share their work with each other. When using computers, students also tend to make revisions while producing, rather than after producing, text. Between initial and final drafts, students also tend to make more revisions when they write with computers." Use of word processors by students is to be applauded, not denigrated. Similarly, Cuban found teachers often used computers to accomplish routine administrative tasks. That's exactly what one would expect and even hope for. (Chapter 6 will discuss this topic in greater depth.)

- If Cuban is right that many teachers use computers only occasionally (and his data match other research findings), then Oppenheimer's claim that technology is "gradually altering and choking its surroundings" is just not credible. If one visited a classroom at random in the United States, chances are there would be little use of technology and that the principal, teachers, students, and parents at the school would not identify technology as something that was "choking its surroundings," or anything like it. Similarly, Healy sets up a false dichotomy, claiming that a good education without technology trumps "technological fads." Good education and technology are compatible, and to suggest that computers and the Internet are a fad is to completely misunderstand how deeply they have become embedded in society. We aren't going back, and it's time we get used to it.

It is worth repeating that Healy, Cuban, and Oppenheimer make many salient observations about educational technology. Healy, for example, notes that research in the field is not well funded and is of uneven quality, and she bemoans the fact that insufficient effort has been made to provide teachers with professional development to help them better use technology (although that situation has improved greatly since 1998, when her book was written). One must also agree with the school principal who told her, "We're really careful to use technology not just for the sake of technology. The teachers make it a seamless part of the learning process. We stress the importance of choosing the right tool for the job; sometimes it's the computer, often it isn't." Good! That is as it should be.

Still, as previously noted, a significant problem with the skeptics' books is that they are outdated. Recent developments include virtual schools, the increasing adoption of 1-to-1 (one-to-one) computing in schools (as in Maine, where every public middle school student is provided with a laptop to use for schoolwork), and computer-based testing, which promises to change the purpose of standardized testing—to mention only a few significant examples. The skeptics also focus too much attention on illustrating poor uses of technology, which are often due to inadequate teacher professional development, and too little on the positive applications of digital technology that will transform schools. As the president of Stanford University said more than ten years ago, referring to information technology, "The first few decades of this [coming] millennium may bring more changes to universities than their first thousand years."[36] Like it or not, the same is true of schools—but one would never know it from reading the skeptics' books. Finally, the skeptics frame discussion of educational technology in a shortsighted way, not identifying the characteristics of technology, roughly what experts call its "affordances," that enable transformational change to take place. Technology allows people to redefine the physical and temporal boundaries of schools, for example. By comparing the characteristics of technology with the needs of students, teachers, and schools, as done in this book, one can learn about the ways that technology enables and supports education reform.

It is worth saying again, and again, that educational technology is not a panacea. Improving schools is a complex, difficult process. It takes many elements to create excellence, including talented leadership at all levels, qualified teachers, high but reasonable standards, a fine curriculum, support from parents, politicians, and the wider community, adequate funding, and so forth. The reasons why it is necessary to improve schools are social, economic, and cultural. This is a book about transforming schools *with* technology, not *only with* technology, and not merely *because* it is useful for students to be able to use computers and other technology. Those who want to transform schools into more effective institutions need to understand schools and the contexts in which they operate and then set appropriate goals. They need to harness political will and work constructively with many constituencies. Although what is required is much more than technological savvy, technology will be a *necessary* part of education reform, for reasons that are explored throughout the book.

Talented teachers are the most important single component of good schools. Schools need more of them. Undoubtedly a few excellent teachers choose not to use technology, or to use it sparingly. But survey after survey shows that the great majority of teachers and principals understand that digital technology—including wireless access to the Internet, which is now potentially available in every classroom—is here to stay and ought to be harnessed to improve schools. Teachers need powerful tools in their toolkit—they know it—and technology provides them with many of these. According to a national survey commissioned by the U.S. Department of Education, by 2001 a majority of teachers used computers and other digital technology for professional purposes at least a few times a week. It is true that teachers need a variety of supports to make effective use of educational technology—a theme developed throughout the book—but teachers are by no means opposed to using educational technology, as is sometimes suggested.

To be as clear as possible: The thesis of this book is that digital technology has enabled schools to change the way they operate in significant ways; that technology is an essential component of the transformation of schools that most people believe is necessary; and, that the impacts of technology will depend partly on technical factors but also, importantly, on the choices many people make about how to use technology.

TECHNOLOGY UTOPIANS

At the other end of the scale from the skeptics are the promoters and popularizers of educational technology. The most notable example is Seymour Papert, a visionary professor at MIT who cofounded MIT's Artificial Intelligence Laboratory and was a founding faculty member of the MIT Media Lab. He was one of the developers of Logo, the computer language for children, and had high hopes that it would be very widely used. Papert also wrote a number of books that influenced a generation of education leaders, including *Mindstorms: Children, Computers, and Powerful Ideas* (1983), *The Children's Machine: Rethinking Schools in the Age of the Computer* (1993), and *The Connected Family: Bridging the Digital Generation Gap* (1996). However, all three were written before the World Wide Web, which is now so significant, blossomed and became so important.

There is no doubt that Papert has been influential; for one thing, he played an important role in persuading then governor Angus King to begin Maine's laptop program in 2001. Visionaries like Papert should probably be forgiven for painting pictures of the future in broad brushstrokes—pictures that are not entirely accurate. Still, Papert too often adopted a utopian view, a characteristic that for decades has run through a substantial, and influential, portion of the literature about technology in schools.

The utopian view is that computers will change everything, and for the better. In the mid-1980s Papert wrote, "There won't be schools in the future. I think the computer will blow up the school. That is, the school defined as something where there are classes, teachers running exams, people structured in groups by age, following a curriculum—all of that. . . ."[37] In another article he wrote, "Nothing is more ridiculous than the idea that this technology can be used to improve school. It's going to displace school and the way we have understood school . . . I think that the very nature, the fundamental nature, of school that we see in this process is coming to an end."[38]

This utopian vision—Papert approved of the idea of doing away with schools—is also illustrated more recently by the title of the 2004 national technology plan published by the U.S. Department of Education, *Toward a New Golden Age in Education*. Newsflash! Reports that technology will soon bring educational utopia to a nation very near you are both unwarranted and simplistic. Publications like *Toward a New Golden Age in Education* and the periodical *edutopia* (produced by the George Lucas Educational Foundation, and which often focuses on educational technology) contain interesting information, but many readers won't get further than the titles. The notion that computers, or any other device, will bring about a marvelous new world of education is naive, and the titles make the authors appear naive. In fact, computers, like any other technological innovation, provide people and social institutions with both opportunities *and* problems.

Realizing the opportunities that new technologies can bring to schools is not an inevitable outcome of technological innovation. In fact, helping to spread the types of benefits described in these pages, and to use new opportunities wisely, requires hard work from thousands of people, including teachers, principals, school technology coordinators, parents, students, legislators, and others. I hope this book proves informative to many of them.

THE PROLIFERATION OF TECHNOLOGY

One reason this is an important moment in the history of technology in schools is because what has arguably been the biggest barrier to educational computer use is beginning to crumble. In large numbers of schools, computers are finally prevalent enough that they can be used routinely, like a textbook or other basic education resource. In Maine, for example, every middle school student in the state is issued a laptop computer to use for the year, and all of the middle schools provide wireless connections to the Internet throughout the school. Henrico County, Virginia (greater Richmond), provides more than 20,000 laptops with wireless Internet access to students in grades 6–12. Chapter 4 discusses these programs and others like them that are cropping up all over the country. The day when every student has a personal computing device to use is not far off.

The computer is at the center of the digital technology revolution, both in schools and out. A computer is "a machine that imitates other machines." When we buy a personal computer we have purchased a word processor, a fax machine, an e-mail terminal, an Internet radio, and an information appliance that connects to libraries worldwide. We have in our hands a machine that can help teach keyboarding skills, mathematics facts, and foreign languages, including the pronunciation of words. We can watch movies with our computer and use it as a telephone answering machine or as a video recorder. We can do a good job of typesetting and create beautiful letters, brochures, and other documents, complete with illustrations. The computer will touch up photographs and send them to our friends, and it will do nonlinear editing of movies and videos. It will keep our calendar and our address book. A list of computer applications appropriate for schools could be extended virtually without limit, and it is this versatility, at lower and lower prices, in smaller and smaller packages, which makes the computer such a revolutionary force for change.

Students, appropriately, have a sense that technology is changing quickly, and when asked what they would like to see invented that would help kids learn, they say things like:

- A Palm Pilot that had all the school textbooks downloaded into it, with Internet access and school schedules, so you could do your homework on it and that would be all that you had to carry around.
- A cell phone that has a calculator, organizer, and a computer built in.
- A Palm Pilot/dictionary/textbook/thesaurus put all together.[39]

Tomorrow's computers will be even more flexible than today's typical laptop. Already, some cell phones come with large-capacity hard drives, as well as a camera that can take still or moving pictures; some music players are equipped with video screens to play movies; and some graphing calculators—handheld computers, specialized for doing mathematics, that display graphs and tables—can be networked together in classroom sets. In other words, digital media are converging, and becoming more powerful, all at lower and lower prices. One visionary has developed a so-called $100 laptop especially for use in developing countries.[40] It may be difficult to predict what common personal computing devices in schools will look like in five or ten years—some, for instance, may have flexible screens that roll up to more easily fit in a pocket—but the long-term trend that has resulted in greater capabilities at lower costs will continue for decades.

Fast, highly capable computers can be purchased for a fraction of what they cost a few years ago. Wireless networks that provide access to the Internet are affordable and will soon blanket entire cities. While labor costs and the price of bricks and mortar continue to rise, and increases in the cost of higher education routinely outstrip the rate of inflation, technology is more affordable and thus more prevalent than ever. It would be foolish for schools not to make effective use of what technology offers, for reasons that will be explored throughout the book.

CHARACTERISTICS OF DIGITAL TECHNOLOGY

There is little room for utopian thinking in today's world, and it is not my purpose to suggest that an educational utopia is going to be created. On the other hand, there *is* reason to be optimistic about the role of technology in transforming schools, and certainly reason to expect *substantial* change in education, good and bad. A survey in late 2004 of more than 1,000 people with extensive knowledge of the Internet asked how much change they expected the Internet would bring to various institutions during the next decade. Respondents were asked to indicate the degree of change on a 10-point scale, with 10 representing the most radical change. Education ranked second highest among 11 institutions, with an average rating of 7.98. Only news organizations and publishing, at 8.46 out of 10, ranked higher than education.[41]

Apart from such expert opinion, which should not be discounted, why would you expect digital technology to substantially change education? These are some of the key characteristics of today's digital technology. It is these characteristics that will or will not enable technology to help transform schools. The technology is:

- **Inexpensive and pervasive**. Digital technology is increasingly inexpensive and therefore increasingly pervasive. The fact that parents, teachers, students, and others already use computers and other digital technology means that they find it much easier to use these technologies in a school setting.

- **Scalable**. Thousands of people, or even millions, can use the technology within a particular system or entity, such as a business or a school district. Automobiles, in contrast, scale in an entirely different way, causing massive traffic jams, for example.
- **Flexible, all-purpose**. Computers can substitute for machines that once were stand-alone, single-purpose devices, as word processors once were. Some school districts, for instance, now distribute instructional film and video through their local area network, obviating the need to store and distribute individual tapes. Pictures, video, and sound can be processed by computers in addition to text, numbers, equations, and other symbols.
- **Interactive**. Users interact with digital technology; it is not a "passive" technology, as television is said to be. Students or other users are able to receive instant feedback (e.g., from applets, simulations, tutorials, or other software).
- **Customizable and able to keep records**. Computer software and Internet services (e.g., Amazon.com) can be tailored to individual needs and can store information about users. For schools, tailoring might involve students' special needs (e.g., software can speak to blind students), particular interests, their grade levels, etc.
- **Democratizing**. The World Wide Web provides access to vast amounts of information, in many forms (e.g., sound, pictures, text), that was once far more difficult to obtain, if it was even possible. From historical documents and early Edison sound recordings, to the latest pictures from the Hubble Space Telescope, to up-to-date medical information, the Web "levels the playing field" in a remarkable and unique way.
- **Immediate**. Unlike television and radio, specific information is available whenever you want it, and often (say, with the weather) in an up-to-date form.
- **Dynamic.** Because of the speed and flexibility of computers, many representations, such as drawings or pictures, can respond in special ways to the user dragging or clicking a mouse. One can zoom in on photos, rotate figures to look at them from different perspectives, play with simulated planets of different sizes in different orbits, and so on.
- **Insensitive to distance.** Using e-mail, online courses, discussion groups, and other formats, the Internet easily and inexpensively bridges the world.

- **Community-friendly.** New forms of community have developed because of digital technology. At one extreme, social networking groups such as myspace.com and facebook.com are used by more than 100 million people, especially students, while Internet-based support groups for people with rare diseases and their families might include only a few hundred but be of great importance to those few.
- **Less sensitive to time than other communication technologies.** E-mail, threaded discussions, and other digital techniques are time-independent (asynchronous), allowing people in different time zones, or who respond on different days or at different times, to interact with one another more easily than other media, such as the telephone.
- **Service-oriented.** The Internet provides a huge variety of services, free of charge or for a fee. Government agencies, for example, provide searchable databases of information once available only in a static form. School districts are using websites to provide parents with access to password-protected information about students (see chapter 7).
- **Evolving.** Not only are more data, as well as new services, being added all the time, but also users themselves are part of that evolution. An example is the online encyclopedia Wikipedia, constructed by users, and there are also many other websites to which ordinary people contribute, or which they create.
- **Complementary.** Rather than only displace old forms of communication, new media may be used to complement the older forms. Newspapers, for instance, often include special online features; textbooks may include website references.
- **Extensible**. A wide variety of devices can be physically attached to and used with computers and the Internet, ranging from music keyboards, to digital cameras, to sensors and probes for gathering scientific data, to graphing calculators into and from which data or software can be downloaded or uploaded. Even some telescopes and other scientific devices can be controlled through the Internet.

This remarkable set of characteristics helps explain why computers, the Internet, and the World Wide Web have become pervasive so quickly. What is more, digital technology will become even more remarkable as prices continue to drop, new capabilities become feasible, and, as noted above, various media converge.

If Cuban is right in his assertion that many schools and many teachers have yet to make full use of digital technology—and he is—we should not be surprised. Incorporating new technology can be a challenge to any institution. The vaunted private sector is sometimes slow to incorporate new technology, as the history of automobile manufacturing in Detroit and Japan shows. Consumers perceived Japanese cars to be superior to American cars for many years, largely because the Japanese had developed much better quality control. And that "little problem" (which cost Americans thousands of jobs and a continuing loss of leadership in the automotive industry) arose despite the billions of dollars available in the private sector for research and development. There is no clear counterpart in public schools commensurate with the size of the elementary and secondary school enterprise (about $400 billion annually[42]). The fact is, the private sector has in many cases been too slow to react to technological change. Look at what happened to Wang, Digital Equipment Corporation, or Prime Computer.

But the fact that schools have been slow to change should not obscure the reality that the transformation of schools is now well begun. The list of characteristics above provides a few suggestions of how digital technology can transform schools. Matching these characteristics with the needs of schools is the subject of the next chapter. First, it is valuable to understand the concept of transformation.

TRANSFORMATION

As noted above, technology visionaries sometimes suggest that almost anything that happens in current schools doesn't work and should be changed. But transforming schools ought not to mean they would become unrecognizable. Most schools will certainly look like schools for decades—and that's not a bad thing. Even if more people from other age groups used schools, even if students spent more time in internships or learning in museums, even if schools expanded their function to include, for instance, more health-care services for children, society is likely to continue to want and need an institution and a place that specializes in educating young people. We will almost certainly continue to call that place *school*, not "the learning center" or some other term.

What does it mean, then, to transform schools? There is no dictionary definition that distinguishes a revolution from a transformation, or a transformation from a modest change. It seems right to say that aviation has been transformed since the days of the Wright brothers—it is now pervasive, used by millions of people, much cheaper and safer, engrained in society in ways that would cripple us if it were suddenly unavailable, uses new technologies that were inconceivable 100 years ago, and so forth. Still, the Wright brothers would recognize a modern jumbo jet as an aircraft. Aviation remains recognizable as aviation. As the aviation example shows, when there are many changes and some or many of them are substantial, *transformation* is the appropriate way to describe the totality of the changes.

Have there been *fundamental* changes in aviation? (This *is* germane; bear with me.) Possibly so, although again, the dictionary isn't of great help in deciding the question. Most air travel is done on jet airplanes, which operate on different physical principles than propeller aircraft; perhaps that is a fundamental change. However, one could as easily argue that an aircraft is an aircraft; we don't travel between cities on rocket ships, or by teleportation as on *Star Trek*. In any case, the shift from the era of the Wright brothers to today's system of commercial air travel is a profound, extensive, socially significant *transformation* of aviation, from a primitive to a mature state.

Recall that Cuban is concerned that educational technology is not engendering "fundamental" changes in schools. The term is difficult to define—and, curiously, Cuban does not offer a definition. Will we ever see *fundamental* changes in the way people learn, which is what schools are for? A plausible answer is no. Despite the existence of new media, people learn as they always have—through practice, direct instruction, projects, inquiry, hands-on experience, apprenticeships, positive and negative reinforcement, metaphors, images, life experience, and so forth.

Cuban's *Oversold and Underused* is, in my opinion, the most useful of the books by the skeptics, and certainly the most concise, but nonetheless, in the final pages Cuban unfairly defines his way to success as a skeptic when he writes, disparagingly, that even if all teachers and students had laptops, teachers ". . . would use the laptops to sustain existing practices." Even with personal computers at home and in school, Cuban says he believes "that core teaching and learning practices—shaped by internal and external contexts—would remain very familiar to those who would visit mid-twenty-first-century schools."[43]

Cuban is suggesting computers ought to result in "fundamental" change, and since they haven't, and will not ever do so (or so he believes), the nation's investment in technology is not worthwhile. Yet Cuban never explains what is wrong with many of the "core practices" in schools (such as writing papers, doing practice problems, taking notes, completing homework assignments, and taking tests), or why, exactly, he expects that computers and other technology should eliminate these age-old practices. Ironically, he is using the utopian thinkers as a kind of benchmark, reminding his readers that "the ardent promoters' chain of logic that access . . . will transform teaching and learning has yet to be realized. . . ." Cuban is saying, in effect, "You see, schools have not been fundamentally changed as we were told to expect, so the investment is a failure."

Quite frankly, many people never believed the utopian rhetoric in the first place, and to them, Cuban's finding that schools have not been turned inside out and upside down is neither a surprise nor an appropriate benchmark by which to measure the impacts of technology. A far more appropriate outlook is to assume that no matter how powerful computers become, how rich are the resources on the World Wide Web, and how talented teachers may be, technology will transform some education practices while others will not change, and indeed should not. So I say to readers—let others argue about what is "fundamental" change in schools and whether that is needed; it will be enough if schools are significantly *transformed*, as aviation has been.

Education is not exactly like aviation, of course, so what would a transformation of schools look like? We see the beginning of transformation already as digital technology has an impact on:

- *Where and when* **students learn**. Michigan, for example, has just become the first state to *require* that all high school students gain experience with online learning, a method that enables students to learn from almost anywhere there is a computer and to engage in "class discussions" at any time of day or night.
- *How* **students learn (i.e., the tools they use)**. Students use word processors that help them learn to write better, and software tools like Geometer's Sketchpad and other dynamic games, models, and simulations that make it easier and faster to teach and to learn many scientific and mathematical concepts.

- ***Who* students learn with**. The Internet and the Web make it possible for students, and not just those in online schools, to learn with and from a much larger community.
- ***What* students learn**. For instance, millions of high school students learn computer skills ranging from programming, to computer animation, to network maintenance, that help prepare them for technical careers and other jobs.

Given the breadth and depth of the many changes that technology enables, "transformation" is an appropriate term to use, even if some skeptics and some utopians resist it. The number of students affected in major ways is still modest, but it is growing quickly. In several chapters, the question of the scale of change will be discussed.

THE REMAINDER OF THE BOOK

Chapter 2 continues building a framework for thinking about the role of educational technology. That chapter first provides an overview of current education needs that have caused so many people, ranging from President George W. Bush to Microsoft's Bill Gates, to call for a transformation of American schools, and then goes on to identify six overarching goals for education on which nearly everyone can agree. The chapter also examines several current, well-known efforts to improve schools, including the No Child Left Behind Act.

If we know where we are going as we improve schools, only then can we appreciate whether or not technology is one vehicle to help us get there. Six chapters examine the ways in which technology is contributing to meeting the six education goals discussed in chapter 2. The goal of increasing student achievement using a wide variety of technologies, from word processors to online schools, is the subject of chapter 3. Better engaging students in learning and in schools is the topic of chapter 4, which discusses school laptop programs, blogs and social networks, educational computer games, and other technologies. The goal of making school a successful environment for *all* students is the subject of chapter 5, which focuses on the use of technologies for students with disabilities, English language learners, disadvantaged students, and other groups with special needs. Chapter 6 discusses the role of technology in attracting, preparing, and retaining qualified teachers. Increasing out-of-school support for children by parents and communities is the topic of chapter 7. And chapter 8 focuses on the goal of increasing schools' accountability for results and the many ways that technology is vital to meeting that goal.

Chapter 9 explores another important theme, one that is too often invisible: the roles of nonprofit organizations in educational technology research and development (R&D). These organizations have a vital role in conducting many of the studies of technology use that help inform policymakers about what is really happening in schools. Nonprofits also play a significant role in developing applications of educational technology for schools, including: one of the first online schools in the nation, the Virtual High School; one of the most popular sets of educational games used in schools, the Zoombinis; and many of the models, simulations, and interactive learning tools that are found on the Internet. This chapter identifies several important lessons that school systems can learn about the process of innovation.

Finally, chapter 10 reconsiders some of the skeptics' concerns and offers a set of principles and policies needed to ensure that technology is used wisely as part of overall school improvement efforts. Whether in local communities, in political contexts, or at home, there are useful steps that readers can take.

Readers might wonder whether this book will soon be out-of-date. After all, new technologies seem to be constantly available, and today's headlines become familiar facts of life very quickly. But the fact is, the trends described throughout the book will not slow down. If anything, these trends—online schooling, 1-to-1 computing, and many others—will only accelerate. Although it is a pleasant utopian dream to believe that we will soon have the school systems we need, the reality is that an education system for 50 million students does not change quickly. For decades there will be a pressing need to make schools better, and for decades, educational technology is going to provide essential tools for improving them.

CHAPTER 2

Key Education Goals

To merit widespread use, educational technology needs to meet a simple test: Will it help schools succeed in their core mission—providing students with the skills, knowledge, and dispositions they need to be productive, responsible, well-informed citizens living in a democracy that is part of a small, "flat" world. To see how educational technology meets this test, we need to better understand schools' performance and the goals that have been established for them.

THE PARADOX OF ACHIEVEMENT IN TODAY'S SCHOOLS

It may come as a surprise to many people to learn that schools are in many ways more successful than ever.[1] Overall, students are taking more difficult courses than they did 20 years ago, they are achieving at higher levels, and the scale of these improvements is large. For example, while only 26 percent of 1982 high school graduates had taken an advanced math course, by the year 2000 that percentage almost doubled, to 45 percent; and, over the 20-year period beginning in 1983, the number of Advanced Placement tests taken by high school students grew from 240,000 to 1,888,000, a staggering 686 percent increase. The proportion of American adults who have been awarded high school and college degrees has grown over the past 20 years, as it did for decades before. Meanwhile, from 1992 to 2002, school-related crime and violence actually declined by 50 percent.

Somehow, amid the drumbeat of negative news stories about education, it has been too easy to lose sight of the many accomplishments of our schools, which have occurred—amazingly—during a time of almost unprecedented growth in the percentage of students who are members of racial or ethnic minority groups, or whose first language is not English, or who live in homes with only one parent or guardian, or whose families are poor. By many measures, in other words, today's students come from groups that historically have proven *harder* to educate, and yet numerous indicators of school achievement and success have been *rising*.

It would be wonderful if this were the whole story. But it is not. Far too many of America's schools fail to provide students with the education they need. High school dropout rates, especially in America's cities, are appallingly high. The situation for students from poor families, and for ethnic or racial minority groups, is especially bleak. Exact figures don't exist, but by some estimates only about half of all African American, Hispanic, or Native American students graduate high school in four years with a regular diploma and many of them never graduate. This underperformance will have implications for the whole society, because by 2020 about 30 percent of the working-age population will be African American or Hispanic, a figure nearly double the percentage in 1980.[2] Unless minority students do better, the average education level of the American workforce in 2020 will be *lower* than it is today[3]—at the same time that other nations are doing a better job of educating their students.

On the one hand, schools are more successful than ever. On the other hand, we are more concerned than ever about schools' performance because many schools are failing to serve students well. How is it possible that both statements are true?

The reason for the paradox is simply that demands on schools have been rising much faster than schools have improved. The collapse of American manufacturing (such as the decline of the automobile industry that used to provide high school dropouts in the Midwest with well-paying jobs), the "flattening" of the world (meaning that money and information flow almost instantly wherever they are needed on the globe, and jobs can easily follow), and the progress of many other nations, such as Japan, China, and Korea, in educating their students—these and other related trends have dramatically changed what we expect from schools. High dropout rates and low skills among many high school graduates may have been acceptable in the United States in the past, but today they are not. In historical terms, the change in demand for more highly educated young people has been sudden, and our whole society has not been able to change quickly enough to meet this challenge—not only the schools, but also health-care and employment policies, afterschool care, and other policies and institutions.

Thus, schools *are* doing better—but not nearly well enough. We cannot forget that there are many excellent teachers and administrators working in America's schools and accomplishing great things. But the system is huge, and we need more excellent people. Bashing the many outstanding people working in schools, as some critics do, is not the solution. In fact, it is demoralizing.

Of course, there isn't just one education system in the United States. Instead, there are more than 95,000 public schools, which educate about 49 million students. These schools are located in more than 14,000 school districts, in 50 states. More than 3 million teachers work in the public schools.[4] It is an understatement to say that transforming an operation of such an enormous scale is challenging! And that is especially true because school governance is thoroughly decentralized, involving thousands and thousands of state and local school boards, as well as the 50 state legislatures, the governors, the Congress, and the president. As it happens, the states and the federal government have played especially important roles during the past quarter-century in efforts to improve American schools.

(A note about the education system: In addition to public school enrollment, about 6 million students attend private and parochial schools. Some people believe that private schools do a better job of educating young people, on average. Actually, there is little evidence to show that attending private schools results in higher achievement.[5] Similarly, although there has been dramatic growth over the past decade in the number of charter schools, which are public schools that are exempted from many school district requirements, the evidence does not show that attending a charter school leads to higher achievement.[6] So, although there are good reasons why private schools and charter schools exist, it is simplistic to think that these alternatives provide the answer to improving public schools.)

EDUCATION GOALS FOR STUDENTS, TEACHERS, AND SCHOOLS

Americans believe that public elementary and secondary education is of vital importance, and therefore for more than a century the United States has established ambitious goals for its schools. And whether the focus is on elementary, middle, or high schools, or on career and technical education, expectations for public schools have been raised even higher in recent years.

In 1989, for example, the governors and the president established ambitious National Education Goals that were later written into law by Congress. The idea was that these goals would be reached by the year 2000; hence, the name of the law, Goals 2000. One goal was that all students would leave grades 4, 8, and 12 having demonstrated competency over challenging academic subject matter in the core academic subjects. Another was that all children in America would start school ready to learn. Five of the six goals discussed below were part of the National Education Goals. These goals are widely accepted—locally and by states, as well as at the national level—and are understood to be important, although the timeline for achieving them was very unrealistic. The sixth goal below—increasing schools' accountability for results—was not clearly adopted as a national goal until more recently, when it became a centerpiece of the No Child Left Behind Act of 2001.

Obstacles make it difficult to achieve the national goals for schools, and bookshelves are filled with informative studies of American schools and cross-national comparisons that describe some of these obstacles. Some of the barriers, or problems, are described below. Focusing on barriers to reaching the goals is not intended to suggest that all American schools have serious problems, or to diminish schools' growing success on many measures. But it is only by focusing on the problems that we can understand how technology contributes to solutions.

Goal: Increase Student Achievement in Academic Subjects

Probably the most frequently cited goal for schools is to improve students' academic achievement. On average, students are not learning nearly as much as we expect nor as much as they need, at all grade levels and in most subjects. For example:

- In 2001, about one-third of fourth graders were not able to identify the state in which they lived and correctly mark its location on a map of the states.[7]
- In 2003, the performance of American 15-year-olds in mathematics problem-solving was lower than the average for most other developed countries.[8]
- In 2005, more than one-third of fourth graders and more than one-quarter of eighth graders were not able to read even at a "basic" level, and only about a third of students in those grades qualified as "proficient" readers.[9]

In order to increase academic achievement, schools must improve curriculum, instruction, and assessment—a huge job, particularly in such a decentralized system.

Make the Curriculum More Challenging

In too many school systems, much of the assigned work is at a low level. For example, a 1999 study in Chicago found that more than 80 percent of the sixth- and eighth-grade math assignments provided minimal or no challenge. Fortunately, the writing assignments showed more evidence of intellectual challenge, but nonetheless, only 48 percent of the assignments in sixth grade demonstrated moderate or extensive challenge, as well as 64 percent of third-grade assignments and 56 percent in eighth grade.[10] The researchers found that "when teachers organize instruction around assignments that demand higher-order thinking, in-depth understanding, elaborated communication, and that make a connection to students' lives beyond school, students produce more intellectually complex work."[11] Furthermore, those students receiving more challenging assignments achieved higher gains than other students on standardized tests.

Strengthen Instruction

The kinds of questions that teachers ask students are one key variable in judging the quality of instruction. Even in classrooms more representative of the whole nation than those in Chicago, American teachers' instruction often focuses far too little attention on problem-solving and critical thinking. According to a 2003 study funded by the National Science Foundation (NSF), only 16 percent of lessons in mathematics and science demonstrated the high-level questioning experts would want to see, while in two-thirds of the lessons, teachers' questioning was inadequate.[12] Cross-national studies have come to similar conclusions: American teachers do not ask enough questions that require students to think carefully and critically.

A related problem is that students are far too passive in most classrooms most of the time. The NSF-sponsored study found that more than half of the science and mathematics lessons they observed failed to engage students with the intellectual content of the material being studied. As an example:

> An eighth-grade science lesson was designed to give the students a great deal of factual information on Newton's Third Law of Motion. The students copied notes from the blackboard for half of the lesson, and the next half of the lesson was spent with the teacher asking them to recall information from the notes. The observer wrote: "The lesson was designed in a way that allowed the students to be very passive, interacting little with each other or the content. The students spent a great deal of time hurriedly copying the notes; only those students who were called on by the teacher during the review time were required to think about the content, and even that was at the basic level of recalling facts they had just written down."[13]

In my opinion—and most experts would agree—there is nothing wrong with a limited amount of rote learning, if it is at the right time and focuses on appropriate topics. But if students are not taught to understand and to use the material they study, especially complex material, while they may learn something (possibly long enough to pass a test), many will quickly forget it.

Develop and Use Better Assessments

To increase accountability, the No Child Left Behind Act of 2001 (NCLB) requires annual testing of students in multiple subjects. As a result, the number and variety of standardized tests now being used in American schools is astounding. Michigan alone uses 216 different test forms in grades 3–8![14]

The testing craze gripping American schools brings with it a number of problems. There is a tendency to test what is easy to pose questions about and cheap to score, meaning that too many tests fail to focus on more challenging, complex content. At the same time, because of NCLB and other pressures, teachers have increasingly strong incentives to "teach to the test," de-emphasizing topics or entire subjects that will not be tested, even if those are important for their students. In fact, perhaps surprisingly, more than 25 percent of teachers report on surveys that they "focus so much on test preparation that real learning is neglected."[15] There is a real danger that testing may undermine schools rather than help them, despite the best intentions of policymakers.

An additional problem with the tests required by NCLB, as well as many other district-mandated standardized tests, is that they are typically given near the end of the year, when it becomes difficult or impossible to use the results to adjust curriculum or instruction to focus on what students have not learned before the students disperse into other classrooms or schools. Apart from teachers' own classroom tests, there has not been a strong tradition of administering school-, district-, or statewide "formative tests," designed to help teachers rethink what or how they teach (a topic further explored in the discussion on accountability, in chapter 8).

Better Prepare Students for Work and/or Higher Education

Each year hundreds of thousands of students leave American high schools without the skills either to go on to higher education or to land a good job. Although nearly everyone agrees that schools can do better, the perceptions of employers, teachers, and parents differ substantially on some issues. For example, when asked whether public school graduates will have the skills to succeed in the work world, 67 percent of parents and 78 percent of teachers said yes, compared to only 41 percent of employers. More than 75 percent of parents would like their child to attend a four-year or a two-year college after high school, and an equal percentage of students say they plan to attend college.[16] Yet fewer than half of college professors believe that public school graduates will have the skills to succeed in college.

Despite what may well be an overoptimistic view of schools' performance on the part of parents, there is nonetheless widespread support for the idea that schools need to change. According to a leading survey organization, more than three-quarters of the public says that America's ability to compete in the world 25 years from now would be weaker if high schools remain unchanged. Americans realize that continued school improvement and reform is crucial if the U.S. is to retain a leading position in an increasingly competitive global marketplace.[17] A greater sense of urgency is needed, but at least there is recognition that a serious problem is looming.

Goal: Make Schools More Engaging and Relevant

Increasing achievement among those students who stay in school will not be enough, because hundreds of thousands of high school students drop out each year. Even the most optimistic estimate is that nearly 20 percent of students drop out before they graduate,[18] and in many cities and states, and among Black and Hispanic youth, the percentage is much higher, up to 50 percent. These are unacceptable numbers, for one thing because there are no longer enough decent jobs for high school dropouts. Although there are multiple reasons why students drop out, surprisingly, the top reason given by dropouts in a recent study is that their classes were not interesting.[19]

If teachers do not challenge students, or if the curriculum is poorly matched to students' needs, it will be hard to keep students focused on learning. National data show students' engagement in school has been declining for many years, and not just among dropouts. For example, while 40 percent of 1983 seniors said their schoolwork was "often or always meaningful," only 28 percent gave this response by the year 2000—an astonishing and disquieting decline. A similar steep decline occurred in the number of students who say their classes are "quite or very interesting."[20] If students are uninterested in school, many of them will opt out in one way or another—and that is exactly what is happening, in far too many cases. Students also report that they do not work very hard in school. More than 70 percent agree, "Most students do the bare minimum they need to get by."[21]

Focus on More than Traditional Academic Skills

At times, as one listens to the political rhetoric about schools, it seems that increasing students' academic achievement is the only goal that matters. However, there are many distinguished panels, commissions, and business groups that make it clear how much more is needed than just traditional academics. We need young people to be responsible individuals who will make good choices not only as workers but also as citizens and as individuals or family members. For these broader purposes of schooling, what the National Education Goals called the "core academic skills" are simply not enough, and that fact is more widely acknowledged than in 1989.

Consider civic knowledge and political participation: In the 2004 election, fewer than half of 18- to 24-year-olds voted (a lower percentage than in the early 1970s), compared to about two-thirds of citizens ages 25 and above.[22] Young people's knowledge of civics is poor, with 75 percent of high school seniors scoring only at the "basic" level or below on the 1998 National Assessment of Educational Progress (NAEP). Yet youth who have taken civics classes are 23 percentage points more likely to believe they are responsible for making things better for society and 14 percentage points more likely to vote than their peers who have not taken civics.[23] Only a few states administer tests on civics; as a result, many policymakers, teachers, and students consider civics less important than subjects that are regularly tested.[24]

One group of about two dozen large businesses and education organizations, the Partnership for 21st Century Skills, believes that core academic skills are only a part of what schools must teach for students to succeed and prosper. Civic literacy, global awareness, and the ability to use information and communications technology for learning and for problem-solving are among the other focal areas the Partnership believes are important for students.[25]

Students also need to develop a better link between academic skills and the real world, whether that is gained through projects, hands-on learning, community service, internships, or in other ways. And with a substantial number of high school students not attending two- or four-year colleges, or dropping out if they do, the United States also needs to strengthen career and technical high schools to help the many students who will not continue in higher education. Such students do not necessarily need an advanced degree, but they do need more critical thinking and problem-solving skills than their counterparts 20, 30, or 40 years ago, because these skills are needed more than before for all sorts of jobs.

Goal: Achieve a High-Quality Education for All

There is a human tendency to romanticize the past and to believe that schools were better in the "good old days." But that ignores historical truths, from racial segregation of schools, which were separate and *unequal*, to the differing goals that have always separated schools for the elite from schools for the masses. A report from the National Research Council written 20 years ago describes how profoundly our goals are changing:

> The goals of increasing thinking and reasoning ability are old ones for educators. Such abilities have been the goals of some schools at least since the time of Plato. But these goals were part of the high literacy tradition; they did not, by and large, apply to the more recent schools for the masses. Although it is not new to include thinking, problem-solving, and reasoning in *someone's* curriculum, it is new to include it in *everyone's* curriculum. It is new to take seriously the aspiration of making thinking and problem-solving a regular part of a school program for all of the population, even minorities, even non-English speakers, even the poor. It is a new challenge to develop educational programs that assume that all individuals, not just an elite, can become competent thinkers.[26]

Where we are especially falling short is in creating high-quality schools for disadvantaged students. The outgoing president of Teachers College, Columbia, Arthur E. Levine, recently said that we have failed by:

> . . . establishing separate and unequal school systems for low-income and more-affluent children. The former too often receive an education that assumes they will not succeed and is substandard. . . . It is a pity that no major urban school system has successfully been turned around in a 20-year school reform movement.[27]

In that regard, one startling finding is that, based on national reading scores, students who earned mostly As in disadvantaged schools achieved only at the level of students earning mostly Ds in affluent schools.[28] Clearly, the expectations in schools serving large numbers of disadvantaged students are too low.

Another factor influences thinking about educating *all* students. Wherever students are located—good schools or bad ones; urban, rural, or suburban schools—the goal of providing a high-quality education for all is made more challenging because of the increasingly diverse group of students being educated in schools.

Effectively Teach an Increasingly Diverse Group of Students

Between 1979 and 2004 the number of school-age children (ages 5–17) who spoke a language other than English at home increased from 3.8 to 9.9 million, or from 9 percent to 19 percent of all children in this age group,[29] and nearly 4 million students receive English language learner services.[30] Similarly, 43 percent of public school students were considered to be part of a racial or ethnic minority group in 2004, an increase from only 22 percent in 1972.[31] At the same time, the fraction of public school students who were White decreased from 78 percent to 57 percent. The minority increase was largely due to the growth in the proportion of students who were Hispanic.

In 1976–77, some 3.7 million youth were served under the Individuals with Disabilities Education Act (IDEA), and those young people made up 8 percent of the total public school enrollment. By 2003–04, 6.6 million youth received IDEA services, 14 percent of the total public school enrollment.[32]

The fraction of children under age 18 who lived with two married parents fell from 77 percent in 1980 to 67 percent in 2005. In that year, 23 percent of children under 18 lived with only their mothers, 5 percent lived with only their fathers, and 4 percent lived with neither of their parents.[33]

Goal: Prepare, Attract, and Retain More Highly Qualified Teachers

Teaching such a diverse group of students in American schools requires highly qualified teachers. Yet those schools serving large numbers of poor and minority students, whatever the students' race or ethnicity, are more likely than others to be staffed by teachers who are not highly qualified to teach. As noted in the section above about instruction, low-quality teaching is an important factor when it comes to explaining poor outcomes.

California data are illustrative of many other states' experiences. In California, the 2002 graduation rates for African American students (57 percent) and Latinos (60 percent) were far below the state average (71 percent), which itself was not high enough.[34] Of the state's 300,000 teachers, more than 20,000 (about 7 percent) were underprepared, meaning they did not hold a full teaching credential. Schools serving high concentrations of minority students (91 to 100 percent) averaged 20 percent underprepared teachers, compared to only 11 percent in schools serving few or no minority students. The problem in the state is particularly acute in subjects with shortages of teachers, such as in special education, where the proportion of underprepared teachers in high-minority schools was more than three times as great as in schools serving few minority students.

The existing staffing problem will be exacerbated because, due to the aging population of teachers, California is expected to experience more severe teacher shortages across the board in future years. The same is true in many other states.

Make Schools Better Places to Work

To be successful, teachers need to work in a supportive environment. Yet compared to teachers in a number of developed countries, American teachers have high teaching loads and fewer opportunities to meet with and learn from their colleagues.

Virtually every study group or commission that has written about school improvement has focused on the need for ongoing, high-quality teacher professional development to increase teachers' knowledge and skills and to improve current curricula and instructional practices. As an example, more than half of school superintendents and principals report that "quite a large number" of teachers need more training on effective ways to teach struggling students.[35] Only about a fifth of American teachers report that they meet regularly with colleagues about teaching,[36] and yet research shows that strengthening teachers' professional communities is vital to creating and maintaining a highly qualified teacher workforce.[37]

Goal: Increase Support of Children by Parents and Communities

More than 80 percent of teachers agree that "parents who fail to set limits and create structure at home for their kids are a serious problem." Given a hypothetical choice between working in a school that pays a significantly higher salary, or a school where student behavior and parental support were significantly better, 86 percent of teachers chose the latter.[38] One example of insufficient parental support is allowing children to watch an excessive amount of television. In 2000, about a quarter of fourth graders watched five or more hours of television every day—too much for their own good.[39]

Of course, children need the right kinds of support long before fourth grade, which is why the National Education Goals focus on children becoming ready to learn *before* they begin school. Because early brain development affects an adult's ability to learn, investing in preschool for disadvantaged students may well provide a greater "return on investment" even than investments in later schooling.[40]

Thoughtful observers of the school reform process also remind us that in impoverished neighborhoods, "schools can't do it alone."[41] They would like to see cities, for example, "include families, neighborhoods, and city agencies in the reform agenda," even if it meant "reorganizing city cultural, civic, medical, housing, employment, and social services." To borrow an aphorism from military affairs, education is too important to leave it to schools alone.

Another dimension of parental support for schooling is setting an example for children. Yet among adults, reading *any* literature for pleasure declined from about 57 percent of the population in 1982 to less than half (47 percent) in 2002.[42] Neither parents nor other members of the public should expect schools to do all the education of children that is typically done at home, including reading to children often and modeling desirable behaviors, such as reading for pleasure.

These and other deficiencies in parents' and communities' preparation of children for school need to be separated from parental and public opinions of schools themselves. In fact, increasing percentages of public school parents give their local schools a "report card" letter grade of A or B (61 percent in 2004, up from 52 percent in 1998)[43], which is further evidence of ongoing improvements in the schools. The public wants public schools to succeed and says they are willing to pay more to achieve that goal.

Goal: Require Greater Accountability by Schools

Policymakers are insisting on greater accountability than in the past. Accountability can take many forms, from requiring that students pass tests before moving to the next grade level, or graduate, to publishing "school report cards" that provide a wide variety of data allowing members of the public to better understand their local education system. The No Child Left Behind Act (discussed below) includes important accountability provisions for schools.

Although the public has misgivings about some of the ways that tests are used, there is widespread public support for all sorts of accountability provisions. For example, even parents of children in school support measures such as sending more students to summer school or having them repeat a grade if they are not able to perform well enough to move up to the next grade.[44]

Control Costs

Part of the pressure for greater accountability comes from greater concerns about costs than in the past. Between 1961–62 and 2002–03, per-pupil expenditures in public elementary and secondary schools grew substantially. Measured in constant 2004–05 dollars (that is, adjusted for inflation), per-pupil expenditures rose from $2,507 to $8,468, or by a factor of more than three.[45] One of the many reasons for this growth is almost certainly that the current highly diverse population of students is more expensive to educate than earlier cohorts, who were more homogeneous. Providing extra help to special needs students, and to students whose first language is not English, costs money.

One reason this is an issue is because such a growth rate cannot be sustained, particularly with other large fiscal demands, such as Social Security and Medicare, competing for funding. Federal and state policymakers, business leaders, parents, and the public are more concerned about spending pressures and taxes. Expenditures for elementary and secondary education are about $400 billion annually. Although that figure will increase, it is not credible that hundreds of billions of dollars of additional funding will be available for education every year. Solutions to the problems facing schools may require modest increases in spending, but they cannot be predicated on steep increases like those that have taken place during the past forty years.

STRATEGIES AND PROGRAMS FOR SCHOOL IMPROVEMENT

It is clear from the preceding discussion of goals for schools and the problems that need to be solved to reach those goals, that there is no "silver bullet," no single program or approach that can address all the goals and problems, let alone ensure that we achieve these goals. Indeed, during the past decade or two, hundreds of laws have been passed that were intended to improve education, and hundreds of programs have been designed and implemented by federal, state, or local policymakers.

At the national level, for example, a popular approach to school improvement, called "Success for All," has been implemented in more than 1,300 schools (a bit more than 1 percent of all schools), largely elementary schools.[46] This program focuses on implementing the Success for All curricula and improving instruction, and includes about five weeks of teacher training. One unusual feature of the program is that more than 80 percent of teachers in the school must vote, in a secret ballot, to adopt it.

There are countless other ways in which various groups of reformers envision that schools can be improved. These range from creating smaller high schools and implementing an "early college" model* for at-risk students, both of which are initiatives that have been supported by the Gates Foundation, to providing higher salaries for teachers who earn advanced certification from a nonprofit institution called the National Board for Professional Teaching Standards, as a way to improve the teaching profession. A few school districts are literally redesigning schools from the

---

*Early college high schools provide opportunities for at-risk students to earn both a high school diploma and two years of college credit.

ground up, as in Philadelphia's School of the Future. A common element among the great majority of school improvement programs is that they conform to an approach called standards-based reform.

Standards-Based Reform

Standards-based reform is a way of thinking about education reform that grew out of dissatisfaction with uncoordinated programs and policies. The idea is to align all of the important components of education, including curriculum, instruction, teacher preparation, and assessment of student learning. Curriculum standards are typically the central component, describing what students should know and be able to do in a given field. Once these standards are established, the theory suggests, other elements of the education system should be aligned with them. Although this is easier said than done, especially in a decentralized system, there has been progress over the past 20 years in creating curriculum standards and aligning components.

Under the U. S. constitution, and as a matter of tradition, states have primary responsibility for education. As a result, the states have been key to implementing standards-based reform, such as developing 50 sets of state curriculum standards. In practice, state standards in a given subject area are typically similar; in mathematics, for example, all states have been heavily influenced by the standards developed by the National Council of Teachers of Mathematics, first published in 1989 and then revised in 2000.[47] However, there are some important variations in the approaches that states have taken. New York State, for example, is one of only a few mandating that all students learn about technology, in the sense of engineering and design.[48]

No Child Left Behind

Beginning in 2001, the most important program for school improvement, especially for elementary schools, has been a piece of national legislation called the No Child Left Behind Act (NCLB). Because the law itself is more than 600 pages long, it is not possible to describe it fully here, but some of its major features are as follows:

- NCLB requires states to assess students in grades 3–8 annually in multiple subjects. The tests are created by the states, not by the federal government. Data from the tests must be made available as part of school report cards, which also provide information about the qualifications of teachers, and about children's progress in key subjects.
- When states report student achievement data, the information must be disaggregated by race, gender, special education status, and other criteria. The purpose is to show how well different groups of students are achieving, and to provide data about achievement gaps, especially those between disadvantaged students and others.
- If schools do not make Adequate Yearly Progress (AYP) for several years, as measured by student achievement on tests, then parents of students in those schools have recourse to certain alternatives, including transferring their child to a better-performing public or charter school, or providing their child with supplemental education services, such as tutoring.
- States are required to have a highly qualified teacher in every classroom. To be "highly qualified," a teacher must: hold a bachelor's degree; hold a certification or licensure to teach in the state of his or her employment; and have proven knowledge of the subjects he or she teaches. Alternatively, states are given latitude to construct a different definition of "highly qualified," but each state's definitions are reviewed and approved by the U. S. Department of Education.
- All limited English proficient students must be taught English quickly and are tested for reading and language arts in English after they have attended school in the United States for three consecutive years.
- NCLB requires that the teaching methods used to implement the law be proven using so-called "scientifically based research," which is defined in the law.

NCLB is the most sweeping piece of federal legislation affecting elementary and secondary schools ever enacted. Not surprisingly, then, the Act, and various provisions in it, is controversial. Although reauthorization of the law may well bring about some significant changes, it seems very unlikely that NCLB's sharp focus on improving student achievement and its increased emphasis on states' accountability for results will disappear.

How Well are NCLB and Standards-Based Reform Working?

States have been actively using the principles of standards-based reform for a decade and a half or longer. In some areas, such as creating workable standards documents, there has been substantial progress. However, the bottom line for policymakers is improving student achievement, and progress in that regard has been modest, at best. Policymakers' impatience with standards-based reform without clear accountability was one major factor leading to passage of the No Child Left Behind Act of 2001 and its strong accountability provisions.

One positive consequence of standards-based reform has been the growing recognition that because there are so many parts of education systems (setting standards; improving curricula; recruiting, training, and retaining highly qualified teachers; designing better assessments; etc.), making substantial improvements to schools is a complex, challenging job that calls for expertise in many areas.

Perhaps the best aspect of the No Child Left Behind Act is its clear focus on underachieving schools. NCLB shines a bright light on failing urban school systems and other schools that have a very difficult job to do and have not yet been able to do that job well. Similarly, by requiring schools to "disaggregate data"—namely, report their student test scores by various racial and ethnic groups, students enrolled in special education, and other subgroups—NCLB promotes greater attention to problems in schools that would not be apparent if all attention were on raising averages.

Although the extent to which NCLB has been a success is a matter of debate (the Los Angeles Times has written that "the law needs a rewrite, not touches of administrative relief"[49]), and also depends on which portions of the law are discussed, it is clear that the law's timetable requiring that all children be proficient in core academic subjects by 2014 is as unachievable as were the goals in Goals 2000. A past president of the American Educational Research Association, an expert on tests and measurement, declared that achieving this goal would be nothing short of "miraculous."[50] At some grades, rates of improvement in test scores between 1990 and 2000 would have to improve by a factor of 12 to meet the goal set in NCLB by 2014! Enacting laws that establish clearly unachievable goals, yet which are full of requirements, including mandating serious consequences for lower-than-expected performance ("Adequate Yearly Progress"), may strike reasonable people as an excellent reason for modifying the law, and possibly an indication that parts of the law were unwise to begin with. At least in the political sphere, Americans are an impatient people. We want results and we want them quickly. In the case of NCLB, that is not likely to happen. Jane David and Larry Cuban view the problem partly as a case of not doing what standards-based reform called for:

> Instead of broad agreement on a few ambitious standards, most states have lengthy lists that enumerate every skill, reinforcing the frequent criticism of American education: a mile wide and an inch deep. Instead of new tests that show what students know and can do, most states use the same old ones. Instead of trading flexibility for accountability, schools actually have less discretion, more testing, and stiffer penalties for low test scores than they once did. In fact, under No Child Left Behind, these schools can improve substantially and still be penalized. Finally, the idea that schools would have the resources and training needed to teach to high standards never completely gained traction among state and federal policymakers.[51]

NCLB has focused attention primarily on elementary schools. Reform of high schools has not been as high a priority, although that situation is beginning to change. Achieve, Inc., a group created by the nation's governors and business leaders to help raise academic standards and student achievement, has been tracking reform efforts in the states and finds that to date, only a small number have aligned high school standards, including graduation requirements, with the expectations of colleges and the workplace.[52]

For decades, the federal government has had important roles identifying, documenting, and addressing problems in elementary and secondary schools, despite the fact that states and localities contribute much more money to schools than the federal government does. Yet even now, federal and state policymakers have to walk a fine line between calling so much attention to the serious problems facing education that people become pessimistic about fixing them or being so supportive of schools that nothing changes. Viewed in that context, NCLB can be seen as an unusual bipartisan effort to identify and solve real and important problems.

Choice in Public Schools

The No Child Left Behind Act includes provisions that provide parents of students in "failing" schools with choices, including, as noted above, transferring their child to a better-performing public or charter school, or providing their child with supplemental education services, such as tutoring. These provisions have not yet been widely used by parents.

For many more years, since the early 1990s, increasing parental choice has been a goal of the charter school movement. Charter schools are public schools that operate under a contract ("charter") with an authorizing body. The schools must meet the terms of their charter, as well as requirements in the No Child Left Behind Act, or face closure. In return for greater autonomy and flexibility—they are freed of many requirements of regular public schools—charter schools are supposed to be more accountable for students' performance. Students are enrolled in charter schools because their parents make the choice to do so.

In 1990 there were no charter schools. By the 2002–2003 school year, there were 2,700.[53] By then 39 states, as well as the District of Columbia, had passed charter school laws. Since 1995, the federal Public Charter Schools Program, first proposed by President Clinton's administration, and administered by the U.S. Department of Education, has invested more than $1 billion in charter schools, demonstrating the national interest in programs for school choice.

There has also been some interest nationally in voucher programs, which allow parents to use public dollars to enroll a child in a private school. However, only a few states have passed voucher laws.

One theory behind increasing parental choice is that greater competition among schools is healthy and will lead to better schools. The extent to which that is the case is still unknown; there is as yet no evidence, for example, that charter schools are significantly better than regular public schools.

Programs to Incorporate Technology

Taken as a group, local, state, and federal education policymakers have had an ambivalent stance about the role of technology in school improvement. There is hardly a mention of technology in a book of case studies about six major cities' decade-long efforts to improve schools.[54]

The National Science Foundation, a federal agency, spent more than $250 million in the 1990s on efforts to improve mathematics and science education in 25 states through curriculum reform, teacher professional development, and other means, and very few states included technology as part of their strategy.[55] Montana, which incorporated powerful computers into the secondary school mathematics curriculum, was an exception.

Nonetheless, the federal government established several important programs to help schools purchase technology, and to train teachers to use it well, and spent tens of billions of dollars in this effort. The E-Rate program, administered by the Universal Service Administrative Company on behalf of the Federal Communications Commission (FCC), provides discounts to assist most schools and libraries in the United States to obtain affordable telecommunications and Internet access. A fee on telephone bills funds the program. The amount of funding available to schools depends on the poverty rate of the students served, and ranges as high as 90 percent of eligible costs. Vice president Al Gore first had the idea for creating the E-Rate program. E-Rate funds may be used only for equipment and fees related to telecommunications and the Internet, and not for software or teacher training. Since 1998, the program has spent about $19 billion.[56] One result is that almost every school in the United States, and nearly every classroom, is now connected to the Internet,[57] goals set by President Clinton when the E-Rate program was created.

The U.S. Department of Education has also administered several programs that have provided states and districts with billions of dollars earmarked for educational technology and teacher professional development, to learn how to use technology. The Technology Literacy Challenge Fund was the first federal grants program designed to bring computers and other digital technologies into elementary and secondary classrooms.[58] A successor program, created by the No Child Left Behind Act, is called Enhancing Education Through Technology. Under both programs, allowable expenditures include both hardware and teacher professional development, with the latter program actually requiring that schools spend at least 25 percent of the program funds on teacher training. (At the time this book was written, the Bush administration proposed eliminating the Enhancing Education Through Technology program, claiming that other federal programs, such as those to improve the teaching of reading, permit funds to be spent on educational technology.)

The result of these federal technology programs, combined with programs in many, but not all, states and districts, is that the capacity of school systems and teachers to use technology as a routine part of instruction is far greater than it was a decade ago. However, the distribution of technology in schools is uneven, with some states and schools far better equipped than others.

MEETING SCHOOLS' NEEDS WITH TECHNOLOGY

To gain more widespread acceptance and use, educational technology must add value by helping schools achieve the important goals discussed above. Although business leaders, employers, and the public agree that students need to have reasonable computer skills, little mention of technology has been made in this chapter in discussing the needs of schools. Nonetheless, there are a great many ways that digital technologies assist schools and students to meet national goals. Each of the six goals identified above is the subject of one chapter of the book and each of those chapters provides answers to the question, How does educational technology help schools meet their goals?

Using technology is most certainly not the only way to help schools meet their goals, but that is to be expected. No other approach or strategy to improving schools could make that claim either. Yet educational technology is a necessary part of efforts to improve schools. It is impossible to envision any way that schools will meet their accountability and cost-effectiveness goals unless they apply technology wisely. Just as businesses have invested in technology in order to improve their day-to-day operations, and to save money, for schools to respond to today's and tomorrow's needs, to become more clearly accountable for results, and to become more cost-effective (more positive outcomes per dollar spent), the increased use of educational technology will be a requirement, not an option. The necessity of using technology seems clearest in the area of accountability, but digital technologies will also add significant value when used to meet all of the national education goals.

Still, in discussions about educational technology it is important to reemphasize that people—teachers, parents, school administrators, and others—are the biggest key to improving education, not technology. The same can be said of businesses improving their procedures, even Web-based businesses; any technology is only as good as the people who design it, build it, use it, and keep it working.

Recently, the secretary of education for Pennsylvania, Gerald L. Zahorchak, said his state must do a better job of preparing its students for work and college. To do so, he said:

> . . . adults must help students see the explicit connections between what they do in high school and what comes after. *Students are unlikely to gain that awareness unless they have strong relationships at school with adults who know and advise them.*[59] [emphasis added]

Is it contradictory, then, to point to the importance of technology? No, not at all, because to do their jobs well, teachers, administrators, and students themselves need the effective tools that can only be provided by computers and other digital technologies.

Providing and Sharing a Vision for Better Schools

The Internet provides increasing numbers of case studies and video vignettes that offer exemplars of how technology can be used well in schools. This book also includes references to many websites that readers can explore and judge for themselves.

The attributes of digital technology provided in chapter 1 virtually guarantee that an increasing use of technology will be part of any successful approach to school improvement. Moreover, as digital technologies become ubiquitous in homes and the workplace, it is clear that policymakers, teachers, and the public are insisting that these technologies be used as one of the powerful tools to transform schools into more effective, more modern institutions.

CHAPTER 3

Increasing Student Achievement (Goal 1)

Student achievement is King! All bow to the King. The King's name is No Child Left Behind.

You don't want to bow? Perhaps you would prefer the world depicted in one of my favorite education cartoons, which shows a pleasant-looking king on his palace balcony, robed and crowned, addressing the populace. "I want our country to have the most highly educated people in the world," he says. "Therefore, today I am bestowing on all of you a bachelor's degree from our best university."

We can do better than to frame education debates as a choice between extremes like these. Everyone is in favor of higher student achievement. But sadly, in this No Child Left Behind era, student achievement is equated with high scores on standardized tests in reading, mathematics, and science. Such a narrow view is absurd. Schools exist for many other reasons than to increase test scores. We want to raise good people—honest, thoughtful, and unselfish. We want young people to *want* to learn, we want them to vote and participate in civic life, and we want large numbers of young people to be creative, entrepreneurial, and artistic. Clearly, then, many important goals for students are not measured on tests.

Nonetheless, learning reading, math, science, and other school subjects *is* important, and there is no question schools can do better than what is now considered the norm. Although technology is not a silver bullet, it *can* help. There are thousands of software products and websites for teaching and learning, and there are also numerous digital technologies used for teaching and learning, in addition to computers—from graphing calculators to digital cameras to SMART Boards (a whiteboard that acts as a computer display, allowing interaction with the computer by touching or writing on the board). There is space in this chapter to discuss only illustrative examples.

In some cases, there is firm evidence that technology helps students learn. In other cases, there is promise, but the evidence is inconclusive or missing. Occasionally, evidence is simply not needed to reach a reasonable conclusion. It is obvious, for example, that the Web provides more and better information about many current events than is available in printed form in a school building; if recent information is what you need, the Web is perhaps the most excellent source. In one survey, more than two-thirds of social science teachers said that the Internet has improved lessons about current events. Unfortunately, on the same survey teachers reported that current events lessons are more difficult to justify because of the No Child Left Behind Act and other testing mandates.[1]

The fact that there is only modest evidence of the benefits of educational technology should not be surprising because the research base in education is thin, period. The director of the federal government's Institute of Education Sciences (IES) was asked by a school superintendent several years ago to recommend an elementary school mathematics textbook series that would be good for the students in his district. "I had to tell him that there was no rigorous research on the [effectiveness] of widely available elementary mathematics curricula, and that about all I could offer him was my opinion. He said thanks, but he had plenty of opinions already."[2] To say there is "no rigorous research" on mathematics curricula is an exaggeration—but there certainly isn't enough.

Why? Primarily because it costs millions of dollars to do high-quality educational research—just as it takes large sums to do good medical research. For example, a $10 million congressionally mandated study, discussed below, focuses on just 15 education software products used to teach reading and math. The cost of the study will grow to $1 million per product before the work is complete. In the late 1970s, the federal government spent millions of dollars to conduct a rigorous five-year study of just *one* commercial product used to provide elementary students with computer-assisted instruction in several subjects—and the results showed that using the computer only 10 minutes a day led to sizable student gains in reading and math test scores.[3]

The nation hasn't yet invested enough money in credible, high-quality studies of textbooks, computer software, or other instructional materials. The research base is thin for almost *all* education products and services. Reports of research that *has* been done are scattered and of varying quality. In fact, the U.S. Department of Education is spending tens of millions of dollars to review existing studies of education products, programs, and practices; identify the best of these studies; and then summarize their findings.[4]

Improving student achievement using digital technology can mean different things to different people. We might ask: If we use digital technology in regular classrooms, does that increase students' test scores? In some cases it does, and the first section below addresses this question. Or, we can ask: If students don't have access to a particular class in their regular school, how well do online schools do *as a substitute* for regular classrooms? The answer is, remarkably well, and the second section addresses that question. Or, we can ask: Is it important to increase student achievement in using technology itself, for example by teaching computer programming or computer network maintenance? As long ago as 1983, the National Commission on Excellence in Education found that having *some* knowledge of computers is now part of the "new basic skills" for students, and more recently economists have presented evidence that such knowledge is important for students' futures.[5] That issue is discussed in the third section below, as well as in chapter 4. A number of other chapters also include examples of using technology to increase achievement.

HELPING STUDENTS IN REGULAR COURSES IN BRICK-AND-MORTAR SCHOOLS

There are many reasons why digital technology ought to help teachers teach and students learn. For decades it has been clear that school is dominated by teacher talk, with students forced into too passive a role. Educational technology encourages much more student activity and interaction. Students in laptop schools, for example, can imme-diately find answers to many questions arising during class, and they have a sense of ownership of information that is new and different for many of them. (See chapter 4 for a fuller account of laptop programs.) Computers running well-designed software or browsing an appropriate website also offer enormous practice time, providing rapid feedback to students (and to their teachers) as they practice spelling, foreign lan-guages, or other subjects.

Learning to Read and Write

Learning to write is an area in which the benefits of using computers are clear, as noted in chapter 1. In Maine, where every middle school student is provided with a laptop, a student wrote:

> It's helped my writing a lot. That's probably my biggest improvement. . . . now I have spell check and I have a thesaurus right on there. I'm big into poetry and I like writing poetry. It's a lot easier to do that . . . write a little and use the thesaurus to find a better word.[6]

Research supports this observation. In a program focused on teach-ing writing using laptops (including providing teachers with profession-al development on using computers to teach writing), researchers docu-mented gains in student achievement.[7] And a "meta-analysis" (a rigorous reexamination) of more than two dozen studies of learning to write us-ing computers concluded that "computers are a valuable tool for helping students develop writing skills."[8] The "effect size" was calculated at about 0.4 standard deviations, which means that 65 percent of students taught to write with computers scored above the average of students who were taught without computers. (*Effect size* is a measure of how much differ-ence a "treatment" makes; in this case, using word processors.)

These positive findings are not surprising because almost everyone's experience suggests that word processors make it easier to write well. Perhaps the most important advantage is that word processors make it so much easier to revise text, and making revisions is such an important part of good writing. How many writers would willingly give up using word processors, especially for lengthy pieces of writing?

One caveat is that teaching with technology and testing with technol-ogy need to be better linked, especially in those cases where we expect people to use technological tools in the "real world." For example, determining the value of computers for the teaching of writing is affected by whether students are tested with or without computers. Students taught to write using word processors are at a disadvantage if they are tested without one—but in the "real world," students will use a word processor almost anytime that they write anything longer than a paragraph. Testing students' ability to write longer pieces of text without a computer actually discourages teachers from using computers to improve students' writing.[9] (Chapter 8 includes a further discussion of using computers for testing as part of requiring accountability for results.)

Word processors can be a useful part of a writing *program*, but giving students word processors is not the same as—or a replacement for—teaching writing. The same can be said for teaching students to read: a reading program requires more than technology. Reading is a complex skill involving an awareness of and understanding of phonics, the development of vocabulary, and growing sophistication in comprehending text (which is related to genre and subject matter as well as to vocabulary). One recent meta-analysis of reading-software products found evidence that some do help raise students' reading scores, notably writing-to-read and reading management programs.[10] Moreover, computers provide beginning readers and students with disabilities with many kinds of support and assistance, such as by pronouncing unfamiliar words and phrases. (These types of individual supports are discussed in chapter 5.)

Learning Mathematics and Science

One effective, inexpensive, widely accepted technology is the graphing calculator, of which there are millions in schools. Graphing calculators—more powerful and accurate successors to the ubiquitous slide rules of earlier generations—are specialized, pocket-sized computers, costing as little as $60, that include a small screen. They are an effective aid for learning algebra and other mathematical subjects.[11]

In science, students collect data by attaching small devices called "probes" to computers or graphing calculators, which allows the immediate recording and graphing of temperature, pressure, motion, pH, or other scientific data. More than a decade of research shows that students using this approach learn many concepts better than students not using probes.[12] In 2000, about 40 percent of high school science teachers used such devices;[13] almost certainly, the figure is by now considerably more than 50 percent. Hours of precious class time are saved when students use handheld electronic devices to collect science data, instead of making laborious measurements by hand, just as graphing calculators save time creating and using graphs.[14]

Visualizations, Simulations, and Models

Digital technology permits many difficult mathematics and science concepts to be learned more easily.[15] With visualizations, simulations, and models, for example, students can more easily learn how atoms and molecules interact, or how populations affect one another in an ecosystem, faster and at an earlier age. "A picture is worth 1,000 words," according to the old adage, and now, besides static pictures, computers provide dynamic graphs, animations, movies, and simulations that respond to students' input using the mouse and keyboard. For example, Molecular Workbench software, available free on the Internet,[16] allows students to observe how atoms and molecules interact and how those interactions respond to changing key variables, such as temperature. (See chapter 9 for more information.)

In mathematics, one of the software products most highly rated by high school teachers is Geometer's Sketchpad. A gallery of interactive mathematical figures, proofs, and simulated mechanical linkages created using Sketchpad can be seen on Internet.[17]

Tutorial Software

Skeptics might ask whether some of the best institutions in the country use education software. In fact, they do. Physicists at the Massachusetts Institute of Technology (MIT) developed online tutorial software, Mastering Physics, which is used not only in MIT's own physics courses but also by tens of thousands of physics students in colleges and universities across the country. Students log in to a website and use Mastering Physics to do their homework problems. Tutorial assistance is available step-by-step and problem-by-problem. Students who make use of more assistance from the software receive fewer points for correct answers to the problems. On the other hand, when students don't know how to solve a problem, they score more points by obtaining assistance and learning how to solve the problem than they would by skipping it.

A high proportion of all college-level introductory physics students in the entire country use Mastering Physics, and comparable software for high schools is planned. MIT's RELATE program (the acronym stands for REsearch in Learning, Assessing, and Tutoring Effectively), which developed the software, published data showing that use of the software results in greater learning gains than does class participation, or completing written homework as usual, or solving problems as part of a group.[18] On surveys, students report that the software helps them learn physics. The website for the commercial software (www.masteringphysics.com) includes endorsements from physics professors at a wide range of colleges and universities.

Mastering Physics is one of a growing number of software products that are able to tutor students in mathematics, science, or other subjects. Research about Cognitive Algebra Tutor, which is used in grades 6–12, is discussed in the section below on 15 software products.

Student Scientists

Chapter 1 described a website, Valley of the Shadow, which allows students to act as historians by analyzing historical data through the Internet. The Web has also created opportunities for students to contribute to original scientific investigations. In 2000, for example, the National Optical Astronomy Observatory in Tucson, Arizona, announced that high school teachers and their students, working with astronomers, had discovered 73 exploding stars (novae) in the Andromeda galaxy by analyzing images gathered by astronomers and distributed to high schools through the Internet.[19] The GLOBE program, which began to operate on Earth Day in 1995, has allowed students in more than 100 countries to contribute more than 16 million measurements to the GLOBE database.[20] That database, which is used by cooperating scientists, as well as by students and teachers, includes measurements related to soil, climate, atmosphere, and other topics. GLOBE, the stellar novae program, and other projects allow large numbers of students to engage in real science.

Ongoing Evaluative Research

Research is being conducted about dozens of promising digital curric-ulum products for teaching and learning math and science. It is clear that computers and other technologies can increase students' perfor-mance in learning many science concepts (one concept, however, is only a small part of a full-year course).[21] There is also growing evidence of "increases in achievement" in the sense of standardized test scores. As an example, researchers at the University of Michigan have been working for nearly a decade developing and testing Internet-based cur-riculum units for middle school science. A well-designed study of more than 2,000 sixth-grade students in Detroit public schools found that using the materials reduced the gap on the state science test between the statewide average and Detroit middle school students from 30 per-cent to 20 percent.[22]

Fifteen Software Products for Teaching Reading and Mathematics

In April of 2007 a $10 million federal study of 15 software products made news across the country. A headline in the *Washington Post* read SOFT-WARE'S BENEFITS ON TESTS IN DOUBT: STUDY SAYS TOOLS DON'T RAISE SCORES.[23]

The congressionally mandated study, called the Effectiveness of Edu-cational Technology Interventions (EETI), included four sub-studies ex-amining the use of five software products to teach reading in first grade; four software products to teach reading in grade four; three math soft-ware products for sixth grade; and three products for teaching algebra (typically in grade nine).[24] Nearly 10,000 students located in more than 130 schools were included in the study. In each sub-study, teachers within schools were randomly selected either to use one of the software products or to teach as usual, without the software.

The major finding, as the *Post* headline suggested, was that test scores were not significantly higher in classrooms where the software products were used. For each of the four sub-studies, results were reported in ag-gregate, not for individual software products. It is possible that use of some products *did* result in measurable achievement gains, but that those results were washed out by data about other products. A future report, based on additional data collected for the study, will break out results for each software product.

Sadly, there is less to learn from the EETI research than Congress or the public expected. Teachers typically used the 15 software products for about 10 percent of instructional time during the year, which is much less than recommended by the vendors. For example, students used the sixth-grade math products for about 17 hours per year, according to computerized records collected by the products. Over 180 school days, that would be less than six minutes daily, on average—very little time, indeed. Twenty-five years earlier, the federally funded study of computer-assisted instruction conducted by Educational Testing Service examined Los Angeles classrooms in which students used software for either 10 or 20 minutes per day, and found positive effects on both reading and math test scores, in both conditions.[25] For the recent study, it may be that teachers and students simply did not use the software products for enough time to make a difference on tests. Earlier research already had highlighted that concern about use of software. A 2003 review of studies of reading software noted that "in typical implementations students spend only 15 percent to 30 percent of the recommended amount of time on [computer-based] 'integrated learning systems' instruction and that [the] effects would be greater if schools would allot more time to [computer-based] instruction."[26] (That review also found other subjects in which software use *was* effective.) Why did we need to spend $10 million to learn again that it takes significant amounts of time to increase students' test scores in reading and math?

This $10 million study demonstrates that in conducting research, the devil is in the details. Did students use the software as recommended? Answer: No. Were teachers well trained? Answer: Not as well trained as we would want. Did it matter which particular software product students used? Answer: Based on this study, we don't know—but for educators, that is a vital question, perhaps *the* vital question.

One can argue—and many have—that this big, federally funded study ought to have been better designed. The researchers reported that whether taught *with or without the software* products, after a full year of instruction, students in the algebra sub-study were able to answer only "an additional one or two questions correctly" on the 25-question algebra test, and still scored below 40 percent correct at the end of the year.[27] Evidently the test was far too difficult, or instruction was ineffective for the 1,400 algebra students in the study, or both. Unfortunately, there may be a more valuable lesson to learn from the study about the teaching and learning of algebra through *any* means than about the use of certain algebra software products. Growing numbers of states and districts require that *all* students take algebra, yet data such as these show that in many schools, such policies are unlikely to accomplish their goals and may be unwise. In 2004, 44 percent of students taking algebra in Los Angeles flunked and another 17 percent received Ds.[28] That is surely not what it is supposed to mean to leave no child behind!

In spite of the dismal results of this expensive study, it is almost certain that many software products, including some that were included in the EETI study, *are* effective at raising test scores when used properly. Well-designed research about one of the 15 products included in the study, Cognitive Algebra Tutor (distributed by Carnegie Learning, Inc.), was judged in 2004 by the U.S. Department of Education's Institute of Education Sciences to meet the agency's rigorous standards of evidence. The research showed that students who used the product had significantly higher test scores than students who did not.[29] Cognitive Algebra Tutor has been built on an extensive research base and has been demonstrated to be effective. More information about its effectiveness will be provided when the next EETI study report is issued, and another, $6 million, five-year study of Cognitive Algebra Tutor was funded by the Department of Education in 2007.

Meta-Analyses of Instructional Technology

People often wonder whether educational technology, very broadly defined, improves student achievement. Although it's an imprecise question, it is a reasonable one. The question asks about reading, mathematics, music, history, science, and any other subject taught in school. And the technology might be calculators, computers, the Internet, "probes," or many others. Not all uses of digital technologies are the same, and so their effects are unlikely to be the same.

Nonetheless, there are studies that have looked at many technology applications at once. Researchers review reputable journals and collect dozens of articles that are judged to meet certain criteria, such as reporting data about at least two groups of students, one group that uses technology for learning and another that does not. In 2003, a study of this kind examined 29 then-recent articles reporting on learning gains with and without technology, and the authors reported an effect size of .448.[30] That means that about 67 percent of students taught with technology scored above the average of students taught without technology; that is, two-thirds of students instead of the one-half one would usually expect to be above average. In other words, technology used in many different ways helps bring up students' scores by an amount that is educationally significant.

Knowing that many applications of technology have had positive impacts on students' learning is useful, but only to a point. It is studies of *particular* technologies, used in *particular* ways—like using word processors to teach writing—that are the bedrock on which confidence can be built. We know that books are important in education, but that fact would not help a teacher decide which books her students should study or how she should teach using those books. The school principal, department chair, or teacher wants to know *how* to make good use of computers and technology—not just that in some general, unspecified way educational technology is valuable. In this respect, using digital technology is no different than using books: the details matter.

In that vein, there is still a tendency among some people—but one that seems to be diminishing—to believe that using technology is good, period. A teacher may display slides using a computer instead of using an old-fashioned technology like writing on a chalkboard. Slides can be helpful, especially when lecturing to a large group. But using computerized slides is not where one expects digital technology to pay off in schools. Many critics of educational technology highlight such cases to demonstrate impoverished thinking about technology making a difference in schools. If that were all that were happening, they would be right to be skeptical. There are much more effective ways to use digital technologies than showing slides with a computer.

Music

To illustrate the surprising extent to which digital technology has implications for teaching and learning, consider music education. Digital music is pervasive, from the music CDs that have replaced phonograph records and tapes, to iPods and other MP3 players, to the MIDI keyboards that can be made to sound like pianos, organs, or dozens of other instruments. Schools are teaching students to compose, play, and mix music using computer software. Composing music used to be beyond most people's capabilities; now it's far easier, and software exists that will put into musical notation whatever a student plays on a keyboard. Music composition has even been taught successfully over the Internet, by having students exchange MIDI files with their teacher and classmates.[31]

There are many useful music websites on the Internet, including archives providing free access to thousands of pieces of classical music, as well as some websites created specifically for students (e.g., http://www.thsmusic.net/tech.htm, developed at a high school in Connecticut). Using eJamming, a software product, musicians in different locations can play together over the Internet. With other software applications, students can take music lessons on the Internet, or practice playing their instrument as part of a simulated band or orchestra.[32]

However, No Child Left Behind has accelerated the declining enrollments in music and many other subjects because student achievement outside a few subjects doesn't count in calculating schools' "adequate yearly progress" under the law. In California, as an example, the number of students taking music declined from 1.1 million to 589,000 between 1999 and 2004.[33]

ONLINE COURSES AND VIRTUAL SCHOOLS

Whatever the subject, students cannot achieve at high levels in courses not available to them. Online schools that deliver entire courses through the Internet are providing new options to students including, in some cases, replacing brick-and-mortar schools entirely. However, most virtual schools primarily serve students who are enrolled in regular schools but who also take an online course.[34]

Among the most frequent reasons students sign up for an online course is that the course is not available at their local high school. There are thousands of regular high schools that do not offer Advanced Placement (AP) courses, for instance. AP provides opportunities for high school students to take college-level courses and, if students do well on an AP test, many colleges award college credit. Enrollments in online AP courses are surging, and what data exist suggest that students taking on-line AP courses may do *better* than those who take them face-to-face.[35] Virtual schools provide a way for students to enroll in a wide variety of courses that meet their needs and that are aligned to local, state, and national education goals.

In only a decade, half of the states have created their own virtual high schools (e.g., Florida Virtual School, Illinois Virtual High School).[36] K–12 student enrollment in distance education (primarily online learning) is estimated at about 1 million "seats" (not separate students) and is growing quickly.[37] Thin-enrollment courses, such as AP courses that may not be justified at some schools because of low enrollments, and courses for whom qualified instructors are in short supply, are now widely available through virtual schools and programs, thus allowing students to "increase achievement" in these courses. A recent national survey found that in nearly 60 percent of school districts, at least one student in the district had taken an online course in 2005–2006, and nearly 25 percent of the remaining districts expected to have students enrolled in online courses in the future.[38] There were more than 45,000 distance education enrollments in Advanced Placement or college-level classes in 2005–2006, and the number has undoubtedly increased a great deal since then because the fastest-growing area of distance education in public schools is Internet-based courses, and many online schools offer Advanced Placement.

Teachers of online courses are typically people who are qualified in their subject area and have been specially trained to teach using this new medium. Although the online courses make use of computers for communicating and for storing information, computers are not doing the teaching.

Virtual schools have unique benefits for homebound students, and some online schools (including "cyber charter schools") cater to students who are homeschooled. In 2005, thousands of seats in online courses were made available to students displaced from their regular schools by hurricanes Katrina and Rita, demonstrating another advantage to providing virtual alternatives to face-to-face courses. After Katrina, one Louisiana participant in an online course for teachers wrote:

> As a teacher and administrator, I have been interested in integrating technology into both instruction and administration. I feel like the sky is the limit and hope one day every child in the New Orleans Public Schools will be given a laptop, read their assignments and books online. And when

the next big one comes and we are scattered across the country, we can still work online and switch to a virtual campus. It is a vision I think that can become a reality.

For most participants in online schooling, the vision is a less apocalyptic one, namely to expand access to a wide variety of high-quality courses. To better understand this vision, let's briefly examine one online course.

An Online English Course

Martha Easton [a pseudonym], a talented English teacher, was teaching a course in an online high school in 1999. At that early point in the brief history of online education, when it was especially important to monitor course quality, two independent evaluators were contracted to review her course, as well as a number of other online English courses. They had a whole semester's records to examine, including all the discourse among students and teacher, which had occurred as written, online communications. After a thorough review, the expert evaluators concluded:

> This course presents a wonderful learning opportunity for students to study important works in a supportive environment in which they were challenged to apply skills of analysis, creativity, reflection, and abstraction . . . The instructor showed exemplary skill as a teacher [including] personal scholarship and expertise . . . Her love of content, enthusiasm for teaching it, and concern for all students shine through the virtual environment . . . [the course] was creatively designed and taught by the dedicated and readily accessible online teacher. Bravo![39]

The remarkable way Ms. Easton had of understanding and responding to her students was perhaps best illustrated when she noticed that one of the students in her online class did not seem to be well. It turned out that he was severely depressed. Ms. Easton intervened and assisted in getting help for the student. The incident is a testament to this teacher's passion for forging relationships with her students, and the fact that their contact occurred through the Internet vividly illustrates what a student in another online course said: "This is definitely *not* impersonal."

Students taking an online course use a computer to access the course through the Internet. Using a normal Web browser, the students in Ms. Easton's class were able to see and use four online components of the course: the *Schedule*, where class assignments are posted; the *Media Room*, where print documents, as well as links to photographs, video, or other types of media, are stored; the *Course Room*, where the teacher and students interact in written "postings" which are persistent, so they can be accessed at any time; and the *Profiles*, where brief descriptions of all participants are found. Students use a mouse and the keyboard to move around within the course, participate in online class discussions, submit homework assignments, and otherwise take part in the class. (Although different online course-delivery systems, such as Blackboard, eCollege, and Moodle, have different components, they all support the basic features of online courses.)

As in a face-to-face class, much of the work is done outside the classroom, including reading assigned books, taking notes, preparing homework, and studying for quizzes and exams. And, as in a face-to-face class, the quality of an online course depends on many factors, including the teacher, the curriculum, the way that grades are assigned, and the interactions that take place between teacher and students, and among the students themselves.

Online Course Quality

How good are online courses? As just suggested, the answer will depend on many factors, just as with face-to-face courses. The same classroom and subject matter experts who reviewed Ms. Easton's course reviewed a dozen online high school courses in English and language arts, history and social sciences, mathematics and science. Although they had been unfamiliar with online education when they began their review, they were impressed with what they found, writing that:

> Overall, the quality of the courses reviewed was quite high. In our experience, these netcourses compare favorably to similar high-quality courses being delivered through other means.[40]

An analysis of more than a dozen studies of online education for elementary and secondary schools found "no significant difference in performance between students who participated in online programs and those who were taught in face-to-face classrooms."[41] As Internet-based technology improves, a greater variety of online courses is offered. One recent three-year study of a West Virginia program to offer Spanish in middle schools (where qualified Spanish teachers are often unavailable) found that students in the program learned Spanish, had positive attitudes about their experience, and did as well in future Spanish courses as students taught face-to-face.[42] The online students learned to speak Spanish as well as read it and, if anything, had *better* pronunciation.

Online courses are not for every student, however, and dropout rates for online courses are often higher than for face-to-face courses. Students must have sufficient self-discipline to log on regularly and keep up with the assigned work, even though there is rarely any face-to-face interaction with the online teacher. There may be a coordinator of online learning at the local school to work with students if they fall behind, or the distant teacher may telephone. The exact approach used depends on the virtual school. There is more than one approach to organizing online learning in a school, just as there is more than one type of brick-and-mortar school.

Models of Online Education

At one end of the spectrum are full-fledged schools designed so that a student can complete their education entirely online. For the high school, then, that program's goal is student graduation. At the other end of the spectrum is a set of online activities that are used entirely to support face-to-face classes. The most common example involves students in traditional science classes sharing data online, with other students, which they have collected about their local environments, so all the data can be aggregated and studied in the classroom. Such sharing provides a great deal more data (about acid rain, for example) that can cover a larger geographical area than would be possible without the online component to the course. The Maryland Virtual High School project funded by the National Science Foundation supports such sharing. At the elementary school level is the GLOBE program (Global Learning and Observations to Benefit the Environment, www.globe.gov), funded by NASA and the National Science Foundation.

Both the Florida Virtual School and the Virtual High School, two of the oldest and largest online schools, fall in the middle of the spectrum, offering full online courses that students take primarily to supplement the offerings of their traditional high school.

Many online programs offer their courses on a schedule. All students start the course on a specified date, and the course follows a calendar that's similar to the brick-and-mortar school calendar, although students can log on to the online course at any time of the day or night. That arrangement works very nicely for students who are taking online courses in conjunction with face-to-face courses.

Florida Virtual School uses a more flexible calendar, which they emphasize with their tagline: *"any time, any place, any path, any pace."*™ Nonetheless, most students adopt the school's normal academic calendar and progress through courses on the same schedule with their online peers. This more-flexible model provides for open entry and exit, and means that students need not wait until the start of the school year to begin online courses. If they are motivated, they can move through a course and complete their assignments more quickly than their peers. This model also provides for the student who needs more time, whether that's because they have distractions, medical issues, or other personal issues that interfere with completing course work; it also means that they aren't punished for taking more time to complete their course work, and are still able to get credit for it. On the other hand, in courses that stick to a specified calendar, students will have more online peers in the same class with whom they interact, just as in a face-to-face classroom.

As noted above, just because a course is offered online doesn't mean all the student work takes place online. Online course materials vary greatly depending on the particular course. Some courses use textbooks and teachers assign readings in those books. Students would expect to read a number of books in a literature course, probably all in print form. In the Virtual High School physics course, every student was sent a box with the materials they would need to conduct simple, safe lab experiments that were the primary learning activities in the course. Florida Virtual School even includes physical education in its course offerings. The students join formal sport or exercise programs in their area and are granted course credit when they (or their parents or guardians) provide proof of completion of the activities. Advocates of "online" physical education courses note that they can connect students to community activities that lead to lifelong physical activity.

A growing number of teachers are experimenting with blogs (Web logs) and other online additions to regular, face-to-face courses, and these are sometimes included in the eLearning category. Such additions shouldn't be considered online courses, but because they are part of traditional classes, they will be among the fastest-growing uses of online learning. (Chapter 4 includes further discussion of blogs as ways to better engage students and extend their learning outside the school.)

These are not the only variants of online courses and online schools, but it is not feasible to describe all of them; entire books have been written on the subject.[43] If your school system allows students to enroll in online courses, you should do research to find out just what that means—for example, whether students receive full course credit, and what other students have experienced.

Purposes of Online Education

The purposes of online schools vary. In California, for example, the University of California College Prep (UCCP) program began by focusing on the state's neediest high schools, an unusual focus for virtual schools. The UCCP program (www.uccp.org) "was created in 1999 to equalize access to college preparatory courses and materials by providing students and schools with curricula that may not be available otherwise."

Tens of thousands of highly able high school students are benefiting from the opportunity to take online courses directly from colleges and universities. And at least one online school, at Stanford University, was created especially to serve gifted students.

The Kentucky Virtual High School (www.kvhs.org) "offers a range of online or eLearning services to help schools meet their goals for High Student Performance, High Quality Teaching, and a Strong and Supportive Environment for Every Child." The school's website notes that KVHS offers "equal access to expanded learning options, flexible scheduling, and an engaging learning environment that differs from the traditional classroom setting."

Online learning can work for students of all abilities, depending on whether they are motivated, and also on the nature of the online course. Kentucky's reference to flexible scheduling means that virtual courses can appeal to students whose regular schedule is already very full or to students who do not do well in a regular school environment. The Southern Regional Education Board, representing 16 member states, notes that one important function of Web-based courses is to help students who need to retake courses to meet high school graduation requirements.[44]

The Western Pennsylvania Cyber Charter School (www.wpccs.com) caters, in part, to students in the latter category, noting that it "is dedicated to the success of all students who have not had their needs met in a traditional educational setting." However, the largest enrollment in cyber charter schools is comprised of students who previously were homeschooled. As the Pennsylvania school's website says, "Welcome to the Pennsylvania Cyber Charter School, where we help families build their school out of choices, not bricks." In some states, including Pennsylvania, cyber charter schools draw funds from regular public schools.[45] For that and other reasons they have been controversial, and there have been lawsuits challenging the schools. Pennsylvania tightened up its oversight of cyber charter schools after a number of abuses came to light.

Participants

Ideally, most online courses should be designed with the expectation that a diverse student population can be successful in the online environment. Programs designed with that expectation are successful serving a wide variety of students. The stories from online programs telling of the success of former and potential high school dropouts have prompted a growth in online alternative school programs. Special education students, too, can benefit from online courses. Online courses allow students who need more time to process information not to stand out; instead, they're treated as peers. Students with severe physical disabilities can participate in online courses with appropriate adaptations without other students recognizing their physical disabilities.

Some policymakers view experience in online classes in high schools as a way to prepare young people for a future in which they will need to use the Internet in their personal lives, their education, and at work. A great many colleges and universities already offer online bachelor's and graduate degree programs, and the for-profit University of Phoenix is now one of the country's largest universities, offering both undergraduate and graduate programs that are 100 percent online. MIT provides its course materials free on the Web for students and educators worldwide (ocw.mit.edu).

It was with these ideas in mind that in 2006, Michigan became the first state to require online course work as a graduation requirement.[46] To fulfill the requirement, schools and teachers can provide students access to entire online courses, or they can add online components to existing course work. According to Michigan's state superintendent of public instruction,

> The importance of requiring all students to take an online course today can be compared to the efforts to teach young people how to use print resources in a public library 50 years ago.

Dozens of states and thousands of school districts that would not go so far as requiring online learning nonetheless see the value of making these new kinds of options widely available to students. Situated within the context of public schools, virtual schools do not necessarily challenge many common assumptions about schooling (there are still courses, teachers, graduation requirements, and standardized tests), but they *do* overturn other assumptions, including the age-old idea that students in a class meet together at the same time in a physical location called "school." For a virtual class, students and the teacher can be located thousands of miles apart, participate at any time of day or night, and need not be online at the same time in order to take place in class discussions.

Online Course Standards

There are no national standards for online learning or virtual schools (although the American Federation of Teachers has drafted "Guidelines for Good Practice" and the Institute for Higher Education Policy wrote "Benchmarks for Success in Internet-Based Distance Education"), and there are not yet any certification requirements for online teachers. Individual programs have established their own standards for course design and delivery. Many online programs also conduct their own online teacher training programs to prepare teachers for the online environment. In considering a virtual school, it is important to review their standards. If there is a teacher (note that in some online schools, such as K[12] Inc., parents are the intended teacher), training to use the online medium well is essential.

High-quality virtual schools work because they've approached education and learning assuming that the online medium requires a different perspective. These schools did not start simply by putting the teacher's lecture notes, slide presentations, and assignments from a face-to-face course on the Web. Good online courses need to be built with the knowledge that online instruction requires a different approach than face-to-face instruction. Teachers cannot lecture, for one thing, and the teacher's skill in promoting and moderating online discussion is a key ingredient in many virtual courses.

USING TECHNOLOGY TO LEARN HOW TO LEARN

Whether in online or face-to-face courses, "increasing student achievement" too often means raising test scores. However, the chairman of the board at Motorola wrote that the most critical skill required by the workforce is "an ability to learn and keep learning."[47] Yet there are no tests of "learning how to learn," nor is that ability among the standards by which students and schools are judged. Fortunately, the Internet is such an information-rich and dynamic environment that teachers who help students use it appropriately *will* help them to "learn how to learn."

For at least the past century we have lived in an exponentially increasing sea of information. Suddenly the Internet has changed our feelings about and our relationships with this ocean of information as profoundly as the first space-based photographs changed our perceptions of the earth. Anyone who has spent a few hours searching for information online is stunned at the vast resources to be found there. But at the same historical moment that millions of people have personally experienced "information overload" in this visceral way, the astounding capabilities of search engines have provided us with more powerful tools than ever before with which to find, sort, sift, analyze, and make sense of this information and knowledge. As a result, knowledge and information are so much more accessible than in the pre-Internet era that society will never again use information resources in the same way.

Schools owe it to students to use the Internet and other digital technology as one key method for "learning how to learn." More than ever, students must appreciate, in a disciplined way, that almost every significant body of knowledge is changing quickly, including information about basic science, medicine, foreign affairs, environmental science, energy production, space exploration, and cognitive sciences. To a greater extent than ever before, students must learn how to sail on and navigate the vast sea of information—resources that are suddenly available at the touch of a button to every man, woman, and child—in ways that will contribute to their personal success, the well-being of communities and nations, and even the survival of the species. It is hard to imagine how that can be done nearly as well without technology.

DISCUSSION

This chapter presents evidence that technology contributes to increasing student achievement in at least three ways. First, technology provides tools for teaching, learning, and increasing achievement in regular classrooms. In addition, technology has given us a new option for students to learn through online courses and schools. Finally, using technology has become an essential part of the "new basic skills," notably as part of the critical ability to "learn how to learn." In none of these three respects should gauging student achievement be limited to analyzing test scores.

Digital technology is not the "one right answer" to the question of how to increase student achievement. The point is that many policymakers—governors, chief state school officers, and others—realize that it is an essential *part* of the answer. This chapter identifies a few of the ways that technology is used to increase achievement, and the number of possibilities is increasing. Additional examples are found throughout the book.

We could use more research to support claims that technology increases student achievement—just as we could use more research about textbooks, teacher quality, and instructional practices unrelated to technology. Education research is not well funded.

Nonetheless, most people, including many of the responsible skeptics, agree that computers and other digital technologies *can* and often do help increase student achievement. The important questions are *when* to use technology and *how* to use it effectively, including how to encourage teachers not simply to automate existing teaching practices, but instead to incorporate better instructional approaches made possible by technology.[48]

One of the keys to increasing learning is to better engage students. Virtual field trips, online discussions with experts outside school, and many other technology applications can lead to higher achievement because students become more highly motivated and engaged with learning. We turn to that topic in the next chapter.

CHAPTER 4

Making Schools More Engaging and Relevant (Goal 2)

On September 11, 2001, students in a grade 4–8 public school in Harlem had a firsthand view of the World Trade Center as the twin towers collapsed. Like students all over the world, children at the Mott Hall School had many questions about what had happened. For example, did most or all people in Islamic countries harbor such hatred for Americans? What were their peers in these countries really like?

Students at Mott Hall were fortunate to be located in a school that provides every student with a laptop computer. The computers are like textbooks, loaned to the students for use throughout the year. Using their laptops, which are wirelessly connected to the Internet, sixth graders at Mott Hall were able to e-mail students in Egypt as part of the American "Friendship Through Education" initiative, begun soon after the events of 9/11, which connects students with their counterparts in predominantly Muslim countries. One student in Egypt wrote, "I am Amr from Egypt. . . . I want to change the ideas of many people who think that Arabs and Muslims are terrorists." Students exchanged descriptions of games they like to play, as well as other kinds of information that helped put a human face on a nation thousands of miles away.[1]

In another popular activity at Mott Hall that uses the laptops, sixth graders lowered temperature probes into a beaker full of hot water and intently watched a computer screen as the graph of the water's temperature changed while a chip of ice gradually melted. Students recorded details of the science lab on a procedure sheet. Students were engaged in a science unit lasting several days that focused on the heat of fusion, the amount of heat required to melt a solid substance. Science teachers at the school were able to use a variety of probes connected to computers to provide students with easy access to real-world data.[2] Graphs that change in real time in response to the data collected by probes are compelling to students and provide a visual representation that can be saved, analyzed, and compared with graphs created by other students.

These two examples highlight some of the exciting instruction available to students when each one has a computer to use on a routine basis. Programs that provide computers for all students provide a powerful example of how schools use technology to give students more responsibility, to access wonderful resources for learning, and to use the same type of modern tool that they will use as adults.

Computers connected to the Internet provide students with the most flexible "toolkit" for learning ever made—apart from teachers and the human brain itself. It is easy to see why providing every student with a computer increases students' engagement in school, including higher attendance, as many studies show.[3] Engaging students is essential for teachers because "attending to affective issues when considering students' needs is an integral component of instruction, and it can increase teaching effectiveness significantly."[4] Doing a better job of engaging students in schoolwork is essential to reduce high school dropout rates and improve student achievement.

It would be impossible to describe all the ways that using digital technologies is highly engaging to students. But in addition to programs that provide every student with a computer, this chapter highlights three other uses of technology that are making the curriculum more relevant and engaging students: blogs and social networks; Cisco Networking Academies; and educational games.

LAPTOP PROGRAMS

In 2005, at least 100,000 students had access to a school-issued personal computer throughout the academic year, and that number was expected to grow quickly. Sure enough, in 2006 the governor of Pennsylvania announced a high school laptop program for the state.[5] In addition, more than half of all schools own laptops for students to use,[6] including laptops on movable carts, which allow teachers to provide class sets of computers to students for shorter periods of time.[7] By one estimate as many as one-quarter of all school districts are planning 1-to-1 laptop programs.[8]

Good teachers have always talked about having a large and flexible toolkit so that they could use the right instructional approach for a particular class or student. In the examples above, the laptops acted as communication devices and as scientific instruments. Additional examples below and elsewhere in the book illustrate many of the other tools that computers become.

Laptop Programs Are Proliferating

Perhaps the best-known laptop program in the world is the one that began in Maine in 2001. Over a period of two years, all 34,000-plus middle school students and teachers in Maine were given a laptop to use during the academic year, with wireless connections to the Internet provided in each school. About one-third of the high schools have also begun laptop programs, and the state is interested in expanding its program to other high schools. Similarly, more than 25,000 students in grades 6–12 in Henrico County, Virginia (greater Richmond), use personal computers provided by the district. Significantly, each of these programs has survived political transitions from the administration that began the initiative to a successor. In Maine, for example, two successive governors have been key proponents of the laptop program.

Both Maine and Henrico County have economic resources that are lower than average. Each of these long-lived programs demonstrates that providing a computer for every student is feasible even in places that are not wealthy. Being successful with such ubiquitous, or 1-to-1 programs (the name for programs with one computer for each student), is partly a question of setting priorities. Henrico County, for example, sets aside a small percentage of its operating budget each year to sustain the initiative.

While the programs in Maine and Henrico County were the largest in the country as of 2007, interest in this innovation is growing quickly. Illinois, Indiana, Massachusetts, Michigan, New Hampshire, New Mexico, Pennsylvania, Vermont, and Texas are already making investments in 1-to-1 computing, as are hundreds of individual schools and districts.[9] The decreasing costs of laptops and wireless networks increase schools' interest in 1-to-1 computing.

Policymakers are interested in 1-to-1 computing for several reasons. One is economic competitiveness. The former governor of Maine, Angus King, who started the state's laptop program, said:

> For more than 100 years, Maine has always been in the bottom third of states—in prosperity, income, education, and opportunity for our kids. In my 30 years of working on Maine economic issues, no idea has had as much potential for leapfrogging the other states and putting Maine in a position of national leadership as this one—giving our students portable, Internet-ready computers as a basic tool for learning.

Equity concerns are another reason for policymakers' interest. For instance, Mark Edwards, who was the school superintendent when Henrico County began its laptop program, was concerned about the inequitable distribution of computers and access to information between student "haves" and "have-nots" (as was Angus King in Maine). As a result of the Henrico laptop program, thousands of students in the county who did not have easy access to computers, the World Wide Web, and other digital resources now have such access. The NAACP publicly supported the program before the school board because it helps provide computers to families who otherwise would not have them. And because students can take the computers home, they can use them for homework assignments. Other reasons cited by policymakers for implementing 1-to-1 computing are to improve teaching and learning, increase student achievement, and prepare students for the future.

Uses of Laptops

Teachers use the laptops in many ways. One high school biology teacher in Henrico County described how students do online research on infectious diseases and then create pamphlets about those diseases using a word processor. She said that this assignment allows students to use their creativity while also learning important biology content, and she commented that the student brochures are better than any she had seen in a doctor's office.[10]

Such project-based learning is particularly well suited to schools with laptop programs, because so many resources are available to students online. (The term "project-based learning" is used for activities that are long-term, student-centered, integrated with real-world issues and practices, and that are often interdisciplinary.) For example, eight schools in the San Lorenzo Unified School District in California—five elementary schools, one middle school, and two high schools—use laptops for project-based learning. Another laptop program called Tech-Know-Build, which serves thousands of middle school students in both Indianapolis and Crawfordsville, Indiana, is also entirely focused on project-based learning. The academic technology officer in Indianapolis said of the program:

> We have a list that we call the "attributes of an Indianapolis Public School graduate," which is essentially the things we should see in a high school graduate. A lot of what we say our graduates should have—communication and presentation skills, higher-order problem solving, and so forth— we're seeing in the sixth and seventh graders who've been using the iBooks. They're doing things we never thought of. For example, you might think kids would never care to look at an encyclopedia. But we have World Book on the iBook laptops, and some kids know every nook and cranny of that program![11]

Laptops facilitate the use of research projects by students. As one teacher in Maine said:

> The laptops have been an incredible teaching and learning tool. It's like having an interactive textbook that never becomes obsolete. Students have produced quality work that taps into higher level thinking, such as analyzing, comparing, contrasting, evaluating, and integrating.[12]

Laptops are also used for more-traditional and highly structured activities. For instance, sixth graders in Henrico County do an online review of a geometry unit in a format called Rags to Riches, in which the students could win a fictional $1 million prize by answering a series of questions correctly (a format based loosely on a popular television program). The students—many of whom had failed their required state mathematics tests while they were fifth graders—worked intently answering questions about geometry throughout the allotted time. The teacher believed that the immediate feedback from the computer was helpful in maintaining students' attention; she said about the laptop program, "It has helped a lot of kids who want to succeed."[13]

Thousands of teachers across the country also use WebQuests, a Web-based format, which offers students a chance to do online research in a more structured environment than by simply using a search engine like Google or netTrekker (a search engine designed for educational use). There are approximately 15,000 WebQuests available, designed for students of all ages, on just about every conceivable topic.[14] Many Web-Quests have been developed by students for their peers—an excellent example of project-based learning.

The sheer amount of computer use increases dramatically when laptops are introduced. An evaluation of a pilot laptop program in New Hampshire reported that, "in many cases, student-reported technology use increased from being almost nonexistent to nearly every day."[15] In the absence of laptop programs, computers in typical schools are often located in a "computer lab" and are much harder for teachers and students to access on a routine basis. In a laptop program, the easy access to word processors is likely to increase the quality and amount of students' writing.[16]

Students' Experiences

Students in laptop programs use the computers for a wide variety of tasks—for class work, homework (in cases where the schools allow the laptops to go home), and for access to the Internet. In Henrico County, students explained how teachers' supplemental notes, provided in virtual folders on the school network, as well as online tutorials, were helpful methods of reviewing a lesson at home when they needed additional help. (All students in Henrico County's laptop program are allowed to take the laptops home, while about half of the districts in Maine permit this practice.)

Both Henrico County and the state of Maine provide students with access to vast amounts of proprietary information. For example, Henrico County licenses websites, such as BeyondBooks.com and united-streaming.com, providing teachers and students with a wide range of print and video content in academic disciplines. Similarly, thousands of magazines, newspapers, and reference books are available anywhere in Maine through the online resources of MARVEL!, Maine's Virtual Library (libraries.maine.edu/mainedatabases/).

Nearly a dozen states have laws or regulations requiring public schools to offer students virtual dissection as an alternative to dissecting real animals. Animal protection groups have lobbied against dissection and many students have decided that dissecting animals is not for them. Companies such as Biolab, Digital Frog, and DryLab offer dissection software. Henrico County used FrogGuts.com.

Many Henrico County students, especially in high schools, reported in focus groups that they often used their iBooks for non-school-related activities. One student described how her job required her to type, input data, and update her office's website. Having worked with many of these same software programs on her iBook, she found that she was able to transfer what she had learned in school to her job.

In Henrico County, students and parents alike described how obtaining information online about colleges and financial aid facilitated the college application process. An increasing number of colleges are requiring that applications be submitted online.

Teachers in middle and high schools often look at laptop programs through the lens of their own discipline. Physics teachers, for example, might be interested in physics applets that can be used by students, such as those at lectureonline.cl.msu.edu/~mmp/applist/applets.htm, where you can experiment with simple machines, wave phenomena, quantum physics, and many other topics.

On the other hand, students, who typically study in five or six classes at a time, view the laptops in a broader perspective than any single subject. The laptops are a good thing, one middle school student said, "because we can look things up, and we don't have to carry a lot of books around." A high school student said, "I think with having to use a computer in college, I am a lot more prepared." The parent of a high school student said, "I have seen a boost in self-confidence. By that, I mean confidence in the ability to problem-solve, complete tasks, to retrieve data that he knows he needs."

Many of the students, parents, and teachers interviewed in Henrico County (as well as in other locations with laptop programs) agreed that the use of laptops helped students to be more organized. They said that the overall structure and design of the iBooks provided a consistent way for students to keep track of their activities, assignments, and notes, regardless of class or teacher. In particular, the use of virtual shared folders on the school network offered teachers an easy way to provide notes and assignments, reducing the likelihood that students would be unable to work because of lost papers. Students could create folders for each class and arrange their work systematically. As one student said, and others agreed, "What I like is that you can't lose your homework. Also, a notebook can get out of order sometimes. But on the computer you can make a folder for, like, Rome, or the other topics." At the same time, some teachers found that the laptops did not replace paper when used with special needs students, who may have difficulties with organization. For example, one teacher reported that parents of special education students sometimes wanted their children to have a hard copy of every document, regardless of whether or not it was available online.

When considering how laptops affect the level of interaction between teachers and students, the picture is more complicated. Many teachers and students report *more* interactions because of the computer. "Kids are much more willing to ask me individual questions than ever before, and I've been doing this a long time," one teacher said. Another teacher reported that the laptops opened up a channel for additional discussions with her students about course-related content. Similarly, students indicated that they visited teachers' websites or e-mailed teachers with questions. In this way, "teachers are more available to you," one student said. Other students, however, believed that the level of interaction decreased because the laptop gave them opportunities to work independently of their teachers. In answer to the question about how instruction had changed because of the laptops, one student responded: "We do more independent work because everyone has an iBook. In the computer lab, we had to buddy up and do it. We don't interact with the teacher as much because we go on a website and they tell you what to do." Another student in the same focus group said, "The teacher does a little less teaching because the website says exactly how to do it. It's good and bad because the teacher doesn't hassle you as much, but you may not understand."[17]

Teachers' Experiences

Many teachers believe that the use of laptops allows for more engaging activities. One Henrico County teacher said, "It's making us think about what makes things interesting for kids, and instead of just memorizing a bunch of facts, we're learning there are better ways to teach them and they really retain the concept." An algebra teacher, speaking about teaching mathematical functions, was more specific, saying, "by using graphing calculators, using the Internet, and other [computer] resources, you can make it dynamic, showing how changing this one number affects the graph. You can make it more of an exploratory activity where students develop their own thought processes and hopefully retain it better by going through it in that manner." A teacher in a Michigan laptop program responded to a survey by saying,

> Last year when I did this program, I had a class of high-risk students. These laptops made the difference in their education. I saw more excitement and willingness to work, and the quality of the work was greatly improved. I had students turning in work early that had, up to this point, never even completed their work. I am excited about using them for the entire year this year and have spent many hours looking for ways to integrate my lessons with the computer. Thank you for this opportunity to enrich my students' education.[18]

In addition to providing access to engaging material, teachers note that the laptops provide more flexibility in the classroom. One teacher said, "The flexibility that having these laptops . . . provides me in the classroom is phenomenal. I'm teaching a lesson and a spreadsheet is something that would be a good idea to do to enhance this lesson; we can pull that out, do a spreadsheet, five minutes, put it away." Contrast this experience with a teacher who needs to reserve a school computer laboratory days or weeks ahead of time, or who must make do with just one or a few classroom computers.

Teachers in Maine are also enthusiastic about laptops. Language arts teachers note that there are many creative ways the computers can be used to teach reading, writing, and literature. One middle school literature teacher had students log on to a website, nicenet.org, where they engaged other students in their class in online discussions about literature. Among the benefits of this approach reported by the teacher was:

> I found that students that were usually quiet in the groups all of a sudden had a voice. They felt that they could add something in writing and share their opinion, which of course had been there all along. It clearly leveled the playing field.[19]

Many teachers appreciate the instantaneous feedback that laptops can provide to students, such as when they use math programs that indicate when an incorrect answer is submitted. The feedback helps the teachers identify and work with students who need extra attention. A teacher reported, "The major impact for me is the fact the child [using the computer] knows [gets feedback], and as a result, if they're getting them wrong, they call me over and I help them. So it's wonderful. It lets me see where the problems are; it lets me address those quickly instead of when they take a test." An increasing number of districts require that teachers use so-called "formative tests" to help identify students in need of help while there is still time to help them, and computers facilitate this process. (See chapter 8 for more information on technology-facilitated formative assessment.) In a 1-to-1 environment, access to computers is not going to be a barrier to the regular use of computer-based formative assessment.

The availability of up-to-date information is another of the benefits of access to the Internet. Many teachers in laptop programs report no longer having to rely on outdated textbooks for answers to their own and students' questions. How many moons do Jupiter and Saturn have? What did the Supreme Court recently decide about government's "taking" of property to use for private development projects? Answers to thousands of questions requiring up-to-date information are now just a few mouse clicks away. Good teachers use the easy availability of information to enrich the curriculum in virtually any subject. And the process of obtaining information quickly and independently provides students with more "ownership" of that information, and a greater incentive to acquire that information.

Large majorities of teachers in all schools, not just those with laptop programs, report that they use computers to enhance their professional productivity in a variety of ways. Laptops simply make this process easier and less place-bound. Teachers use computers to more efficiently design and create materials, prepare lesson plans, diagnose student weaknesses, and communicate with colleagues, parents, and students. In one school, a technology trainer said that lines at the copy machines had disappeared because teachers were storing documents digitally for students. Some schools with laptop programs have streamlined their administrative processes and require teachers to use e-mail and report attendance via the computer.

To make laptop programs work well, teachers must adjust many of their usual practices. Typically, this pressure to change fosters greater sharing and collaboration among teachers. Teachers in the science department in one school said that the laptop program made them a stronger professional community because they were pushed to have frequent conversations with their colleagues. A social studies teacher in a district with a 1-to-1 program said, "We are all in this together," and that attitude led members of the department to share materials and instructional strategies more often.

At the same time, teaching a class of students, each of whom has a laptop, presents teachers with new challenges. Teachers need to develop new lessons that use the laptops; they need to learn to use the computers, the Internet, and software effectively; and they need to advise students about computer use. If students do not bring a working computer to class, teachers often design paper alternatives for students even though they had planned laptop-based lessons. These and other related issues take a good deal of teachers' time. For a minority of teachers, these increased demands are onerous. According to one teacher, "With the need to have both paper and the iBook assignments available, it's twice as much preparation for the teacher."

Also, laptops can complicate classroom management. Laptop batteries may not last the whole day, and may need to be recharged at school. Also, even with Internet filtering software, it is still possible for students to browse Internet sites that are not germane to the lesson, so teachers need to be aware of what students do with the laptops during class. A teacher in Henrico County noted, "Being the iBook 'police' is hard," adding,

You can't look at 28 iBooks at once. Using Remote Access [a software application], the administration of the school might call you during class and say so-and-so [a student] is on an inappropriate website. But if you're teaching at the front of the room, you don't always know who is on which website.

Given these new demands on teachers, it is significant that teachers are generally supportive of laptop programs in places where they have been implemented. For example, more than 70 percent of 3,000-plus teachers surveyed in Maine in 2003 agreed that laptops helped them meet curricular goals more effectively and individualize curricula to better meet students' needs.[20]

Benefits of 1-to-1 Programs

Students, teachers, administrators, and parents in many locations express satisfaction with 1-to-1 programs. In Henrico County, for example, over 80 percent of more than 28,000 respondents to surveys conducted by an outside company were "satisfied" (52 percent) or "somewhat satisfied" (29 percent) with the instructional use of the laptop computers.[21] These are the people who are most affected, and it is Henrico's taxpayers who foot the bill, after all, so such overwhelming support is not just a nice thing to have, it is of great importance.

Writing is one of the areas in which the academic benefits are clearest. A Maine teacher wrote:

Use of the laptops to enhance writing skills for kids has been a great asset for me. Student ability to draft, revise, and edit written work has been greatly expanded with the laptop program.[22]

More rigorous research focused on using computers for writing supports this teacher's observations. In a 1-to-1 initiative that focused special attention on teaching writing using laptops (including teacher professional development and the creation of new curriculum resources), researchers documented gains in student achievement in that domain.[23] And chapter 3 discussed a "meta-analysis" that examined more than two dozen studies of learning to write using computers and concluded that "computers are a valuable tool for helping students develop writing skills."[24]

But students in 1-to-1 programs use the computers in many ways, not just for writing but also to learn many other subjects and skills. When one considers all the possible benefits that laptop programs might provide, what is the bottom line? Saul Rockman, a senior researcher who has studied these programs for years, summarized the research as follows:

> Our findings, and those of other researchers in this area, are reliable, and the conclusions are clear. We consistently find substantive impacts on teaching and learning, on teachers and students, yet we continue to have difficulty tying full-time access to computers to the outcomes of standardized tests currently in use. Our belief is that, while computers are powerful interventions for both students and teachers, what they do with them is not what is tested.[25]

Rockman writes that there is "more project-based learning, increased student motivation and experimentation, and higher rates of peer mentoring."[26] There is also a shift in teachers' roles, with greater collaboration taking place among teachers, and with teachers more often acting as consultants to students than as the source of all knowledge. The quotes from teachers and students in the earlier part of this chapter represent the kinds of experience that are typical in many different places already implementing 1-to-1 computing.

According to a more recent review of dozens of research studies conducted by an independent research organization (SRI International) for Apple Computer:

> The strongest available research-based evidence for the positive effects of laptop programs comes from researchers who analyzed differences between laptop-program students and comparison-group students using objective tests of some kind. Notably, researchers obtained these results relatively early in the implementation of the programs (within the first three years of the program). Positive effects from these studies include increased technology use, increased technology literacy, and improved writing.[27]

Although it would be wonderful to have even stronger evidence of effectiveness, including connections between 1-to-1 programs and higher student test scores, the programs have usually been structured not to focus exclusively on raising scores in particular academic disciplines, but to spread resources across many grades and subjects. Suppose administrators want to raise test scores in algebra; simply providing students with computers may be a good thing, but that is probably not enough. Special software that helps students learn algebra may need to be licensed. Or, teachers could be provided with professional development to help them identify and use specific resources on the Web to teach algebra. Unless there is a plan for how to use the computers to raise algebra scores, it would be surprising if the simple presence of computers were enough to make a difference.

Over time, as more and better digital resources become available to schools, it may be possible to more strongly link 1-to-1 programs with increases in test scores. Chapter 8, for example, discusses the Web-based Assistments project, which aims to help students in Massachusetts raise their state test scores in math, as well as Summary Street, a commercial program that both assesses writing skills and teaches writing. The "treatment" in those cases is not just access to computers; it is the use of a particular, structured software program for so many minutes each month. For researchers interested in examining impacts of technology on test scores, it is a much better bet to do research on programs like these than to study impacts of overall access to computers.

Of course, focusing so much attention on test scores assumes that high-stakes tests are good for students and for schools. That is a debatable proposition, which depends heavily on the quality and nature of the tests themselves. One study reported that teachers who were able to use computers to help students learn to write were less likely to do so because they believed their students would be at a disadvantage taking paper-based state tests. And the same study reported data to show that the teachers are correct: Paper-based tests underestimate the writing skill of students who are used to using a computer to write.[28]

One should not underestimate the value of the benefits of 1-to-1 computing that are hard to quantify, including energizing administrators, teachers, and students. When done well, as in Maine and in Henrico County, 1-to-1 programs absolutely require dispersed leadership, meaning that school principals, department chairs, school technology coordinators, and individual teachers all must play important roles in making the program a success. The feeling of being part of something new and exciting that involves a large team of people is in itself an important result. One hears stories of teachers on the verge of retirement who were so impressed with 1-to-1 computing that they delayed leaving the profession. School leaders can and should use 1-to-1 computing as a means to infuse a powerful vision of schooling—one that involves more active students, more authentic work products, and a more inclusive view of the learning community. Most administrators, teachers, students, and parents will see and appreciate the importance of such a vision, especially as they gain experience with 1-to-1 computing and overcome any initial anxieties they might have had about providing each student with a computer.

Facilitators and Challenges

Successful implementation of 1-to-1 programs requires more than hardware; it requires a series of actions and investments, beginning with good leadership. Visionary leaders, such as Governor King and Superintendent Edwards, help to set the agenda, but are well aware that others must play key roles. Indeed, that foresight and their understanding of teamwork is one of the reasons they were successful. In Henrico County, for example, teachers report that there has been a lot of administrative support, both in the central office and in local schools, including allocating resources for professional development to help teachers integrate laptops into instruction. Technical support is strong, and includes a cadre of technology support technicians able to fix most hardware and network problems.

At the same time, any serious educational innovation encounters challenges. Some of the challenges facing laptop programs have already been identified, including the limited battery life of current laptops, the additional work by teachers required to integrate computers into instruction in productive ways, and the need to monitor and regulate students' uses of the machines.

Cost is another potential barrier, and the price of buying and maintaining tens or hundreds of thousands of computers slows the spread of 1-to-1 programs to more states and districts. Even as prices of computing devices fall, people recognize that there are other costs, too, such as software, maintenance and technical support, and professional development. There will be some offsetting cost savings; fewer dictionaries, maps, encyclopedias, and even textbooks may be needed, for example. Costs are discussed further in chapter 10.

Despite these challenges, surveys show widespread support for laptop programs. In Henrico County, as previously noted, an independent research firm concluded that each of the several groups surveyed—parents, administrators, teachers, and students—supported the district's laptop program.[29] In Maine, two successive governors and two legislatures have supported the program.

Handheld Computers

It turns out that 1-to-1 laptop programs have captured the imagination of many more policymakers than 1-to-1 handheld computer programs, probably because laptops, particularly those with wireless Internet access, can help students make use of so many more resources and because laptops come with keyboards, as well as larger screens than handhelds. Nonetheless, there are schools with 1-to-1 programs that use handheld computers, which typically run the Palm or Windows CE operating systems. Proponents of handheld programs point out that the devices are both cheaper and more portable than laptops, as well as being very flexible (although adding a keyboard adds to the expense and inhibits mobility). Just as there is a growing literature about laptop programs, there is also an increasing amount of guidance available about using handheld computers with students. One of the more comprehensive sources of information is a book written by Carolyn Staudt, one of my colleagues at the Concord Consortium, called *Changing How We Teach and Learn with Handheld Computers.*[30] The book discusses applications of handhelds across the curriculum, and includes detailed lesson plans.

Hybrid Computers

Vendors have also developed hybrid products that combine features of handhelds and laptops. For example, AlphaSmart makes computers that come with a full keyboard but that are based on simpler operating systems than Windows or Apple OS. Some of these machines are able to run thousands of software titles, just like a Palm, and boot up almost instantly. Their screens are smaller than those of laptop computers and are black-and-white, not color.

AlphaSmart computers have the capability to beam information from one machine to another, and some of the devices also include wireless network connectivity for accessing the Internet. The machines are lighter than typical laptops and are built to be very rugged. According to news reports, more than a million AlphaSmart devices are used in American schools. The top-of-the-line Dana, based on the Palm operating system, sells for about $350 (mid-2007), making it more affordable than laptops—but laptop prices keep dropping, and new devices are being developed.

Further Innovation

As pointed out in chapter 1, the nature of electronic devices—not only computers, but cell phones, music players, calculators, and other digital machines—is changing rapidly, making it difficult to predict what technology in the schools will look like in the future. Several years ago, the cover of *Scientific American* showed a conception of one futuristic device, which combines a cell phone with a computer in a small, handheld package that has a flexible, paper-like, retractable screen.[31] Such a device would combine the portability of today's handheld computers and cell phones with the computing power and larger screens of laptops.

One intriguing possibility is the development of additional computing devices that are designed especially for educational settings. Graphing calculators already fit that description, and millions of them are used in schools; however, they are used almost exclusively for advanced mathematics and science courses, not for more general purposes.

In the United States, Project Inkwell (www.projectinkwell.com) has developed standards for general-purpose computing devices especially suited for use in schools. They hope that this will help improve the match between what vendors offer and what schools need. Nearly all current general-purpose computing devices are developed more for business users than for students and teachers.

Nicholas Negroponte, a visionary at the Massachusetts Institute of Technology, designed a laptop computer for education, especially to be used in developing nations, which he plans to sell, without profit, for only $100 to $200.[32] The device is designed to be very rugged, so that it can withstand constant handling by young people. The screen folds more than one way, so that the device can be used either as a laptop or as a slate on which text can be read. The display is also dual-purpose, so it can either be in color or in high-contrast black-and-white, the latter providing for better display of eBooks and other print documents and for use outdoors in bright light. The new laptop uses an open-source operating system, based on Linux, partly as a way to keep costs down. Intel has also developed a low-cost computer, the Classmate, especially for developing countries.

Assuming these kinds of computers are sold at low prices, there will almost certainly be wide interest in using them. Thailand has announced a plan to provide all primary school students with laptop computers.

Many other developing nations may also be interested in 1-to-1 computing, and there will be pressure to make low-cost computers available in developed nations, too. Singapore, a much more wealthy and developed nation than Thailand, has already adopted an ambitious plan for integrating information technology into its schools, because its leaders believe that computers are a key to economic competitiveness.

More and more districts and states in the U.S. are likely to adopt 1-to-1 computing programs. As they do, textbooks and other print media will be more tightly linked with interactive digital materials thoughtfully chosen to be part of the curriculum—animations, movies, demonstrations, tests, maps, historical documents, and so forth. At present, teachers, who have thousands of possibilities to choose from, are typically the ones who select digital materials. Making these choices teacher-by-teacher and resource-by-resource is both inefficient and often less effective than it might be if curriculum developers chose or created digital materials to complement print materials.

There are some efforts to more closely integrate printed textbooks with the Web. SciLinks, a collaboration between the National Science Teachers Association and publishers, is a website providing users with electronic links, vetted by expert teachers, corresponding to the particular page that students are studying in a regular, printed textbook (www.nsta.org/scilinks). These links can be updated periodically, without waiting for new editions of a book to be published. Many textbook publishers also create websites especially for their textbooks, and a few are beginning to sell digital versions of their print textbooks.

Ultimately, textbooks may be digitized, so that they are viewed most often not on paper but on the better, easier-to-read, more paper-like computer screens that are likely to become common. (One vendor is eInk, www.eink.com.) In that case, not only would students' bulky backpacks become much lighter, but the advantages of greater interaction with instructional materials would become routine, instead of the exception. If curriculum developers could assume that students have computers available, they would likely make very different choices about curriculum materials. Students could mark up their textbooks on a laptop screen without damaging them, and would be able to use all sorts of additional resources in the textbook at the click of a mouse, whenever they needed them. Textbooks might come on a chip or memory card and schools could provide students with mobile computers and textbooks in a single device.

However, there is a chicken-and-egg problem in developing digital textbooks. Unless there is a market for them, publishers are loath to invest the millions of dollars it would take to do an excellent job. At the same time, unless such materials exist, fewer schools may find 1-to-1 computing compelling, because it adds to the costs and requirements for the schools. In such a situation, progress may be slow for a while, until a tipping point is reached when there are enough digital instructional resources, or enough computers, or both, so that further progress takes place much more rapidly. People have been writing about the possibility of computer-based textbooks for decades, but it is only now that computers are beginning to be prevalent enough in schools to make what was once a dream seem a realistic scenario.

Another barrier to developing digital textbooks is that state textbook adoption rules and regulations in some cases are inadvertently written in ways that discriminate against electronic materials.[33] For example, in states that require state adoption of textbooks, the reviewers may not be experienced with interactive, digital materials, or with the use of electronic learning resources in the classroom. Also, pricing of textbooks is seldom on a lease or rental basis, which may be a more appropriate economic model for electronic materials, especially if they are frequently updated.

Nonetheless, a few schools are going "all-digital." At an elementary school in the Dallas suburb of Forney, students get computers with thousands of digitized literature books. A public high school in Vail, Arizona, is foregoing print-based textbooks, as is St. James Academy, a Catholic High School in the Kansas City area. Many other schools are sure to follow.

How 1-to-1 Computing Helps Transform Schools

The characteristics of technology identified in chapter 1 are what give 1-to-1 computing its power. In these programs the technology is *pervasive*, *flexible*, and *interactive*. Access to information is *democratized*, and some of the differences between students from wealthy and poor families in accessing information and software tools are reduced. Teachers are able to use the *immediacy* of technology to take advantage of the "teachable moment," instead of scheduling use of a computer lab ahead of time. The *flexible, all-purpose* nature of computers provides students with a great many powerful tools, such as word processors, spreadsheets, dictionaries, thesauruses, e-mail programs, and others. As discussed in chapter 2, these and other characteristics of technology are an excellent match with the needs expressed by many proponents of education reform, such as doing a much better job of engaging students in schoolwork.

Although the number of students per computer in schools has been dropping steadily for years, there is nonetheless a significant increase in the frequency of use of computers once every student has his or her own device. Only then can teachers and curriculum developers make computer use a routine part of instruction. As prices continue to fall, and as more and more policymakers show interest in 1-to-1 computing, it seems inevitable that one day every student will have a computer to use in school. Because the research on 1-to-1 programs in Maine, Henrico County (Virginia), and elsewhere shows largely positive outcomes, continuing growth in the number of 1-to-1 programs in districts and states across the country should be expected.

Is your school or district ready for 1-to-1 computing? For those interested, there are publications that summarize what has been learned about starting 1-to-1 computing programs.[34] There are even teacher blogs (online Web logs) that document individuals' experiences with 1-to-1 programs. In one of them, a teacher in Maine, Kelly Fitz-Randolph, made the case for using e-mail as a learning tool, writing that:

> E-mail is now the tool of choice to get started with. . . . The biggest mistake I've seen with e-mail in schools around the state is when the kids are given their e-mail accounts and the teachers don't use it. To me, this is like giving the kids the keys to the school and all of the teachers going out to lunch. Hmmm, not a bad idea, but can you imagine what that would look like? Scary!!! One of the things I stressed with my teaching team yesterday was the importance of us all using it for educational purposes with kids so they, in turn, will know how to use it appropriately. How do you use it with kids? . . . Some suggestions we discussed were:

> 1. At the end of class have the kids send a quick note on what they learned or need to know. A quick "check in." You then have the e-mail and can quickly respond.

2. It is a great way for kids to share files for cooperative projects they are working on.

3. E-mail is an easy way to return graded work—work that has been passed in digitally and corrected digitally.

4. Have kids who never speak? This is a great way to get information from them and have them share their thoughts with you.

5. Create a folder or discussion group where kids can post ideas and thoughts on particular topics. Maybe have one for asking general questions. I created a "Tech Folder" for the kids when I was at Lyman Moore. Yeah, there were some not so educationally oriented tech tips in there, but a lot of postings were VERY helpful for kids in completing assignments and presentations.

6. How about a quick, "Hey, I'm missing your homework assignment" from you, the teacher, just after you've found a hole or two in your gradebook. It is a great reminder for the student and a quick e-mail for you.

Alas, I could probably go on, but I'll stop for now.[35]

I, too, could extend this exploration of 1-to-1 computing by many pages. Instead, I turn to another technology that is both highly engaging to students and allows them to learn in new ways.

BLOGS AND SOCIAL NETWORKS

The power of the Internet to build new forms of social networks and learning communities is vividly brought home by the experience of the daughter of a colleague at the Concord Consortium. By the end of elementary school she had become quite a capable writer; however, in middle school there was no opportunity to do the long-form fiction she liked to write. When she turned 13, she became a member of the website www. fanfiction.net. The term "fan-fiction" refers to original writing about existing characters in commercially published books. This particular website allows members to read, comment on, and post stories in many different genres.

Over the next seven months she published "Turns of Time," an original story about the manga characters in *InuYasha* (a Japanese story with elements of action, adventure, romantic comedy, and fantasy), consisting of 34 chapters and 75,000 words! Along the way, she developed her own fan base of 25 regular readers, who posted critiques and encouragement. Two months later, she was well into another story, with nine chapters finished, and started outlining the prequel and sequel to "Turns of Time."

This is a very powerful experience for a 13-year-old girl, and one that would be impossible to duplicate at her middle school. There is little or no room in current schools for a project that takes seven months. Also, classes are not usually structured in a way that encourages authentic feedback from interested peers, or members of the public. If the topic of the project were of limited interest to most of the class, then generating this kind of feedback from classmates would be impossible. Yet fanfiction.net is increasingly popular; it has almost 2,000 separate sections, and *InuY-asha*, one of the most popular genres, has almost 50,000 stories posted. And fanfiction.net is hardly the only example one can find of a very active, positive social network that especially appeals to young people.

The Internet makes it possible for students to interact with a much larger community than ever before, including scientists, students in other cities or countries, or their own schoolmates outside of school hours. In this connected world, students are seeking out authentic experience wherever they can find it. Like it or not, students view opportunities offered by schools through different lenses than once used to be the case. Educators with vision, who want to use technology to help create meaningful school experiences, understand the value and strength, not only the dangers, of computers and the Internet. In Liberty, Missouri, an eighth-grade teacher provided 300 students with the opportunity to "blog" (have an online discussion) with the author of a novel about a 15-year-old living in that state during the Civil War. According to one of the students, "I love being able to communicate with the author because it makes me feel like I can ask anything."[36]

Another powerful example is TakingITGlobal.org, which aims to connect youth from all over the world and help them find ways to take action in their local and global communities. Every month, this website has hundreds of thousands of distinct visitors. On one recent visit, more than 500 people were simultaneously online, participating in dozens of online discussions. In addition to discussions, TakingITGlobal.org includes a large number of articles, newsletters, projects, and stories. As an example, in late 2006 the website showcased an upcoming Youth Employment Summit in Kenya, part of the YES campaign, described as "a youth-led response to the enormous challenge of youth unemployment." Many dozens of other events are listed, as well, including opportunities to speak and to write.

States and districts are beginning to take advantage of these opportunities. New Jersey, for example, is teaming with a nonprofit organization, International Education and Resource Network (IEARN), to teach students about other countries and cultures through online collaborations with their peers in thousands of schools around the world.[37]

Schools can create their own technology-enabled social networks, with rules about appropriate and inappropriate postings and limitations on who is able to access the network. One can limit elementary school students' interactions to a safe network of participants, such as peers, teachers, parents, grandparents, and a few others. For example, nicenet. org provides networking tools for schools to use free of charge (and other groups also license these tools), and Intel Corporation supports online communities especially for students and teachers (www.think.com).

But creative teachers do not need any special, school-related websites at all. One fourth-grade teacher whose students read a popular children's book, *Sadako and the Thousand Paper Cranes*, later had the students read online book reviews to learn about that genre. Students were then assigned to write their own brief reviews. After the teacher's critiques, and students' revisions, the reviews were posted at an online bookstore's website.[38] The authentic nature of the assignment—writing for a real and possibly large audience outside of school—is very unusual for elementary school. Such an assignment also models for students appropriate uses of the Internet, both as a source of information and as a way to express oneself constructively. And it reinforces the notion that new media (the Internet) and old media (books) often complement one another.

CISCO NETWORKING ACADEMIES

Students are more engaged when school curricula are relevant and up-to-date. From government to history to science, curricula can now be adapted and updated far more quickly and easily using the Web than by waiting five to seven years for a new set of textbooks to be purchased. Most publishers maintain websites with dozens of links to current information, and national teachers' organizations, such as the National Science Teachers Association, also provide teachers and students with useful online resources.

Technology itself is a subject that can help students become employable, and large numbers of students across the country have taken courses created to teach computer-related skills. More than 2,000 high schools in the U.S. offered Advanced Placement courses in Computer Science in 2005, typically to students who are college bound.

The Cisco Networking Academy, on the other hand, appeals particularly to students who are not college bound but who need the skills to get a decent job. In Philadelphia, for example, thousands of students have successfully completed courses offered as part of the Cisco Networking Academy, learning about topics such as network topologies, IP addressing, Frame Relays, and technologies for local area networks and wide area networks.[39] The Academy offers 16 different courses on a variety of information technology–related topics.

Over the past decade, the Networking Academy program has grown to more than 10,000 Academies in every state and more than 150 countries. Over 400,000 students participate in high schools, colleges, universities, and other educational settings. The program blends traditional, face-to-face teaching with an online curriculum, hands-on lab exercises, and Web-based assessment. "It's had a huge impact. There is not a governor in the 50 states who doesn't know about the Cisco Networking Academy," according to John Morgridge, chairman of the board of Cisco. "I think we've clearly demonstrated the impact and the leverage of using technology in an education and training environment."[40]

The United States clearly needs to do a better job educating students who are not college bound. The Cisco Networking Academy provides one example of how technology can help.

EDUCATIONAL GAMES

By 2004, the sale of computer and video games in the United States reached more than $7 billion annually.[41] The amount spent on video games (about $31 annually per capita) is steadily gaining each year on the amount spent on movie tickets ($41).[42] Currently, few games designed specifically for education are widely used in schools, but there is a growing interest in expanding this genre. Developers of so-called "serious games" hope to capitalize on the popularity of the medium and its capacity to engage people, especially youth, in detailed and compelling scenarios created on the computer.

For simple drill and practice, games like Math Blaster have been popular for many years. But developers have not been content to focus only on helping students learn basic skills such as arithmetic. One popular series of educational games embeds learning more advanced mathematical concepts (including networks, permutations, logic, and binary numbers) in a variety of stories and adventures that use engaging cartoon characters know as the Zoombinis. The Zoombinis series has now sold more than 1 million copies. The games were developed by TERC, a nonprofit organization that specializes in research and development to improve mathematics and science education. Chapter 9 describes the important role of nonprofits in educational technology R&D.

The United Nations developed a free online game called Food Force (www.food-force.com/), which has been downloaded more than 4 million times—a very impressive number even compared to commercially successful video games.[43] Food Force puts users in the position of delivering food to people living in a war zone on the fictitious island of Sheylan and offers a choice of six different "missions." Materials are available online to teachers who want to incorporate Food Force into the curriculum, whether to focus on the causes of hunger, basic facts about nutrition, the role of the UN, or other topics.

A cofounder of the Serbian youth resistance movement that helped to topple Slobodan Milosevic, Ivan Marovic, has also worked on A Force More Powerful, a video game designed to teach principles of nonviolent strategy. Policies of the fictional resistance movement involve dozens of issues, including women's rights, taxes, and voting rights. The positions taken by the resistance movement affect how many people join the cause. The goal is to foment democratic uprisings. However, the game provides many possible obstacles, including getting arrested by the police.

Because many video games are violent, it is especially noteworthy that games like A Force More Powerful and Food Force focus young people's attention on nonviolence and on helping people caught up in war. One father said, "As I've watched three sons grow through some questionable digital gaming experiences . . . I've been waiting for something like [*A Force More Powerful*] to come along."[44]

There are educational games on subjects ranging from biology and immunology to ancient history.[45] In some schools, students are provided with the rudiments of an educational game and are challenged to do additional programming, as part of their computer science class, to make the game work exactly the way they want it to. There are also efforts to adapt or create "massive, multiplayer online role-playing games," which are used by millions of young people, so that they serve educational purposes.[46]

Philanthropic foundations and universities, as well as game developers, are showing a growing interest in applying video-game technology to learning. Corporations, the U.S. military, and government agencies are using "serious games" to meet their needs because they are engaging and can simulate complex situations in ways that paper-and-pencil or other technologies cannot.

CHAPTER 5

Providing a High-Quality Education for All Students (Goal 3)

A president of the United States once defined the ideal college as a brilliant teacher at one end of a log and a student on the other.[1] Public schools, on the other hand, serve tens of millions of students who comprise an astonishingly diverse group (as discussed in chapter 2) and who can only occasionally be given individual attention by their teachers. Contending with the increasing diversity in American schools presents multiple challenges for teachers, including providing individualized education plans and services to millions of students with disabilities; working with students achieving at high, average, and low levels; helping millions of English language learners; and providing compensatory education to economically disadvantaged students.

SPECIAL EDUCATION STUDENTS

By 2003–2004, 14 percent of all students, or more than 6 million young people, were receiving services under IDEA. When we think of someone with a disability we might think of the renowned physicist Stephen Hawking who has won many prestigious scientific awards and has 12

honorary degrees. His accomplishments are all the more remarkable because he is severely disabled. Hawking developed ALS when he was 21
years old and as a result is confined to a wheelchair and cannot speak, at
least not without a computer-synthesized voice. But in fact the most frequent handicapping condition among students is "specific learning disabilities" (43 percent of the total) including dyslexia, perceptual difficulties, and brain injuries. The next largest group (22 percent) has speech
or language impairments.[2] Deaf, blind, and other students whose handicaps are physical, like Hawking's, comprise much smaller groups.

As a group, special education teachers have been enthusiastic users
of computers since they appeared in classrooms decades ago. Schools
quickly began using the first generation of personal computers for students with special needs and also used then-primitive modems to allow
homebound students to communicate and participate in education over
telephone lines.

Computers provide students who have disabilities with greater independence, immediate feedback, and a patient and nonthreatening environment. One state legislator spoke about the difference computers
made in improving the writing of her son, who has a learning disability,
and hers is a common experience. A special education teacher in Maine
reported:

> One student who has historically been a very reluctant writer is now able
> to compose full essays. His essays have been shared with his last year's spe-
> cial education teacher, who could not believe it was the same child.[3]

Computer laptop programs have been a particular boon for special
education teachers and students. A study in Maine found that "special
education teachers viewed the laptops as highly beneficial to their students with few exceptions."[4] In one school, access to various modes of
learning through laptops—visual, auditory, kinesthetic—was identified
by the special education teacher as particularly advantageous for students
with special needs. A Maine teacher wrote:

> As a special education teacher, the benefits from the implementation of
> the laptops into our curriculum have been overwhelming. The students
> are writing more, are becoming more independent in their researching
> and editing techniques, and have taken an overall improved interest in
> learning. I can't imagine going back to the days when my entire caseload

shared one computer in the back of the resource room. The electronic roadblocks and technical difficulties pale in comparison to the tremendous payoffs of this program.[5]

Ann Luginbuhl, a teacher in a rural school in Maine, wrote that "it was my most needy students who benefited the most" from the laptop program.[6] The laptops were "pivotal in their lives" and allowed one student to progress "from non-participatory and almost illiterate to producing an incredible iMovie that told the story of a bomber run in World War II."

For many students with disabilities, computers help not only with writing but also with organizational skills. Dozens of documents can be stored in one place on the student's computer. They are easily filed in electronic folders and retrieved as needed.

There are countless websites that offer teachers and students flash cards, quizzes, and other learning aids. On many of the sites, subject matter content can be customized by teachers. Students' responses can be graded automatically and, in some cases, the websites will maintain password-protected records for the teacher and the student. Because students can proceed at their own pace and get immediate feedback, such tools are especially useful for students with disabilities.

Online courses also provide benefits for special education, allowing students with disabilities to participate without necessarily disclosing their handicaps. Early in the history of the Virtual High School, for example, 10 students enrolled from the Model Secondary School for the Deaf (MSSD) in Washington, D.C. At the beginning of the term the school's site coordinator contacted the online teachers and explained where the students came from. The coordinator and the teachers left it to the students whether to divulge their deafness to classmates online. Some did; others did not. The local site coordinator explained, "One of the great benefits for deaf students of participating in the VHS class is that communication with hearing teachers and peers is much more direct than using interpreters."[7]

There are dozens of software products designed specifically for students with special needs. An example is Thinking Reader, which uses seven comprehension strategies (such as summarizing text or asking questions about the meaning of what was read), as well as a variety of prompts and hints, to help struggling readers understand a set of literature books commonly assigned in grades 5 to 8.[8] In a similar genre, Kurzweil 3000—a software product whose roots go back to the 1970s, when federal grants were used to develop a machine called the Kurzweil Reader—helps teachers provide differentiated reading instruction to students with special needs.[9] The software can read almost any text aloud, has a built-in dictionary and thesaurus, and provides assistance with study skills. Premier Assistive Technologies, Texthelp, IntelliTools, and CAST also offer related products.

In addition, significant new products are being developed. For example, the University of Memphis Institute for Intelligent Systems created and is further improving an online program to help students through the use of animated characters ("agents") that provide training in using various strategies to make sense of text, specifically including science textbooks, which many students who have reading problems find hard to understand.[10]

Products that are designed for all users often have features useful to special education teachers. Software with graphics capabilities, like Kidspiration and Inspiration, or drawing programs such as Kid Pix, can be used to provide graphic organizers that help students with weak language skills to visually organize and understand complex ideas. Most normal word processors include grammar checkers (which can be tailored to look only for specific types of errors, such as punctuation, if that is what is needed), as well as spell checkers, colored fonts and highlights, and the capability for a teacher to embed comments that become visible only when text (such as a new word or concept) is highlighted. Any of these features can be used to help students with disabilities. Information about using commonly available technology to support a wide range of learners is available at websites such as www.cast.org and others.[11]

Text stored digitally can be used far more flexibly than printed text. The capability to convert text to speech is built into some computer operating systems, and there are also software programs, some of them free or inexpensive, which will read stored documents or websites aloud to struggling readers. A teacher in Maine reported that a student with very poor reading skills "can type in the instructions on the board and have the computer read them to him."[12] With some software, students learning to read are able to highlight a word or phrase and hear it spoken or have it translated (in case English is not their first language). Free websites feature children's books being read aloud, in some cases by well-known actors, as the illustrations are displayed on the screen.[13] There are even websites especially for youth with disabilities where they can have some of the questions about their disability answered or engage in discussions with other students in similar situations.[14] One student wondered if dyslexia is contagious. It would be very troubling for a child not to know the answer to that question. These and other digital tools are useful to students with learning disabilities, when used appropriately.

Guidance in using digital tools for students with disabilities can be found online. For example, the National Center on Accessible Information Technology in Education at the University of Washington has a website to help schools and other institutions use digital tools with students or employees who have disabilities,[15] and the Consortium for School Networking maintains a website to help schools use technology to raise the achievement of *all* students.[16]

Beginning in 2004, a National Instructional Materials Accessibility Standard (NIMAS) was supported by federal law. NIMAS sets standards for electronic files that publishers create to make instructional materials, including textbooks, available to students who have print disabilities, such as blind students. Using these files, and the flexibility of digital tools, text can more easily be presented in a wide variety of formats, including audio and Braille.[17] Similarly, more than half the states have "Braille laws," making it easier to translate instructional materials into Braille.

Increasingly, publishers are making digital instructional materials available online because that is what school systems want or, in some cases, require. In 2006, for example, Pearson PLC entered into a $70 million contract with the State of California to provide digital history curricula to more than 1.5 million students in elementary schools.[18] In a few instances, companies specializing in digital media have purchased traditional textbook publishers, such as when Riverdeep Holdings Limited purchased Houghton Mifflin in 2006. The term "textbook" may even become obsolete as more instructional materials are sold or licensed in digital form rather than in print.

Assistive Technology

A requirement under the IDEA legislation is that Assistive Technology be considered for all students with Individualized Education Plans (IEPs); that is, for all students served under IDEA. Assistive technology (AT) is defined as "any item, piece of equipment, or product system . . . that is used to increase, maintain, or improve the functional capabilities of an individual with a disability."[19] In practice this requirement is challenging. Rapid changes in technology make it hard to know what is possible, and it often takes years for teachers to learn how to effectively teach students with disabilities, especially in light of the wide range of students they are expected to teach today. Ideally, assistive technology should be one part of a coherent system that connects technology with the people providing assistance, such as special education teachers. The system should also include clear learning goals and, whenever possible, individual assessment of students prior to selecting appropriate AT.[20]

In some cases AT means special devices to help students see, hear, talk, or move. There are special switches making it feasible for students with disabilities to access a computer keyboard using only their mouth, foot, or head. Stephen Hawking uses a computer-synthesized voice.

But the largest need for assistive technology is for students with learning disabilities, not for students with physical handicaps. Ironically, more students with low-incidence disabilities, such as physically handicapped students, use appropriate AT than do students with higher-incidence disabilities, such as dyslexia,[21] despite the fact that technology can act as a type of cognitive prosthesis as well as a physical one.

A recent report indicated that "more than 50 percent of adults who use computers use AT every day."[22] These are people making use of many built-in features, such as enlarging text, that are part of their office suite software or computer operating system. By contrast, classroom teachers are not often enough taking advantage of these commonly available technologies, although it is true that AT is used more frequently in special education than in regular classrooms.

As computers, computer projectors, and electronic whiteboards become more prevalent in regular classrooms, it is easier for teachers to make more routine use of software to help accommodate students' needs. Schools with laptop programs instantly have more AT options available to students. Most of us don't think of eyeglasses as assistive technology; they are just part of the normal environment. When computers are ubiquitous a similar transformation takes place. A researcher studying laptop schools in Maine found students using text-to-speech software to listen to words they were having difficulty reading, and referring to online dictionaries and other reference materials to understand text.[23] In a laptop program such accommodations can become routine.

Planning for Special Education Technology

It is a challenge to select, purchase, and then train teachers and students to use appropriate technologies to help students with disabilities, especially in light of the rapid rate at which digital technology is changing. Schools and districts sometimes compartmentalize decision-making so that those in charge of technology budgets, those in charge of special education budgets, and experts who manage subject-matter budgets are not communicating effectively enough. In part, this problem is a result of federal, state, or local budget lines being earmarked or compartmentalized.

Ideally, and especially in larger districts where decisionmaking is more complex, a technology plan should be in place to guide decisions about purchases and training. Although the number of students in special education has grown, the great majority of children are not, and so school and district decisions are frequently made without regard for the needs of *all* students. Yet decisions to help students with disabilities can help others as well. Many students benefit from hearing an unfamiliar word read aloud by a computer or being able to quickly refer to a digital dictionary.

When schools purchase specialized technology, such as software to read aloud whatever is on a computer screen, the costs can be spread across a large number of students if planners conceive that the technology will be used by many students, not just a few. The same principle applies in architecture. Curb cuts were originally intended for people in wheelchairs, but we now realize that curb cuts are great for someone pushing a baby carriage, riding a bike, and others.

ACCOMMODATING LOW AND HIGH ACHIEVERS

Many students besides those with disabilities need individual attention. Nearly one-third of students begin ninth grade reading two or more years below grade level, and a number of others read at only a "basic" level. Yet high school teachers are typically hired for their knowledge of subject matter, not to teach reading. Whether in English, mathematics, or other subjects, schools and teachers need to be able to help low achievers without shortchanging the rest of the class. Certainly there are tested approaches to teach reading and other basic skills to high school students that do not use digital tools.[24] But digital tools offer unique advantages, such as being able to present material at each student's level, pace instruction individually, automatically maintain detailed records, and even reduce the amount of time teachers need to devote to remediation. According to the director of a high school language arts program, "There are potentially huge gaps in student proficiency in any one classroom. Only use of a computer program can address those different levels efficiently."[25]

Many companies claim research validates the use of their products for helping low achievers. Academy of Reading, as an example, is among the most popular software programs for teaching reading. The company's literature reports studies based in dozens of high schools showing that students using the software for only 10 to 20 hours gain about 1.6 grade levels in reading.[26] Similarly, a California school district serving students in grades K–8 developed an afterschool program that makes use of various software programs; reports indicate they successfully raised students' reading skills by two grade levels or more.[27] But at the same time, the study of 15 software products cited in chapter 3 found no significant increase in test scores as a result of using those products—at least, in the particular ways that they were used. It would be useful to policymakers to have more independent, high-quality, peer-reviewed studies of software on which to base decisions. Falling behind in school puts children at risk; low achievers and students with disabilities are more likely to drop out of school than their peers.

At the other end of the achievement spectrum, academically gifted students may be bored and unchallenged by school. Gifted students appear to drop out of school at about the same rate as non-gifted students.[28] To better serve their needs, Stanford University recently began the first online high school especially for gifted students.[29] The three-year school will award high school diplomas to those completing its program and students will have the option of attending Stanford University in person for up to eight weeks during the summer. But students will also be allowed to enroll in the online high school part-time, supplementing the courses in their regular high school with more challenging courses not available locally. University-level courses will be offered in many subjects. Scholarship money will be made available to students through a multimillion-dollar gift from the Malone Family Foundation.[30] The online school will serve students from across the United States and from other countries. The Stanford program is not the only one that serves these students' needs; a number of other online high schools, as well as many colleges and universities, offer courses that are appropriate for gifted students.

Under rules governing the No Child Left Behind Act, online schools are also an alternative for students who choose to transfer out of an "underperforming" public school. The Arkansas Virtual School, for example, was created to provide options for students wanting to transfer but who had no higher-performing school in their local district.[31] Similarly, the University of California's online College Prep program, which is based at UC Santa Cruz, focuses especially on "underserved schools," which in practice means the program works with large numbers of students whose first language is not English, or who have other special needs.[32]

ENGLISH LANGUAGE LEARNERS

Teachers use digital tools to help the millions of English language learners (ELL students) in public schools. According to a school superintendent in Illinois, "many of our special needs students and many of our limited English speaking students need some type of technology to support their learning."[33] The Web now provides services that in an earlier generation were available only in a specialized language laboratory. There are regular and picture dictionaries available online in different languages, as well as websites where students can build their vocabulary or practice speaking or writing their second language with others, here or abroad.[34] Some sites (e.g., babelfish.altavista.com) do a rudimentary job of translating text from one language to another at no cost; higher-quality translation services are available on the Web for a fee. Through a grant program, IBM is providing schools with free access to a special version of its WebSphere Translation Server. The service, Tradúcelo Ahora (Translate Now), translates English to Spanish or vice versa, and can be used to translate websites or, importantly, to help Spanish-speaking parents and children communicate via e-mail with English-speaking teachers and administrators.[35]

Schools are using the Internet to make translations of important documents available to teachers, parents, or others by putting them on the Web or intranet sites. Teachers of ELL students use the Web to learn about the culture and language of their students. Organizations and clearinghouses specializing in teaching English to foreign students maintain sites on the Web,[36] and districts provide suggestions for using technology to teach ELL students.[37]

MERLOT (the Multimedia Educational Resource for Learning and Online Teaching) provides references to useful websites in its World Languages collection.[38] Many of the sites use audio and video segments to teach students who are learning English as a second language (ESL).[39]

It's not just in the United States that teachers use digital tools to teach language. Mexico and the European Union support initiatives to teach English using electronic learning tools.[40] And for nearly 50 years the Voice of America (VOA) has broadcast radio programs using so-called Special English, a limited vocabulary used to communicate in clear, simple sentences with people abroad who are not yet fluent in English. The VOA programs, including news and information about the United States, are now available for free on the Internet and can be used in schools or homes.[41]

A variety of software products are used to teach English as a second language and product reviews can be found on the Web. The Southern Regional Education Board, a nonprofit organization that works in 16 states, maintains an Educational Technology Cooperative to help schools use digital tools effectively. The Cooperative reviewed a heavily advertised product called Rosetta Stone, reporting:

> The repetition and patterned format makes the program easy to use. Useful with a wide range of learners and ages, the program is extremely versatile. The ability to turn off the scoring may motivate reluctant learners. Tutorials monitor and re-quiz users on screens answered incorrectly. The Rosetta Stone: English I and English II (American) is an outstanding program to teach English as a second language to students who are at the novice to intermediate-high level. The program would work best with paired-use (student with volunteer, adult, or peer) or independent student use.[42]

About 80 percent of the students in Chelsea, Massachusetts, come from families where English is not the first language. Schools there are using Soliloquy Reading Assistant, computer software that listens to students read a story aloud and uses speech-recognition technology to show progress on mastery of English, allow students to compare their reading to a professional's, and even correct students' pronunciation. Marilyn

Jager Adams, a reading specialist who designed the software, said, "I decided . . . basically, to make an electronic lap. Children learn incredibly quickly if you can get them to pay attention, but [for many] there's not somebody at home [to help] . . . and if you look at the classroom, it's not set up for one-on-one time."[43] According to Chelsea's literacy program director and other district staff, using the software has helped many students.

With millions of English language learners in schools it is often necessary to provide appropriate accommodations to students so that they can understand tests, including those required under the No Child Left Behind Act. Tests frequently have important stakes for the students themselves and for their schools. State and federal laws permit accommodations to be made to students who are learning English. In 2005, for example, more than 1,200 students with disabilities or designated ELL were tested online in the State of Kentucky. CATS, Kentucky's online test system, can read text aloud as an accommodation.[44] In addition to reading directions or test items aloud, other possible accommodations include providing bilingual glossaries to students or giving them added time to take the test. There are so many possibilities that schools may have difficulty choosing the right accommodations, or may use them inconsistently. To help schools make better choices, a computerized system has been developed to help decide which accommodations ELL students should be provided as part of large-scale assessments, such as state or national tests. Software called the Selection Taxonomy for English Language Learner Accommodations (STELLA) has been developed with millions of dollars of funds from the U.S. Department of Education.[45]

In addition to specialized applications of technology, schools with high concentrations of ELL students benefit from the same uses of digital tools as other schools. For example, a recent study found that higher-performing schools serving ELL students made better use of student assessment data to improve teaching and learning than lower-performing counterparts.[46] Thus one expects that the growing use of online testing and improved data systems will help ELL students, as will training more teachers and administrators to use student assessment data effectively. These kinds of initiatives and tools, which are designed to help all students, are further described in chapter 8.

Similarly, school administrators in El Paso, Texas, decided that a technology-rich environment is important for teaching their students research and problem-solving skills despite the fact that many are still learning English. At Ysleta Middle School, for example, more than 90 percent of the students are Hispanic, and few of them had access to computers at home.[47] The school's technology coordinator said that when students use the Internet to do research, it "really helps them with their English."[48] Ysleta is a high-achieving school. Just because students are English language learners does not mean they should not be challenged.

BRIDGING THE "DIGITAL DIVIDE"

Children from low-income families have less access to computers at home than those from higher-income families. School computers are important for bridging the digital divide, as noted in the previous chapter, because they provide young people with access to countless educational resources that would otherwise not be available to them.

Low-income families are unlikely to have access to telescopes, for instance. Even if they do, for those who live in an urban area the nighttime sky may not be dark enough for good viewing. Harvard's Smithsonian Astrophysical Observatory has developed a network of small, automated telescopes used for education, called microObservatory. The telescopes are accessed and controlled through the Web and are available regardless of students' family income or where they live.[49] During the past decade students have recorded more than a half-million images of stars, planets, and the moon. Similarly, the Bugscope project allows students to remotely operate a scanning electron microscope to take pictures of bugs at high magnification.[50] Some adults may turn away at the prospect of looking at bugs, but many students are fascinated. Other examples of ways that the Web helps to level the playing field for students can be found throughout the book.

Simply being able to routinely use a computer is a big step for children in many low-income families, with or without access to the Internet. One parent said, "In the eastern region [of Henrico County], the iBook may be the only technology available [to families]. [And] not every parent can take their child to the library." Henrico County made inexpensive Internet subscriptions available to families that did not previously have access, with prices ranging from $9.75 to $12.50 per month. Speaking about students who did not have Internet access at home, one parent reported, "They come to the school parking lot early to get onto the AirPort [wireless network]."

Wealthy families often have multiple computers available in the home. Because of 1-to-1 computing programs, that situation becomes feasible for more families. As one Henrico County parent told a researcher, "Having your own computer makes a big difference [to students], especially if you have several children." A principal made the same point, noting, "Every child is on a level playing field. Every child has the same potential for achieving. The computers are used at home and at school; there are no more haves and have-nots." In Henrico County, parents received training to use the computer and the Internet, in some cases for the first time, which also opened the door for their further involvement in the school. Several parents reported that when their children each had their own laptop to work on, it freed up other computers at home to be used by additional members of the family, making it easier for families with multiple children to complete homework assignments and to do other work in a more amicable way.

Laptop programs and e-mail facilitate communication between teachers and families. A biology teacher in Henrico County stated that sending e-mail proved valuable for increasing contact with her students' parents. Another teacher said she was pleased that the Internet allowed her to have conferences with parents whose schedules made it difficult for them to come to school during regular hours. According to a high school administrator, the laptop program was responsible for linking more parents than ever to the school through the use of K12Planet[*] (part of Mac School[*], the student information system adopted by Henrico County). She reported that as many as 85 percent of parents used it regularly, supporting a constant stream of communication between teachers and parents about student academic progress. Not everyone was pleased with this development; one student wryly observed that her parents became more "in touch" with her assignments and grades, reminding her of due dates for projects and becoming better able to track her progress. (See chapter 7 for additional information about increasing parent-school communication.)

A handful of Henrico County parents were so concerned that their students would lose or damage the laptops that they did not accept them. The school system was willing to help low-income families pay any associated expenses; unwillingness to accept the computers was not primarily a financial concern.

UNIVERSAL DESIGN FOR LEARNING

Digital media provide such improved flexibility for teachers and students than ever before possible that an approach to education has been developed called Universal Design for Learning, or UDL.[51] Proponents of UDL point to a number of principles that they believe should influence the development of curricula and instructional materials:

1. Students with special needs cannot be viewed as a single category of students. Rather, they constitute a wide range of learners with different learning needs and styles.
2. Teachers should be able to adjust for the learning-style differences of *all* students, not just those who are identified with disabilities or other special needs.
3. Instruction should not rely on a single textbook; instead, instructional materials should be varied, diverse, and ought to include digital and online resources as well as printed paper.
4. Instruction should be flexible; remediation for students should not begin with an inflexible curriculum.

UDL is a call for much more individualizing of instruction, something closer to the proverbial student at one end of the log and the brilliant teacher at the other end. It is a call for classrooms to better match the idealized view of the one-room schoolhouse of years past, where students at many different levels each received appropriate instruction.

The most basic principle of UDL, that students with special needs cannot be viewed as a single category, is obviously true. One size does not fit all in the many school districts in the United States serving students who, as a group, speak dozens of languages and come from dozens of cultures. The second principle of UDL is becoming more widely accepted, as a few states accept the challenge of designing "individualized learning plans" for *all* students, not only those with disabilities (a subject discussed further in chapter 7). The third and fourth principles are appealing because we know that we teach an amazingly diverse group of students and need to succeed with more of them. In short, UDL is a philosophy that makes sense, even if achieving it on a wide scale remains a long-term goal rather than something rapidly achievable.

Practically speaking, UDL is a call for a more flexible curriculum, one which is appropriate and accessible to individuals with widely varying backgrounds, interests, capabilities, and disabilities. Clearly, digital media offer much more flexible methods of presenting information than paper, such as by using text of varying size or converting text to speech. Digital tools also provide alternative means of expression, such as the capability to answer a question in writing, by recording a student's spoken response, or by drawing. And because so much more and more varied information can be quickly accessed digitally, there are more ways to engage students in learning by taking advantage of their interests and learning styles. Curricula based on UDL principles are being designed to allow flexible presentation *and* alternative means of expression *and* various ways to engage students.

UDL depends on taking maximum advantage of digital tools to make curriculum and instruction effective for more students. As with architectural features such as curb cuts and ramps, it is far simpler and less expensive to use principles of universal design at the beginning of a project rather than make changes later. Increasingly, curricula should be designed using principles of UDL. Writing about the Concord, New Hampshire, school district, promoters of universal design for learning said that in their planning, "rather than work from individual students to the curriculum, they work from the curriculum to all students. . . ."[52] This is a departure from past practice.

The proponents of UDL in effect view many current curricula and instructional practices as *themselves* suffering from disabilities because they are too rigid to accommodate a wide range of learners. They are not calling for lower standards, just for differentiation in the means of reaching the standards. Similarly, supporters of UDL are not opposed to assessment, but they believe that more assessment practices than at present should be designed to improve learning and instruction, not only to evaluate whether students have or have not met standards. Rather than wait, sometimes for years, until students have been identified as having a disability, the curriculum should have a system of differentiated supports matched to individuals' needs.

UDL and a Software Publisher

Just as many television productions aimed at a general audience now include closed captions, which help both hearing and hearing-impaired people in a wide variety of settings, education publishers are designing instructional materials that can from the outset be more easily used by students with special needs. UDL is becoming part of mainstream thinking about education.

An example is provided by Tom Snyder Productions, which began publishing education software more than 25 years ago and is now owned by Scholastic, the largest publisher and distributor of children's books in the world. Among its claims to fame, Scholastic publishes the best-selling Harry Potter books and is the leading publisher of Spanish-language books in the United States. Scholastic sells many kinds of products to schools, including popular software such as Read 180. The company's reach is large; Tom Snyder Production's software alone is reported to be used in more than 400,000 classrooms.

David Dockterman, editor in chief at Tom Snyder, says that as older software products are revised, the company routinely includes captions for video (which can be turned on or off), as well as on-screen buttons that allow students greater control. Students who need to stop, go back, and review material are able to do so. Font sizes can be changed. Material is often explained using multiple representations (e.g., text, pictures, and animations) to make concepts understandable to more students. Under No Child Left Behind, Dockterman says, "schools are responsible for all their sub-populations." As a result, "customers want software that will help teach hard-to-reach populations."[53]

Tom Snyder has worked closely with CAST, the nonprofit Center for Applied Special Technology. Developers at Tom Snyder saw a group of students use a prototype of Thinking Reader and were impressed because students who would not otherwise have been able to read and understand the books that are often assigned in middle schools were now able to "get it" without the text having to be simplified. However, the company showed the product to teachers and decisionmakers and learned that some of the features needed to be changed if Thinking Reader was going to be accepted. For example, the prototype used a computer-generated voice to read text, and that voice was not acceptable to potential customers. Instead, Scholastic was able to license high-quality audio book narrations and even developed technology that made it faster and cheaper to highlight words on the screen synchronously with the audio narration. "Meeting the needs of smaller segments of the population is economically challenging," Dockterman said, "but if the software has benefits for the rest of the population, that makes a huge difference."

Thinking Reader includes nine popular books, such as *Bridge to Terabithia* and *Tuck Everlasting*. Words in the books can be translated into

Spanish by the software. Thinking Reader adjusts the help that it provides to readers and withdraws support as readers become more capable and independent. The reading comprehension strategies employed are ones that good teachers normally use, such as having students summarize, clarify, and ask questions about text they have just read. As needed, animated characters provide hints, prompts, and feedback.

"People who see Thinking Reader love it," Dockterman said. Unfortunately, he added, No Child Left Behind seems to be causing schools to put more time into teaching skills and less time, energy, and money into teaching literature. Teachers are also spending more time on basic skills, such as decoding individual words, and less time teaching students to understand longer passages of text, such as by employing the strategies used in Thinking Reader.

Working on products designed for students with disabilities has taught the staff at Tom Snyder lessons that help in designing all their software. Dockterman says, "I spend more time now looking at the research literature about kids in Special Education to find out what some of the underlying needs are. These kids are more representative of the population as a whole than one might think."

Certain of Tom Snyder's products—such as Thinking Reader, or FASTT Math, which helps students learn basic math facts—are well matched to the needs of groups of students with learning disabilities. But products designed for a general audience need to be accessible to students with special needs, too. "UDL is the way we're going," says Dockterman. "That's the way we are thinking about products."

The nonprofit CAST earlier developed Wiggleworks, a Tom Snyder software product designed to support struggling readers in the early grades. And CAST has also worked directly with Tom Snyder's parent company, Scholastic, on its popular Read 180 software, which was first developed at Vanderbilt University. The significant role of nonprofits in educational technology R&D is discussed in chapter 9.

Characteristics of digital media identified in chapter 1—its flexibility, the ability to customize experiences for different students, and its dynamic, interactive nature—have made computer-based instructional materials and curricula a vital tool for helping teachers reach *all* students. Significant steps have already been taken to differentiate instruction for different kinds of learners, but more work clearly needs to be done.

CHAPTER 6

Attracting, Preparing, and Retaining High-Quality Teachers (Goal 4)

People have known since antiquity that good teachers make a big difference in students' lives. Yet it is only recently that research has been able to quantify the effect by showing, for example, that low-achieving fourth-grade students assigned to effective teachers for three years in a row were more than twice as likely to pass a seventh-grade math test as those who had ineffective teachers three years in a row—90 percent passing versus 42 percent.[1] That's a huge difference.

Although we know that teachers matter, we also know what an enormous challenge it is to attract hundreds of thousands of highly qualified teacher-applicants to the profession, do a good job preparing them to teach before they enter the classroom, and provide them with ongoing support (including strong school leaders, healthy professional communities, and high quality in-service professional development). One indicator of how far we need to go is that nearly half of all new teachers leave the profession within five years, with many of them feeling frustrated. Those who leave have higher measured academic ability than those who remain.[2] Furthermore, teacher turnover costs schools about $7 billion annually, according to one report.[3]

An array of new and improved policies and practices are needed to attract, prepare, and retain high-quality teachers, and this certainly includes smarter use of digital tools. Providing teachers and administrators with the digital tools they need to do their job well is essential to strengthen the teaching force. Imagine that you are a well-trained doctor without access to antibiotics, ultrasound, or dozens of other basic tools of the trade. This would be a frustrating situation, to say the least. Teachers without access to today's digital tools (which keep getting better, like medical technologies) are likely to feel frustrated, too, especially as these tools become more powerful and better used.

This chapter first focuses on the growing use of digital technology to recruit teachers. The second section discusses the use of technology in preparing and supporting new teachers. The themes of the following sections are teachers' increasing use of technology for instruction, and uses of technology to support teachers' many administrative duties, including testing and grading students. Technology is also proving to be vital in building and sustaining teachers' professional communities, including through online professional development, and those are the focal points of the last two sections.

RECRUITING TEACHERS

There is a surprisingly high amount of teacher mobility in the United States. In the 1999–2000 school year, for example, 17 percent of all teachers were "new hires" at their school. Of this group, 9 percent were teachers who moved from one school to another, 4 percent were teachers who had left the workforce but were returning, and 5 percent were individuals who had never taught before.[4] (Rounding accounts for the apparent error in the total of percents.) Finding and hiring "new" teachers every year—more than a half million of them—is clearly a major enterprise for schools.

As an interesting aside, the strongest sources of dissatisfaction among teachers who left teaching or moved from one school to another were "not enough time for planning/preparation" and "teaching workload too heavy." It turns out that American teachers have heavy workloads compared to their counterparts in other nations. Where technology can help teachers become more efficient—keeping track of grades and averages, for example, or reporting daily attendance, or administering early reading assessments—there is a natural appeal, even though there is an unavoidable time investment required at the outset to learn a new system.

Technology is changing the process of recruitment and hiring in schools, just as it is in many other professions. Florida, for example, has the fourth-highest student enrollment of any state (more than 2 million students), and the number of students grows by more than 40,000 a year.[5] Combined with the fact that large numbers of Florida teachers are approaching retirement age, the state calls the demand for teachers "unprecedented." TeachInFlorida.com was created in 2000 to help meet this need. Districts post job openings to the website. Teachers looking for work in Florida can make their resumes available on the site, and are also able to search for job openings using a variety of search criteria, such as geographic area of the state, subject matter specialty, and grade level. This process is more comprehensive and faster than any paper-based system could be.

TeachInFlorida.com also provides a gateway for teachers in the state to access a wide variety of resources, including lesson plans that have been vetted for quality, and a "teacher's lounge" that provides a discussion forum and a chat room where teachers can "meet" and discuss issues. In addition, a section of the website is being built so that prospective teachers can find out more about teaching, Florida itself, and different areas within the state.

Resources such as those available through TeachInFlorida.com, and through literally thousands of other education-related websites, make it important that teachers have computers to use for professional purposes. Other states also use websites to recruit—Missouri has www.moteachingjobs.com/, for example. And a wide variety of other websites are also available for people who are looking for a teaching job, including www.teachers-teachers.com, www.recruitingteachers.org/channels/clearinghouse/, and www.k12jobs.com/, to name just a few. There are even specialized websites to help teachers find jobs in overseas schools.

PREPARING TEACHERS

Technology is increasingly being incorporated into teacher-preparation programs. In addition, there have been exciting developments in online mentoring programs for new teachers.

Preservice Teacher-Preparation Programs

Many schools and colleges of education are preparing prospective teachers to use educational technology. The University of Texas at Austin's College of Education is one of the preservice teacher-preparation programs that require students to purchase laptops so that they become better prepared to teach in technology-rich environments. More such programs are needed and, importantly, schools of education themselves should better integrate technology so that beginning teachers learn to teach as they themselves have been taught. Since 2002, for example, Tufts University has used a technology called VideoPaper Builder to help preservice teachers learn to observe their own and others' teaching and to reflect on it. "For me, this was a great exercise in self-reflection," said one teacher after using VideoPaper Builder. "In putting this [assignment] together, I did a lot of thinking about how I did a lesson and what I wanted to accomplish by doing it."[6]

Although there are now thousands of websites and software applications designed for K–12 students, there are fewer digital tools designed specifically for preservice teachers. An intriguing approach is simulation software, roughly analogous to the use of flight simulators for pilots. Simulation software can provide an environment for learning how to manage a large group of students. Or, prospective teachers can learn how to pose questions and how to respond when students answer questions. One company is developing a simulator, based on artificial intelligence, that will help teachers learn the key concepts in a subject, identify areas that often are difficult for students to learn, and practice responding to students' questions.

The FBI, the Defense Department, and other mainstream organizations already use simulations for training. For example, SIMmersion, a company in Maryland, developed software to help army chaplains identify people with suicidal tendencies and learn how to treat them. In such situations, according to the president of SIMmersion, "You can't necessarily practice dealing with real people because if you do, you will harm people."[7] The military sees so much potential in simulations that it supports an ongoing partnership among the entertainment industry, academia, and the armed forces, called the Institute for Creative Technology, to develop what the Institute calls "synthetic experiences" for learning.[8] In some cases, realistic, full-sized animated images of soldiers have been created that give oral responses to a user's spoken questions in a particular domain of knowledge.

With the high rate of teacher turnover, simulations may better prepare prospective or new teachers. As it stands, many feel they have been tossed into the pool and must "sink or swim" with inadequate preparation. Too many sink.

Mentoring New Teachers

An important component of induction into the teacher profession—but one that is much less common than one would wish—is the mentoring of new teachers. Mentoring is intended to strengthen the skills of beginning teachers and to increase the likelihood that they will stay in teaching and be successful.

Schools that provide mentoring have lower turnover among beginning teachers;[9] however, face-to-face mentoring is not always feasible. For example, a high school science teacher in a rural school may have few (or no) colleagues teaching science in the same school. Also, using the Internet for mentoring has certain advantages, including the fact that participants can log in at different times and still interact effectively; the written dialogue is persistent, so it can be referenced when needed (and also studied by researchers and program developers to improve the mentoring system); it is easy to create links to online lesson plans, or to video clips illustrating good teaching practices; and, conversations and other data are searchable, so it is easier to find information. With the right kind of structures, some questions can be asked anonymously, so there may be less embarrassment about asking "stupid questions." Moreover, online mentoring can be designed to take place within a larger community, consisting of hundreds of mentors and mentees, as well as experts in the field (e.g., scientists).

The National Science Teachers Association, working with the New Teacher Center at the University of California and with Montana State University, has developed this approach. In 2002 the National Science Foundation provided a grant to these organizations for a project, eMentoring for Student Success (http://www.emss.nsta.org/), offering new science teachers online mentoring provided by experienced science teachers living in the same state (who are thus familiar with the same state education standards, state tests, and state-specific resources). More than 500 first- to third-year science teachers in 16 states have received assistance from their online mentors through this program, known as eMSS.

Comments from participating beginning teachers show that they find both the one-to-one mentoring and the larger online community valuable. One said,

> I would not be a teacher next year if I had not had access to my mentor who provided educationally sound advice and great insight on the culture and expectations of this field . . . eMSS is a private place where I could go to get solace without fear of reprisals or gossip.

Another teacher said:

> Being able to communicate with the whole eMSS community through posts, I was able to find new activities to try in my classroom and ask questions when I was stuck. I appreciate how I can pose a question and quickly get many different educated responses.[10]

The beginning teachers in eMSS are recent graduates, or are changing careers, or are newly assigned to teach science. They receive a week-long online orientation and then must log in several times a week during the school year, devoting about two to three hours per week to the task. The eMSS mentors participate in an online summer institute designed to prepare them to be effective online facilitators. and they are asked to spend about three or four hours a week on the website during the academic year.[11]

Each mentor-mentee pair has its own private discussion space. In addition, eMSS includes discussion spaces for particular scientific disciplines (e.g., biology and life sciences), where hundreds of mentors, mentees, and scientists can participate. A great deal of thought, training, and research goes into the design and operation of such an environment. One result is that participants report being significantly better prepared after participating in eMSS. Research on the written records maintained online also illuminates some of the challenges in mentoring new teachers, such as balancing their demand for lessons and materials with stimulating and sustaining deeper conversations about content and pedagogical knowledge.[12] As noted in chapter 3, the persistence of dialogue in an online environment makes it especially well suited for research—research that can benefit face-to-face as well as online education programs.

USING TECHNOLOGY FOR INSTRUCTION

Classroom teachers value instructional technology and view digital technologies as effective teaching tools for many reasons, including to increase student achievement, to better engage students with subject matter, including updated curricula, and, to individualize instruction according to students' needs. These uses of technology are discussed at length in chapters 3, 4, and 5.

In one national survey, about 75 percent of teachers indicated that technology helped students attain educational goals and standards.[13] In another survey, about the same percentage reported that educational technology specifically helped students learn reading and writing, as well as other academic skills.[14] More than half of teachers report that digital technology has changed the way that they teach "a great deal," and only 12 percent said it changed their teaching very little or not at all.

It is not surprising that teachers believe technology helps them and their students. There are dozens of studies showing that digital technology is effective in raising student achievement.

Teachers say that their difficulty accessing computers and other digital technologies is the biggest barrier inhibiting their greater use of these devices for teaching. An elementary school in a quiet New England town provides an example of what many teachers face. The principal—a young, easygoing former science teacher, who has a doctoral degree as well as common sense—would love to see the school's teachers make greater use of computers. He has made sure that each classroom has a computer in it, obtained a grant to provide wireless Internet access to classrooms, and little by little purchased enough computer projectors that there is now one for every grade (that is, one for every three teachers). By connecting a computer and a projector teachers can use the technology for whole-class instruction. And with the principal's enthusiastic support, teams of teachers find or develop ways to use technology well. The good news here is that teachers respect the principal's grass-roots, team-based approach. The bad news is that the principal says that the school board is proud of its low per-pupil expenditures and is not willing to invest more in technology. Teachers bring their own laptops to school, since the school does not provide them. Despite the fact that nearly 20 percent of the students in this relatively affluent school are identified as having "special needs" (manifested most often as significant reading problems), and that the principal is knowledgeable about computer software that would help such students (such as Thinking Reader, described in Chapter 5), it has been difficult for him to advance the school's use of technology into the 21st century. Technology cannot be used whenever needed so long as it is scarce.

There are dozens of examples of teachers using technology well (see earlier chapters), and these instances are not restricted to special subjects or students with special needs. An English teacher at Melville High in California explained to a researcher that he loves being able to introduce his students to diverse poets, even those not included in the student's textbook, because his students can access a wealth of poetry on the Internet.[15] That same researcher received comments about Internet-based computer software that provides students with automated but nonetheless useful comments about their writing (a software application that will be further explored in chapter 8). Aware of how much time it takes to teach writing well, one teacher said:

> I think [the software] makes teaching easier. It's like another pair of eyes, however good or bad those eyes are. It's still much better than what I could do by myself. I have to monitor it, but you have to monitor everything, because I am responsible totally for what goes on in the class.[16]

There are countless other ways in which computers make teachers' lives easier. Simply compare the time it takes to read essays that students have written by hand with those written on a word processor. A high school teacher said that she had read about 100 short printed student essays the evening before in little more than an hour but that it would take as much as half a day to grade the papers if they were handwritten.[17] It's obvious that many tasks are done faster with technology.

USING TECHNOLOGY FOR ADMINISTRATIVE PURPOSES

An overwhelming majority of teachers report that they routinely use computers and the Internet to do research, prepare documents, and for other administrative functions of their job, such as to report student attendance and to keep records of students' grades.

It is rather surprising, then, that schools often do not provide teachers with their own computers. There may be a computer in the classroom, but the classroom is often shared. Besides, the computers in the classroom are usually there, first and foremost, to be used by students. Imagine if doctors, lawyers, and other professionals shared their computers with one another and with their clients!

Slowly, this situation is beginning to change. There is something very strange about schools not providing teachers with basic resources needed to do their job, including computers, easy access to telephones, and private office space. In the 21st century, the computer falls into the category of basic equipment. Fully 95 percent of teachers report using computers to create instructional materials.[18]

One place where the situation is changing is Michigan. In 2000, under the leadership of then governor John Engler, the Michigan legislature appropriated more than $100 million to provide every teacher in the state—more than 80,000 of them—with a computer. Boston is also providing all its teachers and administrators with laptops. Other states and cities need to follow these leaders.

Test Administration

Administering and scoring student tests is one routine part of a teacher's professional life. There is growing use of handheld computers (like the Palm) to automate timing, scoring, and reporting of tests given to students. A company called Wireless Generation, for example, has developed software that allows teachers to better administer a popular reading test called the Dynamic Indicators of Basic Early Literacy Skills, also known as the DIBELS, which is given to students in the early elementary grades. By 2005, Wireless Generation reported that 35,000 teachers in 40 states were using handheld computers to record and analyze data from tests of about 800,000 students.[19]

It takes only a few minutes to test each child using the DIBELS, but when teachers use paper, pencil, and a timer to give the test, and administer it to each student in the class three times during the year, the burden in time and complexity is significant. Researchers who have studied the use of handheld computers for administering the DIBELS found that the teachers reported a number of advantages of using the computer. Benefits include increased efficiency, instantaneous feedback about test results, and enhancing the link between test data and instruction, which is the major reason for giving the test. In addition, use of the computers helped to shape teachers' professional development, as they became more interested in how to use data to guide instruction, and also strengthened home-school communication, because teachers were better able to explain to parents how their children were doing and even how parents could help students become better readers. One Albuquerque teacher told the researchers, "I think it's awesome. . . . Some teachers have struggled, but most everybody has loved it. It has made [testing] so much easier." The software makes it easier not only to administer the test but also to look at students' progress over time, which is easily displayed on the screen of the device.* "The greatest advantage we see," said a researcher, "is that teachers, for the first time, felt like the data was for their own purpose."[20]

Syncing the handheld computer with a desktop computer (by putting the handheld in a specially designed cradle and pushing a button) copies the data onto the desktop, from which it is possible to print reports, view the data on a larger screen, and share data with administrators. In other words, for the DIBELS, the handheld provides the portability, ease of use, and inconspicuousness of a device that easily fits in one hand, while not sacrificing the power and flexibility offered by more powerful computers. Syncing also has the advantage of backing up data, so that it is stored on multiple machines.

Researchers also reported challenges experienced by teachers. Schools with the least-capable technical support, for example, found it more difficult to implement the Wireless Generation system smoothly by providing training, troubleshooting, and maintenance as needed. Time is one of the most precious of teachers' resources, and some teachers reported that it was challenging to find time to study the data and use it to make adjustments to their teaching. For many teachers who were using the

---

* Note that the DIBELS tests such skills as letter naming, initial sound fluency, and word use fluency, but the DIBELS does not test reading comprehension. Whether or not this is the best test for early reading, the fact is that the DIBELS is highly regarded by many people and widely used (especially in connection with a federal program called Reading First). That is why companies are interested in selling software that helps schools improve their administration of the test. The point of the discussion is that computers can be used to improve teachers' administration of tests, not to suggest which particular product or which test of early reading is best to use.

system in the early grades, it was an unfamiliar experience to be asked to use data to inform instruction—yet some schools found it challenging to find or design appropriate professional development for their teachers. The cost of the entire system was another concern.

These challenges are typical of what teachers face using a new technology and thus deserve comment. Challenges should be expected. Any innovation in schools—including the introduction of a new type of reading program that makes no use of digital technology at all—will encounter challenges. The problems of identifying or creating appropriate professional development and finding time in the day for teachers to learn about and practice using a new system or approach are perennial and are hardly unique to technology. Few people would suggest that using paper, pencil, and a timer is a more efficient or a better way to administer the DIBELS test. Therefore, an important question to ask is whether a school system, and ultimately the public, is willing to pay for an innovation such as the use of computers for administering the DIBELS, including paying for technical support and for teacher professional development.

Many students in the United States have trouble with reading, and there is widespread support for improving the teaching of reading, so one would expect that the public is willing to pay for appropriate remedies (and surveys suggest that they are). Some may argue that schools should find the resources within current budgets—but that may not be feasible, especially in the resource-poor districts that are precisely the ones least likely to have capable technical support and excellent professional development in the first place. Using computers to track education data will save money in some cases (chapter 8 provides examples), but it also takes teachers, and administrators, time to use data well (such as by providing more frequent, more useful information to parents about their child's performance and how they might help the child). In any case, if the concern is mainly about dollars and cents, it is not principally about using handhelds. *If the public is ultimately not willing to pay for an efficient system for testing early reading and using those data to improve instruction— and whatever that system is, it is likely to cost more money than the status quo—that difficulty does not belong primarily at the door of technology developers.* Helping teachers to become more expert using technology, on the other hand, is something technology developers and others ought to think about carefully.

Putting a Priority on Professional Uses of Technology

In schools where every teacher and student is given a computer, administrators and teachers alike have learned that the teachers should receive the computers first, so that they have time to learn and become comfortable using them. In Henrico County, Virginia, for example, teachers received their laptops in 2001, a full year before their middle school students did.[21] As part of the process of introducing computers, the Henrico County administrators made sure that using the laptops for professional purposes was expected of teachers and became routine. In 2004 one middle school principal said,

> I started with e-mail years ago. E-mail is an important communication mechanism. We find [e-mail] to be a very helpful way of [handling] filing and documentation, too. It's efficient. Now, I very rarely receive a piece of paper. . . . [These administrative uses are] a plus for the [county's] iBook Teaching and Learning Initiative. I made sure the teachers were trained and comfortable first.

Obviously, other administrative applications of computers are also important to teachers, including creating lesson plans and assignments, doing research on the Internet, and managing information about students. But it is e-mail that makes it possible to communicate more easily with parents, colleagues, and administrators. By 2001 (a long time ago, in "computer years"), more than half of all American teachers were already reporting that they communicated with parents by e-mail.[22] Because the teaching profession has long been characterized by excessive isolation, increasing teachers' ease of communication is vital, whether with parents or with their colleagues.

PROFESSIONAL COMMUNITIES AND
PROFESSIONAL DEVELOPMENT

Collaborative teams are common in many organizations, from automobile factories to research laboratories. Creating and supporting collaborative teams is vital for schools, too, because "the research evidence suggests that schools can achieve higher levels of student performance when teachers form a professional community oriented toward learning."[23] Conversely, as one teacher reported, "My darkest hours of teaching were when I had no one else to talk to about student achievement and effective instruction. It was in those days that I made covert plans to find somewhere else to teach."[24]

Technology is one of the important tools that can help create and sustain professional communities. In many organizations, staff members are provided with computers, e-mail accounts, voicemail, file storage space in an Internet-based file-sharing system, e-mail and file support for teams (e.g., e-mail to one address automatically reaches all team members), access to conference calling from one's desk as well as to speaker telephones, videoconferencing capability, wireless Internet access throughout the work site, computer projectors built into conference rooms, company Wikis (a form of online discussion boards) to share knowledge, and rapid access to a highly capable technology support team. In addition to a typical computer-based office suite, special-purpose computer software is supplied to the staff as needed.

Such technology support is becoming widespread. At the beginning of the 21st century, computers have become ubiquitous on the desks of people for whom information processing is essential. In the offices of doctors, lawyers, insurance agents, government workers, and professors, to name only a few pertinent occupations, the *absence* of computers would be startling. Providing computers and related tools and services to teachers should also be the norm. Whether or not one supports the idea of providing all students with computers, to argue that teachers should not be provided with computers to use as part of their job seems to be merely an argument that teachers and teaching are less valuable than are the people and services in other lines of work where providing personal computers is routine.

The argument is not that technology alone is *sufficient*, but that it is increasingly *necessary*. One expert notes that:

> Effective collaborative teamwork faces many obstacles; the most challenging barriers involve creating a culture of collaboration and conducting collaborative work across distance and time. Technology can be used to enhance the quality and productivity of collaborative teamwork. In particular, it can help teams to organize, plan, and communicate. However, introducing technology into the teamwork process requires careful planning and due regard for the complexities of teamwork, technology, and their interaction. *Teamwork needs technology* [emphasis added], because technology offers tools to diminish threats to efficiency and effectiveness, especially those arising from obstacles of time and distance.[25]

Online Professional Communities

Nearly every professional association for teachers and school administrators provides a rich set of resources on the World Wide Web. The American Historical Association, the National Council for the Social Studies, the National Council of Teachers of English, the National Council of Teachers of Mathematics, the National Science Teachers Association, the National School Boards Association, and many other organizations provide valuable resources and services on the Web, including, but not limited to, online professional development. Mathematics teachers, for example, can find a free library of interactive "applets" designed to help teachers at all grade levels better teach a variety of mathematics topics (illuminations.nctm.org/). There is even an online journal, ON-Math, published by the National Council of Teachers of Mathematics, dedicated to exploring the use of electronic resources.

Simply using the online resources of professional associations is one way of belonging to and benefiting from a professional community. More powerful uses of the Web to foster, develop, and sustain a professional community are illustrated by a "listserv" operated by the National Association for College Admissions Counseling, or NACAC (www.nacacnet.org) that provides a model for teachers and other education professionals.

A listserv distributes e-mail messages to a large group of interested people who have signed up for the service. The sender addresses an e-mail to the single listserv address, which distributes the e-mail automatically to the whole group. In the case of the NACAC listserv, recipients can choose to receive daily e-mails, each of which bundles together all of the individual messages sent during the past day. College counselors from around the country who have questions about admissions can ask a question on the listserv and receive answers, often within hours, from experts such as the admissions staff of colleges and universities, who are also members of the community. Using a listserv means that a question-and-answer interchange can provide information to thousands of people, not just the individual asking the question, while at the same time the listserv also helps to create a community in which people "meet" and learn about the views of others all across the country, including those who work in institutions that may be quite different from their own.

Thousands of professionals belong to NACAC—counselors and teachers from public and private schools, independent college counselors, as well as college and university admissions staff—and the listserv provides a place for this diverse community to meet, interact, and learn. Nothing like the immediacy, the reservoir of expertise from across the country, and the continually growing archive of searchable information provided by the NACAC listserv would have been feasible before computers and the Internet became ubiquitous just a few years ago.

School districts and state education agencies are also building professional communities on the Internet. The Massachusetts Department of Education, for example, has created the Massachusetts Online Network for Education (MASSONE, at massone.mass.edu/), a "set of Web-based tools for communication, collaboration, and curriculum planning, designed to support PreK–12 standards-based teaching and learning." From MASSONE's home page a huge array of resources is available, at no cost to participants, including discussion forums for teachers to exchange ideas, a "virtual hard drive" so that teachers and students can store and retrieve information from computers anywhere, tools for teachers to create and share lesson plans, searchable databases with lesson plans and online resources, and survey tools allowing teachers to quickly create and manage their own online survey or quiz. Teachers can set up discussion forums for students and can create and share online calendars for their classes. For administrators, statistical reports about districts in the state can be accessed through MASSONE, which also lists and supports many statewide data collection initiatives. Information for prospective Massachusetts teachers is also provided online, including teachers from out of state considering a move to Massachusetts. School districts and other educational organizations can also use MASSONE to support online workshops and courses. The Barnstable Public Schools on Cape Cod, for example, offered its teachers more than a half-dozen online courses in the spring of 2007 through MASSONE.

The American Federation of Teachers and the National Education Association each support online programs or communities for teachers. Also, hundreds of recognized teacher leaders are members of the Teacher Leaders Network, a Web-based organization that provides members with a community and a visible voice in the national conversation about improving schools.[26]

In-Service Professional Development

Providing teachers with courses, workshops, and other forms of in-service professional development is pervasive, expensive (costing American schools many billions of dollars per year), and essential. There are no serious school improvement programs or practices that do not include teacher professional development as one vital component. One important responsibility of education policymakers is to help ensure that there is a system of high-quality professional development in place that supports teachers in meeting key education goals.

Online professional development for teachers is proliferating. More than half of all public schools already report that their teachers access professional development through online courses taken at the school.[27] This figure probably underestimates teachers' participation in online courses because school personnel may not be aware of the courses taken by teachers offered by hundreds of organizations outside schools and districts, such as institutions of higher education, for-profit providers, museums (e.g., the American Museum of Natural History), professional associations, or other nonprofits (e.g., PBS TeacherLine, teacherline.pbs.org, which offers more than 100 online courses for teachers).

Given a choice, teachers might prefer online teacher professional development for a number of reasons, including the fact that an online course fits more easily into a busy schedule or because it eliminates travel time to get to a campus. Online teacher professional development can provide access to content that is not available otherwise, as well as to a more diverse group of teacher colleagues. Online training, especially asynchronous training, has a greater likelihood of meeting the *"any time, any place, any path, any pace*™*"* slogan of the Florida Virtual School.

The business world has seen enormous growth in online training, as much as or more than schools. One of the primary reasons that businesses adopt online staff development is to save commuting time and expense. Also, opportunity costs are a consideration; participants can fit their training around critical events at work. When someone is away from a business being trained, phone calls go unanswered and work doesn't get done.

Similarly, traditional face-to-face teacher professional development has generally taken place after school or on student release days or weekends. Such events have to compete for time with other responsibilities in a teacher's life. Online, asynchronous professional education has the advantage of fitting around a teacher's other activities. Schools, however, should not assume that a teacher's out-of-school time is a cost-free resource.

In well-designed programs, especially those in which teachers can post information at any time of day or night, people engaged in online professional development may be *more* reflective than in a face-to-face environment because there is less pressure to respond quickly to comments or prompts online than there is to normal dialogue in a face-to-face conversation. Similarly, people who are not assertive in person may nonetheless be willing to post their comments online.

A unique aspect of the Internet is the availability of streaming video from any computer that is online. The Rhode Island Department of Education has a website that includes video of lessons, made in Rhode Island classrooms, which are aligned to the state's education goals.[28] At least two commercial companies, LessonLab (a Pearson Education company, www.lessonlab.com) and Teachscape (www.teachscape.com), rely on video vignettes of classroom teaching as a centerpiece of their professional development offerings. Video is a powerful medium for learning about teaching. However, it is by no means sufficient simply to watch a video, even of a good teacher. People need to learn *what* to look for as they watch a classroom in a video vignette, and even *how to talk* thoughtfully about what they see. Analysis is needed, not just observation. Despite these caveats, classroom videos provide a very useful tool for learning about teaching.

One case in point is a set of video studies of mathematics and science teaching conducted in seven nations, including the United States. These studies were conducted in 1999 as part of the Third International Mathematics and Science Study (TIMSS).[29] It is eye-opening to watch and listen to typical lessons from different countries. (Audio tracks on the CD-ROM are translated into English.) For example, one Japanese eighth-grade mathematics teacher posed a far more challenging and mathematically interesting problem to students than any of the American teachers shown and required his students to think for themselves in ways quite different than the American teachers. A single lesson proves nothing, but analysis of hundreds of lessons found that American eighth-grade mathematics teachers spend far more time reviewing what has previously been taught (more than half the class time) than their counterparts in all but one other nation (Czechoslovakia).[30]

The LessonLab company was, in fact, created as an outgrowth of the TIMSS study and related work by researchers. However, LessonLab (as well as Teachscape) has expanded to other subjects besides math and science. Hundreds of hours of video for teachers are available for free online, courtesy of the Annenberg Foundation, both to provide background in subject matter and to increase expertise in teaching methods.[31]

Online professional development will not simply replace traditional, face-to-face professional development. Each has its advantages, and there will always be both effective and ineffective professional development activities to be found in either medium. However, it may be surprising to find that teachers can usefully learn online even how to conduct and learn from hands-on science labs. Lesley University in Massachusetts has developed an online master's degree program in K–8 science education. Teachers are provided with kits of materials to conduct their own science experiments, at home or at school, and they discuss their findings as part of the online courses.[32] Using educational technology in the classroom is another topic of online professional development offerings for teachers. The MASSONE offerings by Barnstable Public Schools, for example, include a course for teachers on Digital Media in the Classroom and another called Creating Assessments Using Online Tools.

Taking courses is not the only form of professional development that is valuable to teachers and administrators. Equally important is "informal" professional development in a professional community, ranging from hallway conversations with colleagues to professional meetings and conferences.

MAKING TEACHING MORE ATTRACTIVE

"The preponderance of psychological evidence indicates that experts are made, not born,"[33] one expert wrote, and indeed, we are learning a great deal about the conditions and the experiences that help typical teachers grow and become better teachers. Creating supportive working conditions for teachers is not only a proven way to contribute to higher student achievement,[34] it is also essential to attract and retain good people. Ted Sizer, an education writer who was a school principal as well as chairman of the Coalition of Essential Schools, has said:

The big problem is: *Good people don't take and stay in jobs that don't entrust them with important things.* [emphasis added] Smart college graduates look at the way the system works now and say, "Well, maybe for a few years, Teach for America or something, but the system doesn't trust me, and there is no way I am going to make this a lifelong career." So any solution to the teacher-quality problem has to reflect the movement of authority *downward.*[35]

Good people also look at the teaching profession and wonder whether teachers are being given the tools they need to do their jobs well. Are they provided with a computer to use for professional purposes—to do their job better? Are they and their students given access to technologies that have been proven to help them achieve important education goals? We know that beginning doctors, soldiers, and many other professionals use state-of-the-art technology. Soon, one would hope, the same statement can honestly be made about beginning teachers' uses of technology.

CHAPTER 7

Increasing Support for Children Outside School (Goal 5)

Digital technology is helping schools meet the needs of many learners—yet only about 10 percent of a child's life from birth to age 18 is spent in school. Young people need support from parents and their communities at other times, too, not just during school hours.

Computers, the Internet, and other digital technologies help provide support for children and parents outside schools in a number of ways. For example:

- Dozens of websites provide services to help students with schoolwork and new online guidance systems are being developed to support young people in planning their future.
- Websites provide busy parents with information about how well their children are doing in school—information easily accessible from anywhere, 24 hours a day.
- Computer Clubhouses, community technology centers, and other out-of-school programs provide students from low-income families with access to high-technology programs.
- The E-Rate program has provided hundreds of millions of dollars to public libraries resulting in 100 percent of libraries now being connected to the Internet—up from 28 percent in 1996—improving access to the Internet outside school hours for children from low-income families.

These and other constructive uses of technology to support children's learning will continue to expand, as described below.

But in what context is change happening? Technology is not magic; it operates in a social milieu. Since 1960, largely because of federal programs, the poverty rate for people over 65 has declined by an amazing 70 percent, from over 35 percent of the elderly in 1960 who were poor to only 10.1 percent in 2005.[1] At the same time, the poverty rate for children under 19 declined far more slowly, and in 2005 it was still 17.6 percent. What is more, the biggest decline in child poverty took place decades ago; since 1970 the poverty rate for children has not been significantly reduced. As a surprising analysis of trends in the federal budget says, "children are a diminishing national priority."[2]

Computers and other digital technologies obviously cannot fix that problem. Policymakers cannot continue to reduce priorities placed on helping children—a more diverse group than in 1960, with greater needs—and simply expect magic to happen because of the increased use of technology. The opposite is true, namely that there are significant negative trends in young people's use of media and technology. If families and communities are not vigilant, excessive use of technology, almost all of it outside school, will create problems for children that outweigh the benefits of many smart uses of technology to support the young.

CHILDREN'S USE OF MEDIA

For generations it has been too easy for older people to complain about the values and behavior of the young. The fact is that most young people are well adjusted and that as a group they establish high goals for themselves, such as attending college. Nonetheless, the excessive use of media by young people, especially television, is cause for concern. And the increasing, pervasive use of digital technology by young people—the Internet, portable music players, video games, cell phones—has not displaced the use of television. Instead, the total time that children ages 8 to 18 use media every day has now grown to almost 6.5 hours per day.[3] That adds up to considerably more than 40 hours per week, a typical full-time job.

Reading is one of the activities that *has* been displaced by media use. In 1946, 92 percent of young people had read a book during the past year. By 2002, the figure was down to 50 percent.[4] This is a shame, and it's not merely a prejudice for books. Print materials contain more complex words and ideas than television and offer a much wider range of subjects.

Young people spend nearly four hours a day watching TV and videos. Television is still the dominant medium for 8- to 18-year-olds, far outstripping the time they spend listening to music (a bit less than 2 hours), using computers (1 hour), or playing video games (49 minutes). In contrast, less than an hour a day (50 minutes) is spent doing homework.[5]

Not all television viewing is bad. But is it a good thing for young people to spend almost 30 hours a week viewing dozens of TV programs, which are too often filled with questionable behavior and unsavory characters? Surely it is not.

Amazingly, more than half of all 8- to 18-year-olds report that their parents *have no rules* about what or how much TV they can watch.[6] The same is true for using the Internet and playing video games; fewer families have rules (let alone rules they enforce) than do not. Even among 8- to 10-year-olds, just slightly more than half reported their parents made rules about watching TV. And the most common family rule is that homework must be done before watching TV, which still allows children an enormous amount of time to watch television.

"The fault, dear Brutus, is not in our stars, but in ourselves. . . ." The average child lives in a home that has 3.5 televisions. Almost two-thirds of children live in homes where the TV is usually on during meals. Two-thirds of children have a TV *in their bedroom* (compared to less than one-third with a computer in their bedroom). Children with a TV in their bedroom watch 50 percent more TV than those without. Conversely, children without a TV in the bedroom spend almost 50 percent more time reading than those with a TV.

This is bad news. Schools do not exist in a vacuum and cannot be expected to make up for all the problems outside schools. Schools can help students to learn appropriate and effective ways to use computers and the Internet, but educators should not be held responsible for the oversaturated, permissive media environment in children's homes.

It is time for a campaign to educate parents and communities about excessive TV viewing. Public service advertising aimed at reducing smoking, drinking, drunk driving, and other dangerous habits *has* had an impact. We need a similar campaign to reduce television viewing, or excessive media use of any kind, among the young. Otherwise, whatever the schools do to help children use digital technology in smart ways will be more than offset by the lack of parental rules for children and people's mindless media habits at home. The responsibility for improving the situation lies first of all with adults, but we should also educate young people to make better choices.

Schools can help educate children about out-of-school media use. One approach would be to survey students regarding their media habits (something the students themselves can do under supervision, perhaps using a free online survey tool) and then use the local results, as well as national data, to raise awareness among students and parents about young people's use of media.

An effort by the federal government 30 years ago to promote "critical television viewing skills" among young people was ridiculed by then-senator William Proxmire, who awarded the project a Golden Fleece award for wasting taxpayers' money. Attitudes have changed, and more people now understand how important it is to educate students to use television, the Internet, and other media intelligently. Dozens of states reportedly support school-based media-literacy education in one form or another;[7] however, current efforts are too weak and primarily focus on using the Internet safely.

USING DIGITAL TOOLS TO SUPPORT CHILDREN

Setting appropriate limits on young people's use of media outside school makes good sense. Fortunately, there are also many valuable applications of technology for students and parents to support young people's education.

Online Tutoring, Homework, and Test Preparation

Students from low-income families cannot afford the same out-of-school services as students from wealthier families. With the Internet, that situation is changing.

For example, in Henrico County, Virginia, where every student in grades 6 to 12 is provided with a laptop computer, the district paid for a service providing online preparation for the SAT college admissions test, thereby leveling the playing field for those who previously could not afford such services. Maine, another site of a 1-to-1 computing program, recently received a donation of more than $4 million allowing every high school junior in the state to register for an online SAT-preparation course.[8] Although *Consumer Reports* expressed some concerns about these services (including, in some cases, an inappropriate blending of advertising and educational content), their review of ten online SAT test-preparation sites concluded that 7 of the 10 were "generally effective in their product delivery and the overall quality of their services."[9]

Dozens of websites offer other forms of tutoring and one-time help with schoolwork, many of them at no charge. The New York public library system, for example, sponsors a homework website (homeworknyc.org/), as well as providing assistance to students via the telephone or through instant-messaging. Students in New York State can obtain help with the Regents exams at www.regentsprep.org.

Youth whose parents are well educated could always ask their parents for help doing homework; parents are used to providing such assistance. That type of help is now available to anyone with a computer connected to the Internet.

Career Guidance Services for Students

States are using the Internet to provide new guidance services to students. Concerned that youth are not thinking ahead about the courses they take and how those courses will prepare them for careers, Kentucky, for example, launched an online system to help students make better plans.[10] Students can learn about different careers, including job descriptions, working conditions, pay scales, and educational requirements. They can watch multimedia interviews of people in different fields and take interest and skill inventories providing feedback, including information about the other skills students may need to qualify for a given occupation. There is also a "career matchmaker" function, for those who want to use it. Students can also create "individual learning plans" with the system, as well as résumés.

Furthermore, Kentucky is linking students' demographic and academic data with their career interests. And the entire pre-college guidance system is linked to information about colleges, including financial aid. "We wanted to take our antiquated paper [system] and take it into the real world," according to a spokesperson for the program.[11]

The online guidance system (www.careercruising.com) offers information in Spanish as well as English. Students log in to the website. There, they can save and access their information, including information about courses they have already taken and community service experiences, from any computer linked to the Internet. "I've already had more kids in the last week say things about this than I've ever had in 13 years of education," according to one guidance counselor.[12]

Putting More and Better Information about Schools into Parents' Hands

Parents and communities usually want the best for their students. Members of the public are keenly interested in how well schools are doing, but for decades most information about schools was paper-based and not easily accessible. Comparing the characteristics of different schools—such as their demographics, the qualifications of their teachers, or students' test scores—would have taken a considerable amount of research. Now doing research about local schools is as quick as clicking a mouse.

GreatSchools.net, an independent, nonprofit organization started in 1998, contains profiles of more than 100,000 schools across the United States. Data about schools is also compiled by SchoolMatters (a service provided by Standard & Poor's), Just for the Kids California, and other websites, including many run by state departments of education and by local school districts. Similarly, data about thousands of school districts can also be found online at the website of the National Center for Education Statistics, an arm of the United States Department of Education (http://nces.ed.gov/).

Parents are among the heaviest users of sites with information about schools, as are educators themselves. The easy availability of these data is changing the conversation about schools. Principals, for example, can find schools with similar demographic characteristics, but which outperform their own school, and then investigate how the schools obtain better results. As one principal said, "[Even if we can't change our student population], we can look at schools with high results. So let's look at what they are doing."[13]

Parents can use the Web to investigate local options for educating their child. Some websites allow parents to find schools in a particular town, or even within a given number of miles from home. Many provide for side-by-side comparisons of school data, which can help parents choose a school. In fact, the founder of GreatSchools.net, Bill Jackson, said, "What's driving this is an increase in options. It's led to an expectation on the part of parents that they do have choices."[14] And, indeed, that expectation generates a huge demand: There are more than 2 million visitors to the GreatSchools website each month.

In addition, many organizations offer parents information, via the Internet, to help them support their children's education, encouraging them to read to their children, engage in political advocacy to strengthen schools, or help in other ways. The Education Trust, for example, provides links on its website to dozens of resources for parents, including some in Spanish.[15] There are brochures explaining the No Child Left Behind Act, guides aimed especially at African American parents and Hispanic parents, as well as other materials.

Computers are also changing the ways that schools communicate with parents. Websites like K12Planet* and SurfYourWork.com allow teachers to post a variety of information that is then made accessible to students and/or parents. Using a password, parents and students can log in and review important information (in those categories they are permitted to see), such as how well a student is doing in his or her courses, a list of homework assignments, or even access to documents that a student may need to do the homework, such as Word or Adobe Acrobat files. Some websites are also built for other types of transactions, such as allowing students to deliver their completed homework electronically, or permitting administrators to post school events to a calendar available for students and parents to view online.

Interestingly, a high school student developed SurfYourWork.com (which calls itself a School Management System). He reportedly sold the product for $1.25 million.[16] The website includes features that allow students to communicate and collaborate with one another, and it provides some services to schools for free.

Websites that help schools communicate with parents and students are becoming amazingly popular. For example, the Fresno Unified School District, in California, enrolls about 80,000 students and uses a management system called PowerSchool* (a registered trademark of Apple Computer, Inc.). In the 2004–2005 school year, more than 20,000 students and 20,000 parents had log-in codes allowing them to access the district's website, and there were more than a million log-ins.[17] The system was being expanded to allow more parents and students to have access. And this was in just one of the nation's 15,000 school districts.

Greater Lawrence Technical School in Massachusetts uses a Web portal for parents to provide a wide variety of information they would have been entitled to receive in person, but often didn't have time to obtain. The password-protected Web pages offer information from report cards, progress reports, attendance, and discipline records.[18] By the time a student gets home, parents may already know of any disciplinary problems that occurred at school during the day. Having access to specific and up-to-date information about her child's grades led one parent to comment:

> When you log in, there's a contact section. If I have a question about a grade or a comment, I can e-mail the department and they always, always, e-mail me right back or they call me on the phone. Without the portal, I wouldn't know who to call.[19]

So-called school-to-home communications systems are another computer-based innovation designed to improve connections between schools and homes. These systems can automatically place phone calls to hundreds or thousands of homes, delivering messages recorded by administrators. The systems can be used on snow days, or during school emergencies ranging from a bomb scare to a broken-down bus. If a call fails, the system provides that information to the administration, which then knows they need an updated telephone number. Companies that distribute such systems include Connect-Ed, School Messenger, ParentLink, and Instant Alert for Schools.[20] Some systems can send e-mails as well as make telephone calls.

The common feature of all these types of systems—those providing comparative data about schools, school management systems, and school-to-home communications systems—is that they help parents provide better support to their children. These services also help parents and other members of the public better understand schools, and thus make those institutions more accessible and accountable to the people they serve. Rather than having to make an appointment to see a teacher or the school principal, or having to spend hours in the library finding information, or listening to the radio to get an update about what is happening at a school, the information needed becomes available quickly and easily. As a result, people's relationships to schools are changed. Institutions that once may have seemed distant or hard to communicate with become closer and more transparent. Improving communication with the public helps schools garner greater support as well as improving school systems' effectiveness.

Linking Parents and Schools with Other Organizations

Schools alone cannot provide enough support to children to help ensure their success. Health providers, social service agencies, and other organizations are also important in children's lives. Children who are not healthy, for instance, are less likely to do well in school. In Syracuse, New York, the principal of an elementary school that narrowed the gap between test scores of Black and White students said that a health clinic and a prekindergarten program were responsible for the gains.[21]

The Internet enables schools to become better connected with other organizations. Los Angeles is using computer-based discussion forums, and other high-technology tools, to help identify crime problems near school sites and address those problems. New York City has incorporated computer-based tools into its Impact Schools initiative, which reportedly has resulted in a 50 percent reduction in crime in and around targeted schools.[22]

Schools are creating partnerships with and connections to institutions such as health clinics, universities, and city parks departments. The website for the Indianapolis public schools includes links to information for many out-of-school activities, such as opportunities to send at-risk students to summer camp, ways to find help for children with mental health problems, and how to enroll in a university-based summer program to improve elementary school students' reading skills.[23] The website for Boston's public schools includes newsletters about summer opportunities for children. Chicago Public Schools has a Department of External Resources and Partnerships whose newsletter is available online, and the school system's website links directly to the city's website and its vast array of resources.

Increasingly, schools are gateways to a wide range of institutions, services, and community organizations; still, greater efforts need to be made to expand these connections. One program to foster connections is the

National Network of Partnership Schools at Johns Hopkins University.[24] About 1,000 schools are part of the network, which promotes research-based approaches to foster family and community involvement and provides information for schools via the Internet. The Annenberg Institute for School Reform is another organization supporting efforts to help students both in school and out.

Approaching the issue from a different perspective, the American Architectural Foundation, in partnership with Knowledgeworks Foundation, provides the Richard Riley Award to schools that make their facilities more accessible to the community. The award is named for former secretary of education Richard Riley, who promoted the concept of making schools centers for community services. Schools are already important focal points in communities, and increasing their use outside of school hours makes them more vital, more effective institutions. Videos and other information about schools with outstanding connections to the community are available online.[25]

Mentoring

To succeed in school young people need caring relationships with adults both in and outside school. According to a recent study, these relationships are absent for about 20 percent of children, and that percentage is even larger for children from low-income families.[26] Mentoring programs are one way to help address this deficiency. Students in high-quality mentoring programs have fewer school absences, better school attitudes and behavior, higher college participation, and less use of drugs and alcohol.[27]

For educators, parents, or others looking for mentoring programs, or mentors, there are websites to help. Sites provide information about the role of mentors, questions to ask to help decide if a program is of high quality, how to decide if a mentor is a safe person, and research findings about mentoring programs.[28] Mentoring programs can be located online by state, or locally by entering a zip code. Websites also provide opportunities for volunteers to sign up to become mentors.

Online mentoring is not likely to replace face-to-face relationships between young people and adults. Still, for some young people—notably students enrolled in online schools, but others as well—virtual or online mentoring can be useful. In Washington State, for example, students at the University of Washington are available to mentor students in dozens of schools across the state who are members of the Digital Learning Commons (DLC).[29] The DLC is an organization created to provide on-line courses, technology tools, and other educational resources to students and teachers in Washington State.

Afterschool Programs Teaching Technology

There is still a substantial difference in access to home computers depending on such factors as race, poverty, and parents' education. In 2003, 78 percent of White students used computers at home, while the corresponding figures for Hispanic and Black students were 48 percent and 46 percent.[30] Only 35 percent of students used computers at home in families where the parents had less than a high school credential, compared to 82 percent for students in which one or more parent had a college degree. Students with a computer at home are in a much better position to develop basic computer literacy and learn to use common computer software, such as word processors; in 2003, for example, White students used word processors at home at a rate nearly double that of Black students.

There have been efforts to overcome this "digital divide" for decades. In 1980, when hardly anyone owned a personal computer, Antonia (Toni) Stone set up the first community technology center in the United States. The first center (called Playing to Win and located in Harlem, New York) and its successors provided training in computer skills as well as public access to computers. By the year 2000 there were hundreds of community technology centers across the country, most of which served not only adults but also students in afterschool programs.[31] These centers helped provide students attending high-poverty schools an opportunity to access computers and learn about technology in a disciplined way.

The No Child Left Behind Act of 2001 revised the mission of those community technology centers that were federally funded and renamed them 21st Century Community Learning Centers.[32] The purpose of these centers is to provide afterschool programs to students attending high-poverty schools. Some of the centers still offer technology education programs.

In addition to the Community Learning Centers, there are a variety of other afterschool opportunities for students to learn technology skills. Such skills are important because jobs requiring science, technology, engineering, and mathematics skills are projected to increase at a faster rate than other jobs. Besides, computer skills are part of the "new basics" that everyone needs.

Similar to the community technology centers, a Computer Clubhouse for inner-city youth was started in the early 1990s by The Computer Museum, which is now part of the Boston Museum of Science, in collaboration with the MIT Media Lab. Young people come to the Clubhouse to work with adults and create computer-generated art, music, and video; scientific simulations; animations; kinetic sculptures and robots; and Web pages.[33] The goal is for students to become excited about learning and fluent with digital technologies, ultimately developing skills that can help them in their careers or their communities.

The original Computer Clubhouse spawned more than a dozen similar programs in other locations, and then, in 2000, Intel Corporation decided to invest in supporting more clubhouses. Since then, other sponsors have also signed on; now, there are more than 100 clubhouses around the world, including dozens in the United States, supported by a Computer Clubhouse Network.[34]

In some places, the Clubhouses are connected to the Girl Scouts, Boys and Girls Clubs, and other youth organizations. Increasingly those organizations, too, offer young people out-of-school opportunities to learn how to use computers and other technologies. Although there is still a significant "digital divide," progress has been made in narrowing the gap.

CHAPTER 8

Requiring Accountability for Results (Goal 6)

The No Child Left Behind Act requires that schools show "adequate yearly progress" in the form of increases on standardized test scores, or else be subject to a variety of sanctions. More than any federal legislation ever passed, NCLB made accountability an overarching goal of elementary and secondary school reform. But even without NCLB, many states and districts had already increased schools' accountability for results. Governors, school superintendents, and many others are requiring greater accountability from schools.

To be accountable, educators, school systems, policymakers, and the public need accurate and timely information by which progress, or lack thereof, can be measured. Obtaining such information and then making good use of it might seem to be straightforward tasks, but they are actually quite challenging, especially when one is talking about tens of millions of students.

Take the apparently simple issue of raising high school graduation rates. High school dropout rates are surprisingly high, so governors and state legislators might insist that a state's high school graduation rate be improved. But how are such rates measured?

There are many different ways to measure graduation rates, with different states and even different districts within a state historically using measures that are not comparable with one another. A school can count the number of entering twelfth graders and compare that to the number of high school graduates nine months later. However, this approach ignores all the students who drop out of school before twelfth grade, and so it makes the graduation rate look too good. But if one wants to track, say, the incoming ninth graders and find out whether they have graduated four or five years later, the measurement problem is far more complex. Then it becomes important to find out whether students who don't show up in school have moved to a different school, either in the same state or in another, and what happens to them once they are there. Keeping track of the movements of students over a period of many years is simply not the norm in many places. In the pre-computer era one could easily understand what a monumental task it would be to track millions of students. Now, however, it is primarily a question of standardizing definitions and assigning students ID numbers, as well as finding the money and the willpower to do the job. It wasn't until 2005 that all governors signed an agreement to standardize the way that graduation rates are calculated—and, of course, simply reaching such an agreement does not mean that accurate data, or data management systems, are easily and widely available.[1] In fact, as of 2006 only about half the states could calculate high school graduation rates using the definition adopted by all 50 governors![2] This is a surprisingly small fraction of the states, given how important it is that students graduate high school.

Without appropriate use of digital technology and the political will to track important trends, the only information that educators, policymakers, and the public have is a hodgepodge of data of dubious reliability—hardly the stuff of which accountability is made. Computers make it possible not only to gather millions of pieces of data, but also to make sense of it and to use it more wisely. Chapter 6 discussed teachers' use of handheld computers to keep track of students' reading achievement. Three other powerful examples of using digital technology to improve accountability are illustrated and discussed in this chapter: computer-based testing; the use of data to improve instruction; and, putting more and timelier information about schools and students into parents' hands.

COMPUTER-BASED TESTING

Tens of millions of standardized tests are administered every year in schools, and the number is increasing because the No Child Left Behind Act requires that more school subjects be tested annually using "high-stakes" tests—namely tests with consequences for schools. Schools that miss improvement targets are subject to an increasingly tough set of remedial and ultimately punitive steps. You don't have to believe that testing is the only way to measure progress—most people agree it isn't—to understand that NCLB makes standardized tests more important than ever.

To administer and score tens of millions of tests costs billions of dollars annually. Yet despite the cost, the slow turnaround time before test results are ready and while the exams are scored is inefficient. Computer-based testing helps address each of these problems. Computers can dramatically improve schools' efficiency and effectiveness in testing students, just as they have already done for driver's license tests in many states. Many people now know instantly whether or not they have passed their driver's license test. There's no waiting and no extra expense to the Division of Motor Vehicles for scoring the test, which the applicant takes directly in front of a screen on a computer. Even the Graduate Record examination (required for admission into many graduate programs) is now administered on a computer, and the score is available as soon as the test is finished.

Computer-based testing for elementary and secondary students is already taking place in schools in many states. Oregon and Virginia have been among the pioneering states in this field. Oregon alone administers more than 1 million tests online during a school year. The state developed its own testing technology, which it calls the Technology Enhanced Student Assessment, or TESA. During the 2004–2005 school year, about three-quarters of Oregon students sat at computers and used TESA to take tests measuring their progress in meeting state education standards. The state's goal is that 100 percent of students will soon use computers for such tests. In some subjects, other sorts of tests complement computer-based testing. For example, high school science students are required to perform laboratory experiments and write about them, and their results are scored as part of the state's testing requirements.

According to Oregon's state superintendent for instruction, "Our investment in TESA is paying off in both financial and academic terms."[3] Another state official estimated that the state saves $1.30 per student for each test administered electronically instead of using paper and pencil. Savings quickly add up over millions of tests and multiple years.

Virginia, rather than developing its own testing system, teamed up with NCS Pearson to begin experimenting with online testing in the year 2000. Hundreds of thousands of online tests have been administered to Virginia's high school students. As in Oregon, the state's goal is to expand the system. Eventually, all state tests administered to high school students will be delivered online. The online system includes security provisions so that students can't open electronic documents on the computer, or use other software, while they are taking a test. To help its schools, Virginia offers funds to improve districts' network and hardware infrastructure so that schools will be ready when online testing becomes widespread.

When students take tests on computers, data about their performance does not need to be entered into the computer separately; it's already there, item by item. As a result, computer-based testing can help any school system study the performance of its students. So-called "data-driven decisionmaking" (discussed below in this chapter) allows a teacher, a principal, or even a whole school system to adjust curriculum or instruction based on an understanding of what students know and are able to do. Many effective school systems now do just that. Not only districts, but also whole states are working to improve their data systems, and the United States Department of Education is investing more than $50 million in grants to help states improve the nature and quality of their education data and make it easier to use.[4] For states to build "data warehouses," analyze the data, and make it available in timely, useful, convenient forms is expensive, and can cost more than $10 million per state.[5] As yet, some states do not even assign unique ID numbers to identify students and keep track of them if they move from one school or district to another.

Testing on computers does more than increase efficiency. The fast turnaround provided by computer-based testing allows schools to greatly expand the use of tests to improve instruction. If scoring can be done rapidly, computer-based tests can quickly inform teachers and students about areas in which the students need more help. In the past, standardized tests used to measure students' annual progress were typically administered near the end of the school year, but weren't scored and returned until the beginning of the following school year, thus significantly limiting their usefulness for improving instruction. Some states are now changing the timetable for testing, as well as relying more heavily on computers. Many companies are offering computer-based testing for "formative" purposes; that is, to provide information that can guide teachers and students by pinpointing what students know and are able to do. To select two examples among many, Plato Learning, Inc. markets the eduTest Web-based assessment system, which is reportedly used in more than 3,000 schools, and the nonprofit Northwest Evaluation Association has developed Web-based "benchmark" assessments called Measures of Academic Progress (MAP).

Summary Street

Amazingly, schools are beginning to apply Web-based computer testing and scoring even to students' essays. NCS Pearson, for example, markets a product, Summary Street™, that serves as a way to assess and score students' writing *and* as a way to provide feedback to students that helps them improve their writing.[6] Summary Street is provided to students via the Web and is based on having students summarize texts they have read on many different topics in the curriculum, from science to social studies. Because about half of middle and high school students read at only a basic level, or below, improving students' reading comprehension is an important national priority.

The basic idea of Summary Street is that students need to read and understand a piece of writing before they can summarize it effectively. When they get feedback about the summaries they write, they learn to read better and to write better. Grading students' writing is time-consuming for teachers (many of whom teach more than a hundred students), and because Summary Street can provide students with more opportunities to get constructive feedback about what they have written, it helps both the student and the teacher. Surprisingly, scores on students' writing based on the Summary Street technology (also known as the KAT™ engine) are as accurate as human graders' scores, agreeing with the human beings' scores more often than several people's scores agree with each other. The technology also provides reliable information about students' understanding of the content that they have read, making it useful for teaching in different subject areas.[7]

Students using Summary Street improve in general writing skills, summarization skills, and reading comprehension. In one study, the impacts were such that students who initially scored at the 50th percentile (average) would have been able to improve their writing performance with challenging material to the 82nd percentile.[8] This increase is a dramatic and unusually large improvement to report after only a few weeks, for any type of instructional approach. Summary Street was developed at the University of Colorado at Boulder. Students reportedly find it motivating and enjoyable to use.

A variety of other products exist, and more will be developed, to provide students with feedback designed to increase their skills and understanding. The key point is not that one particular product or another is worthwhile (something that changes from year to year, as more good products and new research becomes available), but that computers can provide teachers and students with scores that serve multiple purposes, both assessment *and* instruction, in ways that are powerful and that add significant value to what teachers are typically able to do without computers. When students and teachers are provided with useful information about student performance, it is both easier to improve instruction and more appropriate to hold the teachers and students accountable.

Assistments

Another example of the use of computers to provide feedback to students is a pilot program in Massachusetts called the Assistment project (www. assistment.org), funded by the United States Department of Education. Designed and managed by researchers at Worcester Polytechnic Institute and Carnegie Mellon University, the Assistment system provides Web-based tutoring in mathematics for students in grades 4 through 10. The system combines tutoring—assistance—with reports to teachers about students' skills—assessments. Dozens of skills are tracked for each student, carefully tied to the state's mathematics standards, and to its student assessment system, the Massachusetts Comprehensive Assessment System, or MCAS. About every two weeks, students use computers to access the online system, which automatically provides them with tutoring on items they get wrong. Researchers have demonstrated that the Assistment system can reliably predict students' MCAS scores and track individual skills being learned by students. A teacher can, therefore, use aggregated information about the students in her class to adjust instruction and focus on areas of high need. Researchers have also shown that students learn directly from the system, making it quite different than the usual standardized test.

The project directors, Neil Heffernan and Kenneth Koedinger, hope to expand the Assistment system so that it serves students throughout Massachusetts. It may be possible to apply the same principles to create similar systems in other states and other subjects.

The Use of Computer-Based Tools for Testing

The computer also provides other benefits when used for testing students. An increasing number of students use the computer as an integral tool for learning—such as learning to write by using a word processor, which makes the process of revising text much easier. Yet typically students are tested without computers, so they cannot use the same tools on tests that they use to do their work. This is discouraging not only to students but also to teachers, who wonder whether it makes sense to teach using computers if their students learn to rely on them for certain purposes but can't use the computer on tests.

Both teachers and students understand that what's tested is often what is most valued; if it's not tested, it may not be important. When computers are used for testing, this situation changes by opening up the possibility of using computer-based tools as part of the tests. North Carolina, for example, has used computers to test students' knowledge of basic computer tools, such as spreadsheets and word processors. Doing this with paper and pencil makes little sense, although, unfortunately, it is not uncommon—another example of a dubious way of testing students. Similarly, because most people use word processors for much of their writing, it would make sense to test students' writing using word processors, especially when longer pieces of writing are called for. There is already an important precedent. The use of graphing calculators is now ubiquitous for teaching advanced mathematics, just as the use of slide rules was in an earlier era, and it is natural for students to use these basic tools of the trade when they are tested—just as they will use them later on the job. Already, the College Board and others allow students to use calculators on certain college admissions mathematics tests.

Computers can be programmed to provide many different tools on the screen (including the equivalent of handheld graphing calculators), and the software used for testing can restrict students' use of computer-based tools so that the tools are operable only for certain test items. This capability could have a positive impact on teaching and learning. It is easy to believe, for example, that teachers' and students' use of spreadsheets in mathematics classes will become commonplace only when spreadsheets can be used on selected items on high-stakes mathematics tests, reflecting through the testing process the value that schools and society place on learning to use these ubiquitous tools. Formulas used in spreadsheets are algebraic, so spreadsheets are a useful tool for teaching algebra and applying algebra skills in a commonly used, real-world application.

The National Assessment of Educational Progress (NAEP), also called "the nation's report card," concluded that testing students in technology-rich environments is important in order "to measure skills that cannot be easily measured by conventional paper-and-pencil means," such as students' facility in using computer-based searches and simulations for solving certain types of science problems. An exploratory NAEP study also found that a large majority of students enjoy using computers and reported getting more schoolwork done when they use a computer.[9]

Adaptive Testing

An additional advantage of computers is that they can increase the accuracy of tests through a process known as *adaptive testing*. Rather than providing each student with the same test items, the computer can present new items based on whether the student has gotten previous questions right or wrong. If the student has gotten several questions wrong, the computer presents an easier question; if the student has gotten several questions right, a harder question is posed. By offering each student a greater number of items better matched to their abilities, a more accurate score can be obtained. Unfortunately, the No Child Left Behind Act requires that all students be given the same test items as other students on any tests used to meet requirements of the law, thus discouraging the use of computer-based adaptive testing.

The Importance of Computer-Based Testing

Even if other applications of digital technology were ignored, the advantages of using computers for testing makes these devices as essential to schools as they already are to most other organizations. More than 20 states have followed the examples set by Oregon and Virginia and offer some form of computer-based assessment of student learning.[10] Eventually, computer-based testing will become the norm, not the exception.

Nonetheless, the great emphasis on testing is creating a number of problems. Not only is the number and variety of standardized tests in use almost unbelievable, but also the cost of meeting the testing requirements of the No Child Left Behind Act range to more than $5 billion.[11] The testing industry is having a hard time simply maintaining test quality while keeping up with the relentless demand for new tests.

Because so many tests are being administered to so many students, 15 states use only multiple-choice tests. Although such tests are easy to grade, they typically limit the skills and knowledge that can be tested, putting a premium on facts at the expense of critical thinking, problem-solving, and a host of "soft skills" that are needed by students, such as the ability to work well in groups. There is no technical reason why students can't provide longer, constructed answers to questions posed on a computer. Even students' handwritten sketches can be scanned and stored as computer data. The difficulty is that it's generally more expensive and more time-consuming to grade constructed responses than multiple-choice answers. Sometimes, however, you get what you pay for—and testing may be one of those situations. Many people are rightfully concerned that an overreliance on standardized tests will skew school systems to focus almost exclusively on what is easily and cheaply tested, thus squeezing out valuable parts of the curriculum.

The federal government, the states, and publishers of instructional materials need to invest more money—eventually hundreds of millions of dollars—to develop a new generation of high-quality, computer-based tests. These tests will be more focused on providing students, teachers, and schools with usable data to improve teaching and learning. They will focus on a wider range of important skills and knowledge. New tests will increasingly incorporate computer-based tools when appropriate, just as many tests already allow the use of calculators for certain items or sections. With the power of multimedia computers, new tests can include simulations and other ways of engaging students in complex, realistic situations that pose interesting, educationally significant challenges.

On the one hand school systems are well advised to take greater advantage of computer-based testing. The potential benefits of computer-based testing include: immediate feedback; easier and cheaper data storage, access, and analysis; and increased likelihood that tests will be used to guide learning and instruction. On the other hand, using computers to measure achievement more often and more efficiently in a few selected topics—notably math, reading, and science—does *not necessarily* help students learn, or even *necessarily* lead to teachers developing a better understanding of students' underlying needs. As a way of improving outcomes, effective testing is worthless without effective instruction. And finally, students' needs include much more than merely mastering a set of well-defined skills or a body of factual knowledge that is easily tested on a computer. Students have needs for physical education, art, music, social science, caring adults, good nutrition, the practice of civic responsibility, and many other things that excellent schools help to provide. Nonetheless, although tests cannot measure everything of importance, they are more essential than ever, and they need to be improved, in part by making greater use of computer-based systems.

USING STUDENT PERFORMANCE DATA: DATA-DRIVEN DECISIONMAKING

Once students are tested, there are many ways that teachers, principals, and school systems can make better-informed decisions using data about student learning. There are simple but powerful classroom technologies to help teachers in the classroom, as well as data systems based at the school, district, and state levels.

From the classroom to the statehouse, there is a growing emphasis on using data not only for accountability, like a report card, but also to help students learn, and to help their teachers and school administrators better understand what students know and where they need help. Using data thoughtfully pays handsome dividends by helping schools meet their goals.

Using Data Effectively Helps Schools Meet Education Goals

A study of more than 500 schools in California found that those that were more effective in raising students' academic performance tended to use four strategies:

1. putting a priority on academic achievement;
2. using the principles of standards-based reform to implement a coherent educational program;
3. providing the necessary instructional resources (i.e., the learning tools for teachers and students); and
4. using assessment data to improve instruction.[12]

The importance of the fourth strategy was explained by a school superintendent, who explained that he uses

> a pyramid of intervention. . . . You ask three critical questions: What has the student learned? How do I know that the student has learned it? And what do I do if the student hasn't learned it? That basically focuses our district's whole instructional program. What it means is that you make data-driven instructional decisions.[13]

Not surprisingly, the more-successful schools use *multiple* sources of data about students to inform decisionmaking. Principals review data frequently, both by themselves and with teachers.

Results from this and other studies reinforce the fact that the nature of the students attending a school—such as their family background and the languages they speak—although obviously important is not the only factor that determines how well the school does in measures of academic performance. State, district, and school policies, and in particular, using assessment data effectively, makes a difference. The study also highlighted the contribution of other practices discussed in earlier chapters, such as fostering a culture of teacher collaboration.

Big-city school systems are also beginning to use a variety of data to better understand which students drop out of school.[14] Philadelphia, for example, is developing a profile of its dropouts. In New York City, the data show that the great majority of high school dropouts are older than their classmates and have fewer high school credits than they should. By identifying such students before they drop out, preventive steps can then be taken to help. New York created Transfer Schools, for example, especially to enroll students at risk of dropping out. With accurate, timely data, training to use those data, and resources to provide new options to at-risk students, the appallingly high dropout rates in big cities can be reduced.

But as noted at the outset of this chapter, we cannot yet take for granted that accurate data about dropouts are available in most cities and states. And there is some evidence that No Child Left Behind has created so much pressure to report high test scores that some school systems are allowing or even encouraging low-performing students to drop out.[15] In other words, there is a significant tension among the goals of increasing student achievement, engaging and retaining more students, and making schools accountable for results.

Classroom Response Systems

One interesting way of using computers to test students, hold them accountable, and also improve instruction goes by the name of "clickers." These are handheld devices, something like a television remote control, that use infrared or radio technology to beam to a portable receiving station students' responses to questions posed by the teacher. A computer connected to the receiving station can not only keep track of individual students' answers, but also can aggregate them and display the results to the instructor and the whole class.

Research has shown that, with the right kinds of questions, providing this type of feedback can have powerful results. The public anonymity of the responses protects students from embarrassment if they answer wrong. At the same time, instructors and students alike immediately find out what students do and do not understand. The virtue of using classroom response systems was expressed by a classroom teacher who said, "I have a class of 25 students. [With the technology] I can hear answers from all 25, rather than just two or three of them."[16]

A useful technique to use with clickers is to ask a multiple-choice question that taps students' conceptual understanding, say of a physics concept. As students respond by pressing a button on the clicker, a bar graph appears showing how many students chose each of the answers. Then, after responding, students might be asked to turn to their neighbor and try to persuade them that the particular answer they gave is correct. After this interaction, students can be asked the question again and, typically, a much higher proportion of students will get the right answer. Colleges and universities are beginning to make extensive use of these computer-based systems, which are also expanding into elementary and secondary classrooms. Many vendors offer appropriate hardware and software. There are even graphing calculators that can be used as classroom response systems.[17] Because individual clickers are not expensive, and a system can be put together with only a single computer in the classroom, equipping a classroom need not cost a lot of money. After 20 years of use, the research literature showing the effectiveness of these devices for improving teaching and learning has grown large and persuasive.[18] Classrooms in which all students use laptop computers can also be equipped with hardware and software for the same purpose as clickers.

School-Based Decisionmaking

Clickers are useful for individual teachers. Principals, however, are concerned about schools as a whole, and not just as a collection of teachers operating independently. As a result, faculties in an increasing number of schools are learning about the use of data. Greater understanding of data is intended to help teachers focus on what is most important for students and to reach schoolwide goals. Along the way, learning together about using data can help to build effective school teams.[19]

Some data systems allow teachers to view a "teacher dashboard" on their computer screen. A variety of information might be available to a teacher: academic and attendance histories for all his or her students; results on state and district tests (in some cases including results on individual test items); and estimates of whether or not the students are on a path to pass required tests.

Building such systems and learning to use them effectively does not happen overnight. But what one would like to hear after the months or years of hard work is done is what one sixth-grade teacher in Irvine, California, said about a computer system that makes it easy to search, sort, and analyze data about her students: "This makes my life easier."[20] Teachers who have a better, more-detailed understanding of students' weaknesses can provide extra help where and when it is needed. They can also better collaborate with other teachers to achieve school goals.

To reach that point, school faculties must first prepare to use data (e.g., by working in subject-matter or grade-level teams and identifying important problems), then learn to ask important questions of the data, and only then, finally, act on the information. Districts can provide schools with data systems and training. Or, schools and teachers can figure out for themselves which data are important and how to use them. The authors of a book called *Data Wise: A Step-by-Step Guide to Using Assessment Results to Improve Teaching and Learning*, provide an example of the latter course of action:

> One school we worked with decided to start by looking at the way it collected data from the midterm and end-of-year math and English tests required by the district. When it investigated how results from these assessments, which were delivered by interoffice mail in paper form, were used, it realized that almost no one used the results, except to assign course grades. In response, the school's data team got an electronic version of the test results, transferred the data to an Excel file, and then displayed them to show which skills students struggled with most. The new use and display of these data made it more likely that teachers could use the test results to understand which specific concepts students had mastered and which they had not.[21]

Schools and districts that successfully integrate what is called *data-driven decisionmaking* need to develop a common vision among teachers about what goals and which data are important. These schools help teachers understand data (from specialized vocabulary, like "stanine," to concepts of measurement error and reliability) and how data can be linked to practice. They choose the right assessments. The schools' leaders foster a culture of inquiry and openness rather than one that assigns blame. Administrators understand that the process takes time and costs money, often $10 per student or more.

Computers are essential in these efforts (and it obviously makes sense for all teachers to be provided with personal laptops if schools are serious about using data). But so are leadership, professional development, and an ongoing emphasis on faculty collaboration.

The results are worth the effort. The principal of Lincoln Park High School in Chicago said about teachers in the school:

> After I showed them [how our tests were scored and how to interpret and disaggregate the data], they were shocked; the data had never been broken down and used to show teachers what they were supposed to be doing and on which students they were supposed to be focusing. The teachers said that it was the most powerful professional development they [had ever] had.[22]

Another principal said,

> Last year, we computerized everything. The teachers have access to all of the data . . . and they can see exactly where the kid has scored, where the kid needs to go, and from there teachers look at the benchmark exams, the midterm exams, do the itemized data analysis, and go back and reteach.[23]

This kind of approach may *seem* to be routine business as usual, but it's not. As one superintendent said,

> Education is not [typically] a culture of collaboration. It's a culture of isolation. "Give me my kids, close the door, and let me do my thing." That's enough when you expect some of the kids to succeed. When you expect *all* the kids to succeed, it's not.[24] [emphasis added]

In another district, a coordinator of data assessment and accountability contrasted the thoughtful use of performance data with past practice, when "[they had] always based solutions on hunches," not data.[25] Collaboration among teachers is especially needed when performance trends cut across multiple classrooms (perhaps one gender is not doing well in a particular subject at a particular grade level), and therefore teachers need to develop and implement a common strategy to change instruction in some way. In such situations, teachers may also want to bring parents into the conversation and enlist their support.

State Data Systems

Although billions of dollars are spent by state governments each year to improve education and raise student achievement, it has become increasingly clear to many people that "without quality data, the states are essentially flying blind"[26] when they try to determine which programs or strategies work well and which do not. As a result, in 2005, 10 organizations began a long-term "data quality campaign" to improve the collection, availability, and use of high-quality education data by state governments (www.dataqualitycampaign.org). A particular goal of the campaign is to have states build *longitudinal* data systems, meaning systems that are used to follow students from year to year. One important result would be a better understanding of which schools and programs are working well and which are not.

For example, it would be a good thing if policymakers in states could answer a simple question like, "Which schools in our state show the greatest academic *improvements* for students, and why?" However, as of 2006, fewer than half of the states could identify such schools, because a majority of the states either don't collect the necessary data, or don't have it in a form that allows them to answer the question.

Hurricane Katrina provides another example of why improved data systems are needed. After the disastrous flooding in New Orleans, tens of thousands of students were suddenly displaced from their regular schools. School systems in which these students were then enrolled, wherever located, were not able to use prior education data and information about these students because, in most cases, that type of data didn't exist, or it had been destroyed, or it was no longer accessible. In contrast, immediately after the tragic events of September 11, 2001, millions of financial records associated with organizations that were destroyed in the World Trade Center, and elsewhere, generally *were* available because businesses had built robust data systems and had secure, off-site backups of key data.

Organizations supporting the data quality campaign include: the Council of Chief State School Officers; State Higher Education Executive Officers; Achieve, Inc.; National Governors Association Center for Best Practices; and, Standard & Poor's School Evaluation Services— among others. The first goal of the campaign is that states put in place by 2009 data systems that incorporate 10 essential elements. Later, after these basic elements are in place, further improvements can be made.

The 10 essential elements of a longitudinal data system identified by the campaign are:

1. a unique statewide student identifier;
2. student-level enrollment, demographic, and program participation information;
3. the ability to match individual students' test records from year to year to measure academic growth;
4. information on untested students;
5. a teacher identification system with the ability to match teachers to students;
6. student-level transcript information, including information on courses completed and grades earned;
7. student-level college-readiness test scores;
8. student-level graduation and dropout data;
9. the ability to match student records between the prekindergarten through high school and postsecondary education systems; and
10. a state audit system assessing data quality, validity, and reliability.

Very few states have as many as 8 of these 10 elements in place, and some of the elements are missing in the great majority of states.[27] Maintaining records of students' scores on SAT, ACT, AP, and other college-readiness tests, for example, is done in fewer than 10 states. And few states keep track of students once they leave high school, making it difficult to measure the long-term success of schools and school programs.

Unfortunately, discussions of data and data systems will put many people to sleep—unless they suddenly need access to those data. In that case, new information systems make it clear that millions of parents and other citizens want meaningful data and want it to be easily accessible.

CHAPTER 9

Educational Technology Innovation

If schools are to be transformed, leaders in education need to understand and support the process of innovation. This chapter highlights
several lessons learned about innovation that are applicable to schools,
drawn from the experiences of nonprofits that conduct R&D in educational technology. Readers interested only in those lessons can read the
last section of the chapter, which begins on page 182.

The chapter begins with the question: Where do effective educational
technology innovations come from? An important part of the answer is
that nonprofit organizations have long played a vital role in the development of, and research about, educational technologies used in schools
and homes:

- *Sesame Street*, originally developed by the nonprofit Children's Television Workshop, was built on a novel, powerful partnership among researchers, educators, and TV production staff. Since 1969, when *Sesame Street* first aired, the program has been adapted in 120 nations,
  and as a model it has led to countless other high-quality television
  programs for children, as well as websites and computer games (e.g.,
  www.sesameworkshop.org).

- The Center for Applied Special Technology (CAST) is one in a long line of nonprofit organizations focused on the needs of youth with disabilities. CAST has codeveloped successful software products, such as Thinking Reader, and is a pioneer in the development of national standards for making curricular materials more accessible to special education students.
- The computer languages BASIC and LOGO, each designed for students (and used by tens of millions of them at one time or another), were both developed as part of grants awarded to universities by the National Science Foundation.[1]
- The Virtual High School (described in chapter 3) was started by two nonprofits, the Concord Consortium and Hudson, Massachusetts, Public Schools.

Unfortunately, government funding for innovation by nonprofits, such as in the examples highlighted above, is dwindling when it is badly needed.

NONPROFITS AND INNOVATION

Independent nonprofits—ranging from the American Red Cross, the Boy and Girl Scouts, to the Carnegie, Ford, and Gates foundations—have played a vital role in the United States for more than a century. These organizations use valuable approaches to identifying and solving problems that complement the approaches taken by government or for-profit organizations.

Nonprofits play important roles in education innovations of all kinds. At the state level, for example, nonprofit organizations have been created specifically to improve mathematics and science education, including the Vermont Institute for Science, Mathematics and Technology, the Maine Mathematics and Science Alliance, and the Connecticut Academy for Education in Mathematics, Science, and Technology. At the local level, the nonprofit Knowledge is Power Program (KIPP) supports a network of more than 50 locally run public charter schools aimed especially at helping low-income, minority, and other underserved students on the road to college.[2]

Unlike large technology companies, such as Apple Computer and Microsoft, the nonprofits working in the field of educational technology are often unfamiliar. Nonetheless, many are unusually creative places with long and impressive track records. SRI International, for example, in addition to its work in educational technology R&D (described below), is the company that invented the computer mouse, was the second node on the Internet, and developed the original TTY technology* for deaf communications. Yet most people have never heard of SRI, or many other nonprofits.

Nonprofit organizations are among the most important sources of reliable, objective knowledge about the use of digital technology in education. Besides developing products and services, their staff testify before congressional committees, are members of government advisory groups, pioneer many R&D methods, write books and journal articles, and conduct independent studies for the government and for corporations.

The independence of nonprofit organizations from pressure to make a profit for shareholders and increase stock prices allows them to focus their work differently than for-profit corporations working in the same field. If developing an innovative product or service will make little profit, the private sector is not highly motivated to make the needed investments. To take an example from another field, developing vaccines to treat diseases common in low-income countries offers little hope of bringing in billions of dollars of profit, which is why it is so important that the Gates Foundation is investing billions (most of it in universities and other nonprofits) to develop such vaccines. Conducting basic research—whether in education or the sciences—is another area in which the private sector (even wealthy corporations) is not motivated to make all the necessary investments; government agencies make a lot of the investments in research, typically by making grants to universities and other nonprofit organizations.

To illustrate the vital role of nonprofits in educational technology, and because schools can learn valuable lessons from them about innovation, this chapter focuses on the Concord Consortium and SRI International. The Concord Consortium concentrates heavily on technology development, including open source computer software, and SRI's Center for Technology in Learning (CTL) principally does research and

---

* Originally TTY stood for teletypewriter. Later, people referred to TDD devices (telecommunications devices for the deaf).

evaluation, including large-scale national studies conducted for the U.S. Department of Education. Together, these two organizations have been involved in a full spectrum of sponsored research, development, strategic planning, and consulting in the field of educational technology.

THE CONCORD CONSORTIUM

For most of its life since 1994, the Concord Consortium (CC) has been a small organization, employing 25 to 50 people. But despite its size, CC can point to many singular accomplishments. A partial list shows that CC:

- has been a pioneer in promoting the use of "probes" in science education (devices attached to a computer that measure temperature, sound, motion, or other phenomena), an innovation that spread rapidly and after less than 20 years is used by about half of all high school science teachers;[3]
- in 1996 began the first online high school in the nation, which thrives to this day and whose successful practices have influenced many other virtual schools;
- disseminates hundreds of free online lessons based on complex but easy-to-use models and simulations of the interactions of matter at the atomic and molecular levels;
- is a leader in developing open source science and math education software for schools; and
- is responsible for a half-dozen books and dozens of journal articles about online learning, virtual schools, handheld computers in the classroom, and many other significant innovations involving educational technologies.

In short, CC has been an effective "skunkworks" (a small, loosely structured corporate research and development unit formed to foster innovation).

On its website (www.concord.org), CC describes itself as an organization that "creates interactive materials that exploit the power of information technologies. Our primary goal in all our work is *digital equity*—improving learning opportunities for all students." The group's emphasis on innovation means that CC has resisted becoming a service organization. In 2001, for example, rather than enlarge its core mission, CC spun off the successful Virtual High School, which continues as an independent nonprofit organization (www.govhs.org) with more than 9,000 course enrollments serving students in 30 states and more than a dozen foreign countries.

The Concord Consortium, which like the majority of nonprofits has no endowment, is almost entirely dependent on external funding. Two projects, the Virtual High School and Molecular Workbench, provide contrasting illustrations of how nonprofits obtain the funding needed to develop innovative educational technologies.

The Virtual High School

The Virtual High School (VHS) resulted from several strands of work and ideas being woven together in a creative way. In the mid-1990s, CC won an NSF grant for CC's first online education effort, a three-year project for nearly $3 million called the International Netcourse Teacher Enhancement Coalition (INTEC). INTEC created and taught online courses for middle and high school teachers to learn to use inquiry in their math and science classrooms. Using the Internet proved appealing, especially to teachers who were unable to attend summer or evening courses.

Ray Rose, an experienced manager of educational R&D projects, was hired by CC to direct INTEC. In early 1996, Ray proposed that CC obtain funding to start an online school, most likely a high school. Shelley Berman, then an innovative superintendent of schools in Hudson, Massachusetts, and a founding member of CC's board of directors, proposed that CC team up with accredited schools to create a virtual high school. CC would provide the technical expertise for an online school, while accredited high schools would donate teachers' time in exchange for some of their students being allowed to take courses offered by *any* of the high school teachers in the online school's network.

CC's leader, Bob Tinker, who has a PhD in experimental low-temperature physics from MIT, led the development of a compelling proposal. He and Shelley were proposed as co-principal investigators (PIs) of the winning $7.4 million Technology Innovation Challenge Grant awarded by the U.S. Department of Education late in 1996. The goal of the project was to create a national consortium of schools, each of which would contribute to teaching one or two online courses (called netcourses), and in return for each course would be allowed twenty seats for the school's students to enroll in any of the consortium's online netcourses (almost always ones offered by other schools, not their own). This national consortium approach was and remains an unusual one for online schools.

In 1996, the concept of a national online high school was undeveloped and untested. VHS and its member schools were pioneers. Federal funding provided the seed money needed to convert VHS from an idea to a reality, including:

- bringing together a talented staff of educators, evaluators, and techies;
- developing standards of quality and principles of operation for an online school;
- adapting an existing technology (Lotus Development Corporation's LearningSpace, which was primarily intended for corporate training) to the needs of high school teachers and students;
- developing a syllabus and an online course to train experienced classroom teachers how to teach effectively in the new online medium;
- recruiting participating schools and teachers (including explaining the concept to principals and school boards and persuading them that the experiment would benefit their schools and their students); and
- working with about 30 teachers to develop netcourses for students in a wide variety of subjects.

As expected, creating and managing the Virtual High School was a complex job requiring a team approach. To manage the project the co-PIs turned to Bruce Droste and Liz Pape. Bruce was hired because he had been director of a private high school and had promoted educational technology to other private schools. Liz, who has an MBA degree and had worked in for-profit companies, was hired about a year later. Led by the CC team, VHS quickly became well known and received extensive publicity, including a full-page 1998 article in *U.S. News and World Report*. Educators around the U.S. and the world interested in developing their own online learning programs contacted CC for information.

Beginning in 2001, VHS, Inc. became an independent nonprofit organization in its own right, with Liz as CEO. She also helped to start, and serves on the board of directors of, the North American Council for Online Learning (NACOL), an international organization formed in 2003 "to facilitate collaboration, advocacy, and research to enhance quality K–12 online learning."[4]

Many other talented people also were needed to make VHS a success, including its initial group of 28 outstanding teachers, drawn from dozens of public and a few private schools across the U.S.[5] As a group, these teachers were extraordinarily hardworking, creative, adventurous, and passionate about good teaching and their subject matter. Most continued teaching a course online for years, while devoting the majority of their professional energies to teaching face-to-face in their home schools. A number of this first cohort of teachers took on leadership positions within VHS.

At an early stage, VHS began to support itself. The departments of education in Georgia, North Carolina, and Ohio each paid for training programs. Nearly 60 local school systems also paid for additional training, beyond what was included in the federal grant, and Israel's ministry of education paid to train participants in a VHS workshop in 2000. Between the Challenge Grant and these additional fees for services, Concord spent more than $4 million starting VHS and providing services to students as part of the initial grant, and the Hudson Public Schools spent another $3 million plus.

Nonetheless, additional funds were needed to allow VHS to make the transition from federal funding to its current independent, nonprofit status. The rules governing use of federal funds are strict, and they may not be used to pay the start-up costs of a new organization. Fortunately, Bob was able to interest Penny Noyce (by then a member of CC's board of directors) and the Noyce Foundation, which provided the Concord Consortium a grant of $885,000. Penny, a philanthropist and the daughter of an Intel founder, had been a technology-oriented medical researcher and not only understood CC's work, but also its need for special funding to avoid the constraints of government grants.

Commercial innovations that depend on venture capital typically require much more than the $8 to $9 million that it took to make VHS a self-sufficient organization. The state of Florida invested more than $25 million in public funds to develop and support the Florida Virtual School, which has more than 30,000 enrollments each year. In this context, the $7.4 million federal Technology Innovation Challenge Grant turned out to be a successful, relatively modest-sized investment that created a model from which many other organizations were able to learn. The administrator of the Alabama Online High School, for example, said, "[VHS] really jumped head over heels into the briar patch, and they came out clean and helped the rest of us see the way."[6] Just five years after the Challenge Grant was awarded, in 2001 Virtual High School won a prestigious international award, the Stockholm Challenge Award for Global Excellence in Information Technology.[7]

Fortunately, both VHS and the Florida Virtual School took seriously the responsibility to offer high-quality courses online, to develop standards for online learning, and to commission external evaluations of their pioneering ventures. In the case of VHS, a team of evaluators from SRI International studied the school for more than five years, which included doing annual surveys of participants (students, teachers, principals, and school superintendents) and hiring independent subject matter experts to assess the quality of online courses. A book, *The Virtual High School: Teaching Generation V* (on which I was lead author), summarizing the results of the evaluation and providing detailed information about the school, as well as a variety of other online schools, was published in 2003.[8] VHS's co-principal investigators allowed the evaluators to gather reams of data and to make their own judgments based on those data. As a result, the evaluation and the book provide a balanced account of VHS, including both its strengths and its weaknesses. However, the continued success of VHS and the fact that more than two dozen states are operating their own online schools (often drawing directly on lessons learned by VHS) testify to the fact that the strengths of the new venture greatly outweighed its weaknesses.

Unfortunately, most successful innovations do not take place on such a rapid timetable. Even the now-ubiquitous computer mouse, which was originally developed at SRI International in 1964,[9] didn't take off until about 1990! Development projects typically require many years to reach fruition, as demonstrated by a more typical Concord Consortium project, the Molecular Workbench.

Molecular Workbench

Being able to see or visualize a phenomenon is often an important key to understanding it. Conversely, the fact that we cannot see molecules and atoms, for example, is a barrier to understanding heat, temperature, chemistry and chemical equilibrium, protein folding, and other important scientific phenomena and concepts. "Enabling students to observe the unobservable" is a major goal of developing computer models, which is an important strand of CC's work.

Although common sense tells us that being able to "see" otherwise invisible scientific phenomena will be useful, measuring more precisely the impact of computer simulations on students' learning requires research. According to a large-scale national study of science education, "Eighth graders whose teachers had students use computers for simulations and models or for data analysis scored higher [on the NAEP science test], on average, than eighth graders whose teachers did not."[10] These findings are based on data from tens of thousands of students but are not experimental. Smaller research studies with random assignment of students to the experimental and control groups have reached the same conclusion: Simulations help students learn important concepts in science and mathematics.

Boris Berenfeld and Bob Tinker developed the original idea for Molecular Workbench. Boris, a member of CC's staff, holds a doctorate in radiation biophysics from the University of Moscow in Russia and has extensive research experience in biology, ecology, and the application of technology to education. In May 1998 NSF awarded Boris and CC a Small Grant for Exploratory Research, "Hands-On Molecular Science," to elaborate their idea. Work under that grant led to a series of six additional grants. Grants in other R&D strands have also funded CC work with models, including a $7 million, five-year *research* project called Modeling Across the Curriculum, or MAC, focusing on the impacts of the use of models at the secondary school level.

The total amount awarded for the seven Molecular Workbench–related grants was under $6 million, meaning that CC staff members invested much more time and energy writing proposals for these projects than they did for the Virtual High School—and yet received less funding for development than was provided by the single Technology Innovation Challenge Grant that launched VHS. In this respect, unfortunately, Molecular Workbench is more typical of CC's work and the educational technology work of many other nonprofits. The average grant size is not large enough to allow many ideas to reach fruition with one or even two awards. For Molecular Workbench, seven awards have been needed, stretching over more than a decade. The innovation business, in schools as well as in R&D organizations, requires persistence!

Many person-years of effort by first-rate computer programmers (notably Q. Charles Xie) have resulted in a molecular simulation "engine" that simulates the dynamic interaction of atoms and molecules according to physical laws. With the computer, you can watch as atoms and molecules interact. The engine is a professional tool for generating model-based activities and for annotating and sharing them among students. Working with the tool, hundreds of lessons and activities have been developed for students, each focusing on one or more scientific phenomena (diffusion, liquid crystals, dissolving, distillation, etc.), and all are freely available to download and use (molo.concord.org/). These lessons help students learn by observing the behavior of simulated atoms and molecules and by interacting with computer simulations.

During a decade of work, CC carefully separated the expertise required to build the sophisticated simulation engine from the very different kind of expertise needed to develop interactive educational experiences for teaching and learning science. As a result, Molecular Workbench not only provides a powerful environment for creating interactive molecular models and dynamic simulations, but also an easy-to-use authoring tool for building user interfaces and writing guided student activities that use the simulations. Without becoming computer programmers, teachers and other curriculum developers can either use existing lessons or learn to create additional model-based lessons, including embedded assessments for measuring students' learning with simulations. All of Molecular Workbench's functionalities are integrated through a simple user interface, making it far easier than ever for educators to create sophisticated, realistic model-based student activities in which students can control and observe simulated atoms and molecules in action.

As an open source, extensible modeling platform, Molecular Workbench puts the products of millions of dollars of federal funding directly into the hands of teachers and students. One unit appropriate to a high school or college biology course, for example, is called "Shaping Proteins: From DNA to Amino Acid Conformation." Dynamic simulations in this unit allow students to observe and explore how proteins, the building blocks of life, fold into characteristic shapes with specific biological properties. A pretest, four activities, and a posttest are available online (workbench.concord.org/web_content/unitV/index.html).

Users from more than 60 countries have downloaded over 10,000 copies of the Molecular Workbench software, as well as more than 100,000 copies of models and activities based on the software engine. Because the scientific concepts in Molecular Workbench don't age, and because new activities keep being produced, these numbers will grow for many years to come. It is not clear that a commercial distributor would be able to sell as many copies of a specialized software title. Yet it is quite possible to combine open source and commercial distribution. The Linux operating system, for example, is available free of charge, but can also be purchased by commercial vendors who are selling not only a standardized version of the product but also technical support and documentation. There is no reason why textbook publishers could not make greater use of open source software, and some are beginning to do so.

Open Source

Open source is a philosophy, not a project. Perhaps the best-known open source software product is Linux, a computer operating system the first generation of which was developed by Linus Torvalds, then a Finnish university student. The computer source code for Linux and other open source software is made available for anyone to use, modify, and redistribute at no cost. People making improvements in open source software are encouraged to send them to special Internet-based committees coordinated by volunteer experts for broader sharing. This approach reduces software purchase costs, which is especially important to schools. The open source approach also allows a large community of paid and volunteer developers to add to or improve what was first developed. Wikipedia, an online encyclopedia with more than 1.5 million articles in English (as of 2006), applies this same idea to a different type of product.

CC is committed to developing open source software, as exemplified by Molecular Workbench. A website (source.concord.org/) makes available the great variety of open source software that CC has developed. Most of it is written in Java, a computer language that runs on many different computers and computer-based devices.

The development of the Internet and then the World Wide Web has resulted in a huge volume of free resources easily available to anyone, in many fields. But because *many* digital resources are available at no cost, it does not follow that *all* digital resources ought to be free of charge. For educational materials used in schools, it seems clear that in the foreseeable future teachers and students will want to use both materials that are free of charge and those that are sold or licensed. Each fills a niche. But without question, open source materials provide educators with exciting new possibilities. One website alone provides access to the text of more than 19,000 free books, from Adams, Dante, and Dickens to Yeats and Zola (www.gutenberg.org).

The Concord Consortium has had substantial impacts in educational technology in the space of little more than a decade. In contrast, SRI, which was created in 1946, has been around for more than 60 years.

SRI INTERNATIONAL

The list of SRI's accomplishments is simply amazing. In addition to those listed at the beginning of this chapter, among the 50,000-plus projects that SRI has conducted are: developing the machine-readable numbers on bank checks and other essential work on bank automation for Bank of America in the 1950s; project "Mickey" that helped found Disneyland; the first major conference (1956) on the capture and use of solar energy; the first digital fax machine; development of inkjet printing; the technology for modern air combat training ranges (such as shown in the movie *Top Gun*); anti-malarial and anti-cancer pharmaceuticals; and, ground-breaking work in speech recognition, including a spin-off company, Nuance Communications, formed in 1994 to commercialize the technology.[11] This list could be expanded many, many times over.

SRI is a nonprofit contract research organization, sometimes called a "think tank." SRI's funding (more than $280 million in 2005, or about $400 million including the revenues of Sarnoff Corporation, a wholly owned SRI subsidiary) comes from contracts and grants awarded to the organization by its clients. With these monies, SRI supports a staff of 1,400 people.

SRI was originally a part of Stanford University. Because cooperation in R&D between universities and private companies is now common, it is easy to forget that before World War II, such linkages were unusual. SRI, first called the Stanford Research Institute, was created as a subsidiary to benefit the University, the western United States, and to contribute to the "improvement of the general standard of living and the peace and prosperity of mankind." After nearly 25 years as part of Stanford, SRI International became an independent nonprofit organization in 1970.

SRI is entirely devoted to research, development, and consulting. As a recent history of the organization notes, "This type of environment has a distinct quality to it. Though immersed in a large organization, the researcher is, in a very real sense, working directly for the research client."[12] Although contract research has its challenges, such as the perpetual need to find money to support projects, many researchers are content to spend an entire career in this environment. As at the Concord Consortium, project teams, each with a great deal of independence, do the essential work. Quoting again from the recent history,

> . . . there is an unchanging essence that those who have spent meaningful time here come to know. To experience it requires your having been "in the trenches," so to speak: having lived with the excitement of forming a new concept, solution, or vision; having struggled to find the needed support; and having known the euphoria of bringing an idea to realization. Some of the magic of SRI is the creative atmosphere that pervades the Institute and becomes intensely personal for all principal investigators and those who support them.[13]

Education and Human Services

SRI has supported work in education R&D for more than 60 years. Although it is difficult to characterize a typical SRI education project, SRI has done many national evaluations of federal education programs, beginning with the Follow Through evaluation in 1969 (a program created to "follow through" on the Head Start program). That study involved nearly 10,000 children each year. SRI is far more likely to conduct large-scale R&D projects than a small organization like the Concord Consortium. For more than 25 years, SRI has played a central role in large-scale national studies of children with disabilities and their education. Mary Wagner and her team have conducted longitudinal studies following thousands of children, their parents, teachers, and schools for a decade, in the process producing some of the nation's best and most reliable data about special education and students with disabilities. Typically, national studies are conducted under contract to the federal government rather than under grants. At their best, contracts are productive partnerships between government and contractor, similar to the way that a successful building results from the creative interaction of an architect under contract to a client.

Because the organization has always been interested in solving problems that cross disciplinary lines, some of SRI's education-related projects have been unusual. Douglas Engelbart's pioneering SRI work developing personal computing (including the computer mouse, hyperlinks, online document editing, and cooperative real-time work with distant colleagues) was first supported by the Defense Advanced Research Projects Agency under the title "Augmented Human Intellect," which sounds like the cultivation of human intellect, or education by another name. Engelbart, who won the National Medal of Technology in 2000, helped create the computer and networking revolution that makes technology a transformative force in education, as well as in other fields.

SRI's Center for Technology in Learning

The education and human services programs grew under Marian (Mimi) Stearns, who joined SRI in 1972 and later became a vice president. Prior to joining SRI, Mimi had been the government's first program officer for *Sesame Street*, and then worked for the federal Bureau of Education for the Handicapped. At SRI, she fostered growth in many areas, including educational technology, and was known for thoughtful mentoring of staff. Mimi created the Center for Technology in Learning (CTL) in 1989 (ctl.sri.com). The close connection between CTL and other researchers in the same division of SRI, who work on education issues but not necessarily on educational technology, has been an important contributor to its success.

CTL employs about 70 psychologists, cognitive scientists, computer programmers, evaluators, project managers, experts in math and science, statisticians, and others. Its national studies included a qualitative study of technology and education reform conducted by Barbara Means and colleagues, published in 1995, that was disseminated widely and was frequently cited by educators interested in using computer technology to make learning more active and project-based and to increase the emphasis on teaching critical thinking skills, not simply rote memory.[14]

The Evaluation of Educational Technology Policy and Practice for the 21st Century, completed in 2002, included several sub-studies, including the first formative evaluation of the multibillion-dollar E-Rate program (which awards funds to schools and libraries for connection to the Internet, based on fees collected on everyone's telephone bills), conducted by the Urban Institute, a subcontractor. The evaluation found that the program was accomplishing key goals of the authorizing legislation, notably by increasing access to the Internet among schools and libraries serving low-income populations.[15] (Internet access grew from 3 percent of all classrooms in 1994 to 94 percent in 2005, reaching nearly 100 percent of schools.[16]) Another part of the contract was a national examination of how teachers use and learn to use technology for instruction, based on a sample survey of more than 1,200 teachers nationwide, as well as many site visits and a literature review.[17] Among the important findings was that by 2000, more than half of all public school teachers were using digital technology as part of instruction at least weekly, indicating that the nation's investment in computers and the Internet for schools was starting to be reflected in classroom practices.

The No Child Left Behind Act mandated that the Department of Education sponsor an independent, long-term study of educational technology use. NCLB has also increased the demand for "proven" educational practices, notably programs that have been tested through randomized experimental studies. To meet these needs, SRI became a partner to Mathematica Policy Research for the congressionally mandated experimental study called the National Study of the Effectiveness of Educational Technology Interventions, the three-year evaluation of 15 popular technology applications described in chapter 3.[18] Dozens of districts and more than a hundred schools were recruited for the study, representing a diverse cross section of districts. There have been only a limited number of experimental, large-scale studies of education programs, technology-based or not, because they are expensive and require substantial expertise.

CTL's work has grown since 1989 to include many strands, including the use of handheld computing devices in education (including the "clickers" discussed further in chapter 8), using technology for assessing students' work (especially in mathematics and science), assessing design issues in creating technology-supported learning environments, and evaluating uses of technology to support community centers and families. CTL has a diverse set of clients; in addition to conducting work for foundations, and for federal, state, and local government agencies, CTL does strategic consulting for private sector educational technology firms.

Like other parts of SRI, a hallmark of CTL's work is its collaboration with a wide range of individuals and organizations. Its "ubiquitous computing evaluation consortium," for instance, included researchers from nearly a dozen organizations, each of whom studied and evaluated 1-to-1 computing programs (ubiqcomputing.org). Managing a project involving many organizations can be challenging, but it makes a wider range of projects feasible, including those too complex for one organization to do alone.

LESSONS FOR SCHOOLS ABOUT INNOVATION

Because innovation is so important to business and industry, the literature on innovation is large.[19] But even this brief set of examples of the role of nonprofit organizations in supporting innovation in educational technology provides valuable lessons for schools. Successful innovation, including innovation using digital tools, requires vision, teamwork, resources, and time.

Vision

When persuading funding organizations to invest millions of dollars in a new educational technology application, such as the first online high school, or incorporating novel technological innovations in school systems—as leaders in Maine and Henrico County, Virginia, did when they took a calculated risk and began 1-to-1 computing programs—leaders must develop a compelling vision rooted in an understanding of schools.

Communicating the vision effectively is vital, whether it's for a proposal to potential funders, a presentation to a school board or legislature, or a talk given to parents, teachers, or students. More schools and school systems are beginning to incorporate visions of the role of digital tools into their strategic plans and goal statements. One public charter high school, the Denver School of Science and Technology, describes its vision as follows:

> Technology must not be a simple replacement or enhancement of non-technological methods of learning. Technology is too expensive to be a substitute for the pencil and the chalkboard. Instead it must invite and

enable higher order thinking, more creative thinking, learning, and expression. It must engender more intense investment and engagement by the student. It must enable collaboration, extrapolation, projection, analysis, demonstration, and closer, tangible interaction with the subject under study that is extremely unlikely or even impossible without it. It must transport the student to places, experiences, modes of thinking, cultures, and people otherwise impossible to reach for the normal high school student.

Technology should empower and enable, and never replace or reduce the central human role of the teacher in a liberal arts education. The role of a liberal arts education is to enable and facilitate the creation of leaders who value community, individuals, and the creation of a truly human society. Technology must serve this end.[20]

A compelling vision for increasing the use of digital tools in schools helps persuade others of the value of the innovation. Change is often difficult and risky, but clearly schools need to change. Although history shows there are some extraordinary people whose visions and skills allow them to develop or implement innovations unusually well, the reality is that invention, R&D, and the implementation of educational technology innovations are rarely solitary pursuits.

Teamwork

Nonprofit R&D organizations like the Concord Consortium and SRI rely heavily on teams. It requires teams of people to develop and realize the visions for new projects. Like many other educational technology nonprofits, CC and SRI have been able to hire outstanding staff whose expertise includes computer programming and hardware development, knowledge of science and mathematics, teaching experience (including online teaching), cognitive science, psychology, graphics, project and financial management, writing, editing, and other skills. The multidisciplinary nature of projects and the use of carefully assembled teams (often five to ten people) to carry them out are hallmarks of the contract and grant work done by Concord, SRI, and many other organizations involved in educational technology R&D.

Similarly, changing traditional practices in schools needs to be a multidisciplinary, team-based, long-term effort. Leadership is crucial, but leaders are needed at all levels, not just at the top of an organization. Former Maine governor Angus King, who began the state's 1-to-1 program, was under no illusion that he was an expert at using computers for teaching and learning. The state has relied heavily on local, regional, state, and national leaders to move from a vision to a successful program. Examples such as this illustrate that successful school systems, like businesses, are able to build, motivate, and support teams that can change the organizations in important ways.

Resources

Schools spend almost no money on research and development, despite the fact that these institutions need to adapt to a rapidly changing world—which, for most large businesses, would mean that R&D is required. There are exceptions, of course. Dozens of states have developed online high schools; in most cases, however, this has meant adapting R&D done elsewhere rather than beginning by building their own technology and knowledge base.

Innovation requires resources, including time and money. Even for dedicated R&D organizations it is a challenge to find the necessary resources. In schools, resources are obtained in various ways. In Maine, the legislature provided a special infusion of funds for the 1-to-1 program. And for better and for worse, many schools have become more adept at writing proposals to obtain funding from foundations or government agencies.

One-time solutions, such as grants, can be important. But transforming schools is not a one-time event; it is a process that requires support for years. Schools need to create budgets that support technology over the long term. Similarly, schools need to view innovation not as a one-time event but as a process of continuous improvement. Chapter 8, for example, shows that districts planning to make better use of assessment data to improve teaching and learning are putting together teams of people to work together for at least a year, and often much longer.

Time

Because we live in a time of rapid technological change, there is a tendency to believe that social and organizational changes happen as rapidly as technological changes. Yes, some technological change happens rapidly—such as the majority of households buying their first television sets at almost the same time in the 1940s and 1950s—and some social and organizational changes are rapid, too. But more often, significant changes take substantial time, be that the introduction and spread of kindergarten programs, or, as was mentioned earlier, the increasingly pervasive use of the computer mouse, which took about three decades after the device was invented.

Policymakers and the public should expect deep, broad changes in school systems to take time. Buying and installing digital devices may be accomplished quickly. Changing patterns of teaching, testing, communicating, and doing business will take much longer and require extensive training, teamwork, leadership, and public support. Transforming schools will be a long-term process.

Federal Funds for Innovation

The federal government spends more than $30 billion annually for research in the life sciences at the same time that companies in the private sector, such as pharmaceutical corporations, invest tens of billions more. By contrast, the federal R&D budget in 2005 for education, training, employment, and social services; *and* administration of justice; *and* commerce and housing; *and* community and regional development; *and* income security; *and* international affairs; *and*, veterans' benefits and services was only $2.5 billion altogether. These many categories are reported together by the federal government because even combined they are so small—less than 10 percent of the federal investment for R&D in the life sciences.[21] Compared to the $74 billion government investment in military R&D, the percentage is even less, about 3 percent. These figures tell us what federal R&D priorities are. Unfortunately, more and better education R&D is not high among them.

The private sector is not about to invest billions in education R&D. The total of *all* software sales to schools in 2004 was a little over $2 billion,[22] far less than the sales of many prescription drugs (like Lipitor, which reduces cholesterol). The point is not that using software is like using medication. Rather, the materials used in schools simply have not, and as yet cannot, be based on the kind of R&D expenditures that medicine, agriculture, the military, and many other fields take for granted. The private sector cannot improve that situation substantially, given current market size. Nor are individual states and school districts in a position to support expensive, cutting-edge R&D.

The federal investment for innovation in educational technology R&D is essential—but it has been diminishing. Programs like the Technology Innovation Challenge Grants, which funded Virtual High School and other innovations, take calculated risks. That is what innovation requires. There are fewer opportunities for federal funding of educational innovation than there used to be. "Our greatest concern," Bob Tinker has written, "is that the pipeline of educational innovations in math and science is drying up . . . causing us, and others like us, to dismantle our teams and reduce our capacity for innovation."[23]

The National Science Foundation (NSF), an independent federal agency, has been CC's primary funder. Since its creation in 1950, a core part of NSF's statutory mission has been to support "science education programs at all levels in the mathematical, physical, medical, biological, social, and other sciences."[24] The great majority of its 10,000 or so awards each year are made to support the research of scientists, engineers, and mathematicians. In addition, NSF supports a prestigious program of graduate fellowships for the education of the next generation of scientific researchers, as well as many other grant programs designed to support and improve science, mathematics, engineering, and technology education from kindergarten through graduate school.

Materials developed by a limited number of federal education grants have turned into successful, moneymaking products. The nonprofit TERC (which began as Technical Education Research Centers), for example, licensed the Zoombinis series of educational games to a commercial company, which has sold more than a million units. More lucrative has been an elementary mathematics curriculum developed by TERC called *Investigations in Number, Data, and Space*, which has earned millions of dollars in royalties based on its popularity in schools.

Yet anyone imagining that large income streams are typical of education products would be sorely mistaken. It is the rare company that has been able to make money developing and marketing educational software, for example—and this is one of the reasons why organizations like the Concord Consortium are essential. In fact, the market for such materials has declined dramatically, both in the schools and in homes,[25] no doubt due in part to the growing expectation that interactive materials are freely available on the Web. Yet whether a product is commercially distributed or not, there is so little profit incentive in developing complex materials like Molecular Workbench that without foundation or government support, such materials very likely would not be created. As a report written by the RAND Corporation noted,

> The market for educational materials, as traditionally structured, offers limited incentives for entrepreneurial development of content software. The market is fragmented and governed by a variety of materials adoption practices. Even if a high proportion of schools acquires a product, the volume of sales is small. This is particularly true with the more specialized subject areas characteristic of much of secondary education.[26]

Even rigorous education research is expensive. The study of 15 software products discussed in chapter 3 will eventually cost about $15 million. Although such price tags are the norm, or low, for many health-related studies that one reads about in the news and that help shape national health policies and practices, the nation has invested so little in education research that it may come as unwelcome news to realize that large-scale, high-quality education research is costly, too.

It is true that R&D is no substitute for good teachers, healthy families, or communities that support and nurture young people. But the R&D work done by hundreds of nonprofits—including universities, as well as organizations like the Concord Consortium and SRI International—is vital to understand, improve, and ultimately transform schools. Unless we are content with the schools we have, the nation needs to find a way to increase the inadequate federal allocation for these R&D efforts as well as spend money to support innovation in schools.

CHAPTER 10

Transforming Schools

The days of wondering whether technology can improve elementary and secondary schools are over. Computers and other digital tools are helping schools by increasing student achievement (including giving students new options for distance learning); by making classes more engaging and relevant; tailoring instruction to students with special needs; providing teachers with a wide range of professional tools; helping connect schools with parents and with a variety of services that support young people; and by providing new ways to increase accountability for results.

The responsible skeptics understand that computers and other digital technologies *can* contribute to school improvement and to students' education, as noted in chapter 1. However, skeptics too often focus entirely on "increasing student achievement"—by which they mean raising test scores—as the single goal for using technology, as if no other education goals were important. Because other goals are vital, a single-minded focus on raising student achievement simply reduces the skeptics' credibility. Still, that doesn't mean the skeptics' concerns should be dismissed.

SKEPTICS' QUESTIONS

Perhaps the most important caution raised by the skeptics is to avoid being "seduced by flashy graphics and digital legerdemain," as Jane Healy wrote.[1] Technology advocates agree. Education does not need more fads or an expensive set of initiatives that distract people from the core responsibilities of schools.

Is Technology a Distraction?

The use of technology should be aligned with the six important education goals described in this book. However, applications of technology usually address multiple education goals rather than only one. Online schools, for instance, help meet many students' individual needs, increase access to courses not otherwise available, better distribute services of expert teachers, and support student achievement in core academic subjects. Online classes are also a response to the public's desire for schools to be more flexible, more technology-savvy institutions.

Today's digital tools are works in progress, still changing and improving at a rapid rate. This constant churning can be a problem. Like the rest of us, teachers and students would benefit from more-dependable, easier-to-use digital technology that would better combat computer viruses and worms, and reduce the incidence of computers freezing or crashing. Also, like everyone else, they want protection from hackers and crooks who take advantage of the open environment of the Internet.

In an ideal world teachers would have more control over their electronic environment. They would be able to turn off Internet access in their classroom with the click of a mouse and turn it on again when students are allowed to use it. They could specifically disable instant-messaging, music downloads, or other distractions. Some of this can be done already; it is possible, for example, to prevent students from installing new software on school computers, and there are programs that allow teachers to monitor all computers in the classroom. In the meantime, one of the first lessons that teachers in laptop schools learn is how to say "screens down" or "computers off." Nonetheless, as discussed in chapter 4, most teachers in laptop schools support the continuation of laptop programs because they find that the benefits outweigh the problems.

Yes, it is hard for schools to stay abreast of the constant stream of new technologies, from electronic whiteboards, to smarter telephones, to eInk, to new and better software products. Welcome to the 21st century, a time of extraordinarily rapid change. This rapid pace of change requires well-informed school leaders, including capable technology directors, and systemic thinking. We expect business, universities, government, and the military to adapt to new technologies, so why shouldn't schools do the same? The good news is that many schools and school systems have demonstrated that they can and will adopt digital technology in thoughtful, responsible ways.

A majority of the public supports increasing the use of educational technology. According to a 2007 survey of more than 7,000 Americans, about 60 percent agree that "information technology is a vital tool that can help educate our students by providing access to video and other dynamic content."[2] The public seems willing to pay, too. For example, as noted in chapter 4, parents and other voters in Henrico County, Virginia, and in Maine, where innovative school laptop programs produce a stream of news and information and a well-informed electorate, have supported the programs financially for many years.

It is a lot of work to "keep up" with technology. But anyone who thinks computers, the Internet, MP3 players, and all sorts of other digital tools are simply a distraction that can be ignored until calmer times arrive is indulging in wishful thinking.

Won't Educational Technology Increase Inequity?

Wealthy school systems spend two, three, or more times as much per pupil as poor districts. Will technology reinforce existing educational inequities because it is less affordable to schools serving poor families? Actually the converse is a far more important perspective: If schools do *not* use technology, digital equity will depend largely on home use of computers, which is a great deal more inequitable than the access provided in schools.

Through the E-Rate and other programs, the federal government has played an aggressive role in helping schools and libraries that serve low-income families enter the digital age. The result is that all public libraries and nearly all classrooms in the country are now connected to the Internet. By contrast, there are still wide disparities in the way children of different races and socioeconomic status use computers at home, as noted in chapter 7. Governors, chief state school officers, and other policymakers who advocate providing schools with more technology often point specifically to the "digital divide" that separates the haves from the have-nots. They believe that children growing up without understanding and using technology are being deprived of one of the new basic skills in our society.

A more subtle concern is that schools serving low-income students may use technology only to teach the old basic skills, applying what some people call "drill and kill" software. That danger does exist. One yearlong study of laptop schools found that

> low-SES students and the schools that serve them were often less prepared than higher SES students and schools to take advantage of the full capability of laptops. Students in these schools tended to have fewer language and literacy skills, and this limited what they could accomplish with laptops. For students with low reading or writing skills, even searching for a simple term on the Internet was a challenge. Similarly, working independently with automated essay feedback was difficult for students who could not comprehend the meaning of the feedback or understand the grammatical terms used.[3]

But this problem can be overcome. Castle Middle School in Maine (not its real name) serves students from 17 countries who speak 28 languages. In 1992 Castle became an Expeditionary Learning Outward Bound school, doing away with tracking and making 8- to 12-week interdisciplinary research projects the center of the curriculum. Like other middle schools in Maine, Castle became a laptop school in 2001. Castle's test scores are higher than the state average. The combination of project-based learning and laptop use has worked well, even with this highly diverse group of students.[4] More recently, the Jonas Salk High-Tech Academy in California introduced laptops and a challenging curriculum, and experienced a "sea change in the scores and behavior of its students," many of whom are from low-income families.[5]

The conclusion to reach from Castle, Jonas Salk, the Mott Hall School in Harlem (chapter 4), Ysleta Middle School in El Paso (chapter 5), and many other such examples is that laptops and other digital technologies can be successfully applied in schools serving low-income students, but by themselves do not transform education. Schools need to focus on critical thinking, inquiry, and problem-solving to take full advantage of what computers offer. In many schools, especially but not only those serving low-SES students, this change in focus requires substantial effort—an effort in which technology can help. But digital tools are not magic. Introducing laptops or other tools has to be accompanied by efforts to teach higher-order thinking and by aiming at other challenging goals, not just teaching the old basic skills.

Are Digital Tools Worth the Cost?

The term "educational technology" covers a vast range of products and services. One type of digital tool is the graphing calculator, including those that can now be networked together, linked to a teacher's laptop, and used as classroom response systems. Calculators are very affordable. As a result, there are millions of them in the schools and hardly any responsible person questions their value. E-mail is another digital tool with great educational value. High school teachers use e-mail as a powerful tool to help teach students to write, and second graders have learned science as they e-mailed with scientists in Antarctica about penguins. It would be useful if all teachers had e-mail and voicemail, both of which are affordable and routinely used by millions of people. Are laptop computers for teachers affordable for school systems, and worthwhile? Yes—and increasingly schools provide them to teachers and administrators because computers are essential tools for education professionals.

Some applications of digital tools—such as testing, scoring, and reporting data about student achievement—will result in cost savings. Billions of dollars could also be saved if the smart use of technology helps us attract and retain more good teachers, for example through improved mentoring and support, as described in chapter 6.

Although it would make schools' decisionmaking easier if *all* effective educational technology were beneficial from a financial point of view, the uses of technology in medicine—from heart bypass surgery to improved pharmaceuticals—shows that this is not likely. Better medical technology saves lives and has greatly improved people's health, but one result is that per-capita medical expenditures have gone up. The same is likely to be true in education.

Educational technology will help American schools provide more and better education for students—including for the millions of dropouts and other young people who are poorly served by existing education practices—but the improvements will probably cost schools more than they save. Simply stated, improving schools costs money. For example, suppose that we cut today's high school dropout rate to zero—an educational miracle. Suddenly we would have millions of additional students in school and as a result, school budgets would go up by billions of dollars to pay the costs of educating those students. Presumably that is a price we would be willing to pay because the benefits to society are worth the costs. That is also the proper way to measure the costs of educational technology—not by whether investments in technology save money (some of them will; some won't), but by whether the benefits are worth the costs. Better schools pay off financially in the long term (fewer young people in prison, more tax receipts from more highly educated workers, etc.). This does not mean that improving schools will reduce the cost of education, either per student or overall.

The art and science of weighing education costs and benefits is primitive. Ultimately the benefits of better schools are worth what people are willing to pay. How much is it worth to raise students' college admissions test scores by, say, 10 percent? Some parents spend thousands of dollars for test-preparation courses for their children. Others don't believe that's a good use of money. There is no recognized formula that provides an appropriate price for teaching more students calculus or Arabic, or reducing school dropouts, or for achieving other worthy education goals.

Some policymakers believe it would be reasonable to allocate 3 to 5 percent of school budgets to educational technology. Administrators in Henrico County, Virginia, used that figure for planning the ongoing cost of their school laptop program. Per-pupil costs for elementary and secondary schools in the United States were about $8,000 in school year 2002–2003.[6] Five percent of that amount is $400 per student per year, which is enough to cover the annual cost of leasing a student's laptop, including associated support costs. It is impossible to say whether this is an appropriate figure—at least, not without more information, including what exactly that expenditure pays for and what type of benefits are expected.

The education community, like the business community, wants to better understand the costs and the benefits of technology. The Consortium for School Networking, a national membership organization, has a website providing information about the "total cost of ownership" of technology, an accounting approach that considers the costs of software, labor, and other items besides hardware, as well as another site devoted to calculating the value of these investments.[7] Knowing the price tag is not enough to make a good decision; one needs to consider the benefits, too.

Certainly schools need to be thoughtful about technology expenses. Some school systems, for example, rely heavily on free, open source software to reduce costs. The Saugus Union School District in California, one of the lowest-funded districts in the state, used open source software called ELGG to develop an online teacher community and a separate online student community, a kind of safe substitute for the popular MySpace. San Diego is using Linux as part of its 1-to-1 computing initiative.[8] The State of Indiana uses low-cost computers and open source operating systems for many of its school computers. Indiana's InACCESS project aims at making educational technology affordable in part by using dozens of open source applications for everything from word processing to classroom discussion spaces managed by teachers.[9] For example, Indiana uses Moodle, a course management system that has been especially popular with the state's high school English teachers. The long-range technology plan of the Plano, Texas, school district, serving more than 25,000 students, emphasizes use of open source technologies. States and districts are interested in open source software because the savings resulting from its use can be substantial.

Computers also help schools save money in other ways. One school district in Pennsylvania, with 5,500 students, claims to have saved $30,000 in less than a year by converting school board meetings to electronic media instead of paper.[10] The district is helping parents and families to access the Internet by leasing old computers to families for just $1 a year.

In all organizations, the cost of computers and related technology is by now simply an accepted and essential part of doing business. Because the prices of hardware and Internet access have declined greatly, schools are better able than ever to support an extensive and robust technology infrastructure. This trend will continue.

Will Digital Tools Be Used Effectively?

Neither technology nor books nor any other educational tools are likely to be worth the cost if used poorly. Some applications of educational technology—word processors, say—can be used well with little or no training and without changing current education practices. However, many of the advantages of using educational technology do, in fact, require adapting current practices. That is both a great challenge and an important opportunity.

Current practices in most elementary and secondary schools are simply not good enough when they are measured against the needs of students. As one study of the educational experiences of 1,000 children, supported by the National Institute of Child Health and Human Development, recently reported, "Fifth-grade classrooms are pretty well managed and positive in terms of emotional support. They are not rich and intense in ways that would elicit thinking and learning."[11] This finding is consistent with other studies cited in this book and with the conclusions and recommendations of many policymakers.

It would be a tragic missed opportunity to use educational technology only to support and automate current practices in schools. There are so many ways that digital tools can change current practices for the better. Computers provide students with many more opportunities to practice and receive immediate, patient feedback. Teachers can use technology to foster higher-order thinking, analysis, and inference by students, not simply the recall of facts and procedures. School systems are coupling the use of technology with opportunities for students to do more and more sophisticated project work, thereby encouraging them to become independent, active learners. Computers allow schools to keep better records and measure progress less on the basis of seat time and more based on students' actual accomplishments. Teachers are learning how to better use data about students' learning to improve instruction.

Substantially changing current education practices in elementary and secondary schools is a tall order. However, changes are needed to improve schools in any case, with or without technology. Businesses understand that digital tools both permit *and* require fundamental changes in their operations. For schools, too, these tools allow *and* require substantial change to the status quo. It is inconceivable, for example, that public schools would reject the benefits of online schooling for students and families and leave virtual schools only to the private sector, including companies supporting homeschooling. Public school systems would "lose market share," to use a business term, as well as reinforce some people's opinions that educators are not flexible enough to adapt to the 21st century. No one said adopting educational technology on a large scale would be easy—but for many teachers and students, the changes have turned out to be refreshing and even exhilarating.

It is true, of course, that effective use of digital tools requires talented school leaders and substantial teacher professional development. In one of its larger technology programs, the federal government required that 25 percent or more of program expenditures be devoted to teacher professional development. That was a smart thing to do, even though later research showed that school systems were already reaching that benchmark before the requirements were incorporated into law. Teachers do not primarily need to be taught computer skills; instead, professional development should focus on how to use technology well in schools.[12] Lesson plans, curricula, and daily practices need to change to take advantage of technology. Many of the school systems cited in this book are committed to making these kinds of changes—but fostering them takes vision, leadership, time, money, and support.

It is no surprise that changing accepted practice in nearly 100,000 schools takes many years. But make no mistake, changes *are* happening. In many cases—online schools being one notable example—change is happening surprisingly quickly and effectively.

PRINCIPLES FOR SCHOOL REFORM

Educators have joked for years about the "rising tide of school reports" (a play on the "rising tide of mediocrity" identified by the 1983 National Commission on Excellence in Education in *A Nation at Risk*). During the past decades, there have been dozens of commissions, panels, and expert reports about improving America's schools. Many of them call for transforming schools—that is, changing them in fundamental ways. *Tough Choices or Tough Times*, for example, recommends "a whole new formula" for schools. The panel that developed the report included former governors and mayors, prior cabinet secretaries, school superintendents, business executives, and others. The report says:

The core problem is that our education and training systems were built for another era, an era in which most workers needed only a rudimentary education. It is not possible to get where we have to go by patching that system. There is not enough money available at any level of our intergovernmental system to fix this problem by spending more on the system we have. We can get where we must go only by changing the system itself.[13]

It is not my intention to offer a wholesale endorsement of *Tough Choices or Tough Times*, or of any other report on school improvement. Instead, the first key point to emphasize is that reports from *many* thoughtful sources recommend substantial, transformative changes to existing practices in schools. The second key point is that many of these reports describe principles for school reform that, if states adopt them, will clearly benefit from and, in fact, require the smart use of computers and other digital tools.

The National High School Alliance

The National High School Alliance, for instance, is a partnership of dozens of national organizations committed to "fostering high academic achievement, closing the achievement gap, and promoting civic and personal growth among all high-school-age youth in our high schools and communities." In 2005, the Alliance issued *A Call to Action: Transforming High School for All Youth*, which identifies six core principles for change.[14] These principles sound very familiar. One is to require that leaders be held accountable for the performance of schools. As shown in chapter 8, without much better data and digital data systems, accountability is impossible. Another principle is to "empower educators," for example, the report says, by emphasizing professional collaboration within communities of practice and "building educators' capacity to use data and research to inform instructional practice." These areas, discussed in prior chapters, are ones in which digital technology offers unique and effective tools. Two other Alliance goals emphasize *engagement*: academic engagement of all students, and engaged community and youth. These goals, too, are by now familiar; using digital tools for these purposes was discussed in chapters 4 and 7. Another core principle is "personalized learning environments," including "developing a personal learning plan for each student." How will it be feasible for tens of millions of students to have personal learning plans without the smart use of digital tools? Kentucky is leading the way with its online guidance system for students. Finally, one of the core principles is to support an integrated system of high standards, curriculum, instruction, assessments, and supports. This book has illustrated many ways in which digital tools do a better job of connecting and integrating components of education systems, such as assessment and instruction, than is possible using paper alone.

Teaching the New Basic Skills

Another valuable perspective on principles for school reform can be found in *Teaching the New Basic Skills: Principles for Educating Children to Thrive in a Changing Economy.*[15] The authors, professors Richard Murnane and Frank Levy (of Harvard and MIT, respectively) offer five principles for improving schools. The principles were originally drawn from successful improvement efforts in business and industry but, as Murnane and Levy richly illustrate with examples drawn from schools, they apply equally well to education. The five principles are:

1. Ensure that all frontline workers understand the problem.
2. Design jobs so that all frontline workers have both incentives and opportunities to contribute to solutions.
3. Provide all frontline workers with the training needed to pursue solutions effectively.
4. Measure progress on a regular basis.
5. Persevere and learn from mistakes; there are no magic bullets.

Although these principles are powerful, Murnane and Levy remind us that even successful businesses—the quality of whose products is much easier to measure than schools' success—require time and patience (years in many cases) to pinpoint problems, solve them, and thereby improve products and, ultimately, the company's bottom line.

But something is missing from the list: We must provide workers with the tools needed to do their jobs. Industry does not expect employees to succeed without proper equipment. Yet teachers and students (both being "frontline workers" in the business of education) are routinely expected to do their jobs *without* essential tools. This situation needs to change if we are serious about improving education. Computers, the Internet, and various digital devices, such as graphing calculators, have become basic tools for education, as important for teachers, students, and administrators as paper and pencil or whiteboards and markers. Principle number three in Murnane and Levy's useful list ought to be amended, as follows:

3. Provide all frontline workers with the training *and the tools* needed to pursue solutions effectively.

As we have seen throughout this book, a growing number of governors, chief state school officers, state legislators, and other education policymakers appreciate the importance of this principle. As a result, more states and districts are making the investment in computers, the Internet, and other technology tools needed to improve schools.

Consider Education Reform as a Whole Cloth, Not a Patchwork

It is useful to establish a variety of goals for improving education, as federal and state laws do. In some cases, there is even a tension between goals—for example, reducing the high school dropout rate may mean keeping some low-performing students in school, whose averages and test scores will depress system averages rather than increase them, as required under No Child Left Behind. However, transforming schools requires policymakers to reengineer whole systems, not just endeavor to make changes aimed at one or another goal apart from the others.

Thinking of education as a whole system makes the introduction and use of digital tools more effective than restricted thinking that focuses only on parts of the system. Computer-based testing, for example, may save money in administration and scoring, as discussed in chapter 8. At the same time, computer-based tests also allow much more rapid feedback to teachers and students, thereby providing important opportunities for teachers to provide instruction in those areas where it is most needed. And when schools almost instantly have students' test records in the computer, this can allow them to provide faster, better communication of results to policymakers, parents, and the public, serving to increase accountability. Furthermore, digital testing also allows test accommodations to be made more easily for students with learning disabilities, or for whom English is not their first language. This wide range of possibilities means that policymakers who think of computer-based testing only as a means to save money, or only to serve some other education goal (such as better accommodating students with disabilities), miss the forest for the trees.

It is important to realize that digital tools are providing the opportunity to change school systems as a whole, or so many parts of the system that to focus on just one or two would be a lost opportunity and a shame.

PEOPLE ARE AS ESSENTIAL AS DIGITAL TOOLS

Avoiding "either/or" thinking is important in education. Too many people succumb to impoverished thinking that takes out the middle, such as "either we teach basic skills, including the use of drills and memorization, or we give up those goals and methods and instead teach children to think." Nonsense; schools need to adopt multiple goals and a variety of methods.

Simplistic either/or thinking is often applied to educational technology. *Either* it's the greatest innovation for education ever invented *or* it's a waste of money. We should apply common sense. The facts are that:

- We need to transform American schools into higher-performing organizations whether or not we use technology.
- Digital technology is a powerful tool, offering unique benefits and advantages that can help transform organizations, especially those based on information and knowledge.
- Countless examples illustrate that schools are using technology in smart ways to support key education goals.

While digital tools *are* necessary to transform schools, these tools alone are not sufficient. That same conclusion has been reached about the application of information technology (IT) in business and industry. As one study of economic productivity reported,

> The greatest benefits of computers appear to be realized when computer investment is coupled with other complementary investments, such as new strategies, new business processes, and new organizations. These latter all appear to be important in realizing the maximum benefit of IT.[16]

This finding is worth underlining even if it may not seem surprising—except, perhaps, to some of the technology skeptics.

Business investments in "human capital" are as important as or more important than investments in digital tools—and both are needed. An MIT professor who studies investments in technology by large companies looked at one popular type of investment in computer resource planning systems and found that for every $1 million that companies spent on hardware, $3 million was spent on software, and $16 million was spent on "organization capital," including retraining workers and redesigning practices in the workplace.[17] The exact proportions might differ in schools, or for different digital tools, but the fact is that modern organizations depend on people, processes, *and* technology.

Many policymakers adopting digital tools already understand that lesson. For example, Dan Evans, a former state superintendent of schools in Indiana, recommended that leaders of 1-to-1 computing initiatives:

> . . . put together a team that brings together expertise in curriculum, learning, school change, and technology [to focus] on getting teachers ready to use the tools in powerful ways for learning.[18]

A closely related way of looking at the smart use of digital tools in schools is to ask, Where are the most difficult barriers? Harvard professor Chris Dede says, "The fundamental barriers to employing new technologies effectively for learning are not technical or economic, but psychological, organizational, political, and cultural."[19]

Transforming *any* organization is not simply a matter of finding and implementing the appropriate digital tools. Digital tools are *one* essential component for transforming schools, but the tools cannot stand alone. Good teachers and visionary leaders remain as important as ever.

NEW STRATEGIES FOR SCHOOLS

The policymakers in Maine, Henrico County, Virginia, and in many other places that make intensive use of laptops and other technology understood that we need to transform education, rather than simply make old practices more efficient. As noted in chapter 1, transformation means rethinking *where* and *when* students learn, with *whom* they learn, *how* teaching and learning take place, and *what* students study.

As noted above, too many classrooms today are "not rich and intense in ways that would elicit thinking and learning." They look much the same as they have for decades. The fifth graders observed as part of the recent national study of 1,000 students were engaged in whole-group instruction more than half the time, with the teacher at the front of the room. Individual seatwork was the next most common method of learning. Together, these approaches accounted for more than 91 percent of class time. Collaboration with other students, working with technology, and enrichment activities were rare.[20]

Digital tools allow for more active and varied learning by students. The world can be brought into the classroom through the Internet. Students can visit museums, take field trips—some Web-based programs even allow students to accompany working scientists on their expeditions—collect real-world data, and become more engaged in schoolwork. Students, including those in online courses, can quickly and easily interact with their peers in other nations.

The challenge is to integrate digital tools in a disciplined way that offers students the opportunity for important learning. For decades, many teachers have assigned students to conduct interviews—of immigrants, World War II veterans, grandparents, or others whose experiences and memories can be valuable to young people. Sometimes classes have put together books consisting of such interviews. In the right hands, assignments like this can teach students a great deal. Now consider how technology can be used in this tried-and-true assignment. Word processors make it easier to produce, edit, revise, and grade the interviews. Digital photographs can easily be added to text. Instead of, or in addition to, publishing a paper book, it is possible to distribute the word processing files or put the results on the Internet where a large audience can benefit from the students' work. Password protection or other methods are available to limit who accesses the website, if that is appropriate. In one laptop school, eighth-grade students who interviewed immigrants for an American history class were allowed to create movies, slide shows, or "podcasts" (edited audio recordings made available on the Web) of their interviews. The best of such products can be selected and, with appropriate permissions, shared widely. Allowing students to create products for an audience outside the classroom is highly engaging and provides students with a compelling reason to create a high-quality product. The teacher who asked students to create multimedia presentations says that "exposure to these types of programs allows [students] to take the material and make it come alive."[21]

New Skills for Students

Experts have been saying for decades that schools must teach the "new basic skills," not just the old three Rs (reading, 'riting and 'rithmetic). As noted in earlier chapters, the Partnership for 21st Century Skills and others have identified new skills students require.

One example is information literacy skills, including the skill of finding and judging information on the Internet. People are now able to quickly find more information on almost any subject than was ever before possible. However, this does not necessarily mean that students, in particular, are able to judge the reliability of information they find. As one college faculty member said, "They're citing Joe Schmo's paper in their paper, but who is Joe Schmo? And is he objective?"[22]

To better understand students' information literacy skills, Educational Testing Service (ETS) developed iSkills, a test of information and communication technology literacy. As part of the development process, ETS tested thousands of students at dozens of institutions. The results show that schools still have a long way to go in teaching students to go beyond locating information with a search engine like Google. When it came time to narrow a search or to evaluate a website's objectivity, authority, and timeliness, many students performed poorly. For example, when asked to narrow an online search that was too broad, only 35 percent of students selected the correct revision.[23]

This example illustrates one way that digital technology is changing what we consider "basic skills." In response to changing circumstances created by digital tools, schools have begun to revise and update curriculum, instruction, and assessment. These changes are consistent with the well-recognized goals of teaching critical thinking and problem-solving, but they also reflect the new capabilities provided to everyone, both students and adults, by the ubiquitous presence of computers, search engines, and the Internet. In this example, the changes that are needed are not an extreme makeover—they hearken back to the teaching that good librarians used to do—but neither are they trivial. Because current tests do an inadequate job of assessing whether or not students have developed good information literacy skills, ETS spent millions of dollars to develop a new test.

The example underscores the importance of looking ahead. Schools exist to educate students to lead full and productive lives, especially after they leave school. That means considering the needs of students in tomorrow's world, not yesterday's.

Implementing Technology in Schools

Because there are many useful how-to books about using computers, the Internet, and other digital tools in schools, as well as journals specializing in this area that are aimed at administrators and practicing educators, this book has treaded lightly on implementation questions. However, drawing from those sources and earlier chapters, a few useful principles for policymakers are as follows:

- Transforming organizations requires offering a compelling vision to stakeholders and making them participants in change efforts. Engage teachers, administrators, parents, and others not only because they are in the front lines, but also because dispersed leadership is essential. To integrate digital technology effectively, schools need visionary superintendents, principals, department chairs, and central office staff, as well as outstanding teacher-leaders. Excellent school technology directors are obviously important, but educational principles should drive change efforts, not technology.
- Use digital tools for important educational purposes aligned with schools' key goals. Schools and school systems will, and should, identify a variety of different needs. The State of Iowa, for example, connected its schools, colleges, and libraries with fiber-optic cables more than a decade ago because policymakers decided that communicating more easily over large distances, even routinely using two-way video, was important to support education in a large, rural state.
- It is often valuable to try out ideas in a few schools rather than to immediately implement them throughout an entire state or a large school district.
- Whenever possible, learn from people and places that have more experience. Many organizations have experience and expertise in this field, ranging from the National School Boards Association (which leads site visits to districts that are leaders in using digital tools)

to teachers' organizations like the National Council of Teachers of Mathematics.[24] Two specialized groups, the Consortium for School Networking (www.cosn.org) and the International Society for Technology in Education (www.iste.org), each have years of experience helping schools plan for and use technology effectively.

- Budget for the long-term use of digital tools, not simply for one-time expenditures. School budgets must reflect routine, ongoing costs if the use of digital tools is to be sustainable. States and the federal government need to support their fair share of costs, too, including ongoing research and development to improve the use of digital tools. The private sector cannot do the R&D alone any more than they can do so in the health sciences, where profits are orders of magnitude larger than those in education.

- The most important transformation needed in schools, as documented by many studies and reports, is to engage and challenge more students. We need to move away from the kind of basic-skills-and-nothing-but-the-basic-skills approach that relegates too many children to a dead-end education and to dropping out of school.

- As Murnane and Levy have written, we need to "persevere and learn from mistakes; there are no magic bullets." There are many lessons that the United States can learn from studying schools in other nations, but American schools will never be simply copies of those in other countries. We need to find our own way in uncharted territory.

For centuries, Americans have been pioneers in developing and using new technologies, including the Franklin stove, the interstate highway system, the transistor, space travel, and the Internet. It is natural and appropriate for Americans to use digital technologies to help transform public schools. The six education goals elaborated in this book are widely shared by members of the public and policymakers and, as a result, they provide essential guideposts for using technology to transform schools into more modern, responsive, effective institutions.

NOTES

CHAPTER I

1. Murray, C. (2004). "Study reveals trends in ed-tech spending." *eSchoolNews Online.* Accessed June 28, 2006, from http://www.eschoolnews.com/news/showStory.cfm?ArticleID=5340.

2. U.S. Department of Education. (2003). *Federal funding for educational technology and how it is used in the classroom: A summary of findings from the Integrated Studies of Educational Technology.* Washington, DC: Author. See also CDW-G. (2006). *Teachers talk tech 2006: Fulfilling technology's promise of improved student performance.* Accessed July 21, 2006, from http://newsroom.cdwg.com/features/TeachersTalkTech2006Results.pdf.

3. Friedman, T. (2005). *The world is flat: A brief history of the twenty-first century.* New York: Farrar, Straus and Giroux.

4. I first heard the term "School 2.0" used by Tim Magner, director of the U.S. Department of Education's Office of Educational Technology, and would like to acknowledge his work on this issue.

5. "Educational reference websites spike 22 percent in year-over-year growth, led by Wikipedia and Yahoo! Education, according to Nielsen/NetRatings." (October 13, 2005). New York: Yahoo and PR Newswire, biz.yahoo.com. Accessed October 17, 2005, from http://biz.yahoo.com/prnews/051013/sfth055.html.

6. Potts, J. (November 2005). "Transforming America's schools." *Carnegie Mellon Today*, pp. 2–6.

7. Zucker, A. A., & McGhee, R. (2005). *A study of one-to-one computer use in mathematics and science instruction at the secondary level in Henrico County Public Schools.* Menlo Park, CA: SRI International. Available at http://www.ubiqcomputing.org/FinalReport.pdf, p. 17.

8. Healy, J. (1998). *Failure to connect*. New York: Simon & Schuster.

9. Stoll, C. (1999). *High-tech heretic: Why computers don't belong in the classroom and other reflections by a computer contrarian*. New York: Doubleday.

10. Cuban, L. (2001). *Oversold and underused: Computers in the classroom*. Cambridge, MA: Harvard University Press.

11. Oppenheimer, T. (2003). *The flickering mind: The false promise of technology in the classroom and how learning can be saved*. New York: Random House.

12. Schrage, M. (March 22, 2006). "The 'edutainers' merit a failing grade." *Financial Times*.

13. Greenspan, A. (October 28, 1999). *Information, productivity, and capital investment: Remarks by Chairman Alan Greenspan before the Business Council, Boca Raton, Florida*. Accessed May 9, 2006, from www.federalreserve.gov/Boarddocs/speeches/1999/199910282.htm. Little more than a decade earlier, the Nobel Prize–winning economist Robert Solow famously said, "You can see the computer age everywhere but in the productivity statistics" (http://en.wikipedia.org/wiki/Solow_computer_paradox). Opinions had changed dramatically.

14. Perie, M., Moran, R., Lutkus, A., & Tirre, W. (2005). *NAEP 2004 trends in education progress: Three decades of student performance in reading and mathematics*. Washington, DC: U. S. Department of Education, National Center for Education Statistics.

15. Wenglinsky, H. (2005). *Using technology wisely: The keys to success in schools*. New York: Teachers College Press, p. 77.

16. Wenglinsky, *Using technology wisely*, p. 77.

17. Oppenheimer, *The flickering mind*, p. 411.

18. Healy, *Failure to connect*, p. 130.

19. Cuban, *Oversold and underused*, p. 197.

20. Oppenheimer, *The flickering mind*, p. xiv.

21. Stoll, *High-tech heretic*, p. 32.

22. Healy, *Failure to connect*, p. 205.

23. Healy, *Failure to connect*, p. 89.

24. Healy, *Failure to connect*, p. 88.

25. Cuban, *Oversold and underused*, p. 67.

26. Oppenheimer, *The flickering mind*, p. 395.

27. Oppenheimer, *The flickering mind*, p. 395.

28. Cuban, *Oversold and underused*, p. 133.

29. Zucker, A. A., & Kozma, R., with Yarnall, L., Marder, C., & Associates. (2003). *The Virtual High School: Teaching generation V*. New York: Teachers College Press.

30. Becker, H. J., & Riel, M. M. (2000). *Teacher professional engagement and constructivist-compatible computer use* (Teaching, Learning, and Computing: 1998 National Survey, Report #7). Irvine: University of California, Irvine, Center for Research on Information Technology and Organizations.

31. Cuban, *Oversold and underused*, p. 176.

32. Cuban, *Oversold and underused*, p. 133.

33. Cuban, *Oversold and underused*, p. 91.

34. See Russell, M., Bebell, D., Cowan, J., & Corbelli, M. (2002). *An AlphaSmart for each student: Does teaching and learning change with full access to word processors?* Chestnut Hill, MA: Boston College, Technology and Assessment Study Collaborative; Russell, M., Bebell, D., & Higgins, J. (2003). *Laptop learning: A comparison of teaching and learning in upper elementary classrooms equipped with shared carts of laptops and permanent 1:1 laptops.* Chestnut Hill, MA: Boston College, Technology and Assessment Study Collaborative.

35. Goldberg, A., Russell, M., & Cook, A. (2002). *Meta-analysis: Writing with computers 1992–2002.* Chestnut Hill, MA: Boston College, Technology and Assessment Study Collaborative.

36. Casper, G. (April 18, 1995). *Come the millennium, where the university?* Address to the annual meeting of the American Educational Research Association. Available at http://www.stanford.edu/dept/pres-provost/president/speeches/950418millennium.html.

37. Papert, S. (October 1984). "Trying to predict the future." *Popular Computing*, p. 38. Cited in Oppenheimer, *The flickering mind*, p. 20.

38. "The future of school," a discussion between Seymour Papert and Paolo Friere. Accessed May 10, 2006, from www.papert.org/articles/freire/freirePart1.html and cited in Oppenheimer, *The flickering mind*, p. 20.

39. U.S. Department of Commerce, U.S. Department of Education, & NetDay. (2005). *Visions 2020.2: Student views on transforming education and training through advanced technologies.* Available online at: http://www.nationaledtech-plan.org/.

40. See One Laptop per Child, http://laptop.org/.

41. Fox, S., Anderson, J. Q., & Rainie, L. (2005). *The future of the Internet.* Washington, DC: Pew Internet & American Life Project. Available online at www.pewinternet.org.

42. See http://nces.ed.gov/fastfacts/display.asp?id=66.

43. Cuban, *Oversold and underused*, p. 175.

CHAPTER 2

1. Center on Education Policy. (2005). *Do you know . . . The* latest *good news about American education?* Washington, DC: Author. Available online at http://www.cep-dc.org/.

2. Figure cited in Kolb, C. E. M. (July 12, 2006). "The cracks in our education pipeline." *Education Week*, p. 56.

3. Kolb, "The cracks in our education pipeline."

4. Data from the National Center for Education Statistics (www.nces.ed.gov).

5. National Center for Education Statistics. (2006). *Comparing private schools and public schools using hierarchical linear modeling* (Report No. 2006-461). Washington, DC: U.S. Department of Education.

6. National Center for Education Statistics. (2004). *America's charter schools: Results from the NAEP 2003 pilot study* (Report No. 2005-456). Washington, DC: U.S. Department of Education.

7. National Center for Education Statistics. (2002). *The nation's report card: Geography 2001* (No. 2002-484). Washington, DC: U.S. Department of Education.

8. National Center for Education Statistics. (2005). *International outcomes of learning in mathematics literacy and problem solving: PISA 2003 results from the U.S. perspective* (Highlights Report, No. 2005-003). Washington, DC: U.S. Department of Education.

9. National Center for Education Statistics. (2006). *The nation's report card: Reading 2005* (Report No. 2006-451). Washington, DC: U.S. Department of Education Institute of Education Sciences.

10. Bryk, A. S., Nagoka, J. K., & Newmann, F. M. (2000). "Chicago classroom demands for authentic intellectual work: Trends from 1997–1999" (Data Brief). Chicago: Consortium on Chicago School Research.

11. Newmann, F. M., Bryk, A. S., & Nagoka, J. K. (2001). *Authentic intellectual work and standardized tests: Conflict or coexistence?* Chicago: Consortium on Chicago School Research.

12. Weiss, I. R., Pasley, J. D., Smith, P. S., Banilower, E. R., & Heck, D. J. (2003). *Looking inside the classroom: A study of K–12 mathematics and science education in the United States* (Highlights Report). Chapel Hill, NC: Horizon Research, p. 7.

13. Weiss et al., *Looking inside the classroom*, p. 4.

14. Olson, L. (November 30, 2005). "State test programs mushroom as NCLB mandate kicks in." *Education Week*, p. 10.

15. Johnson, J., & Duffett, A. (2003). *Where we are now: 12 things you need to know about public opinion and public schools (a digest of a decade of survey research)*. New York: Public Agenda, p. 15.
16. Johnson & Duffett, *Where we are now*, p. 19.
17. Educational Testing Service. (2005) *Ready for the real world? Americans speak on high school reform*. Princeton, NJ: Author.
18. http://www.epi.org/content.cfm/book_grad_rates.
19. Paulson, A. (March 3, 2006). "Dropout rates high but fixes under way: 9 of 10 students had passing grades when they left." *Christian Science Monitor*. Accessed August 25, 2006, from http://www.csmonitor.com/2006/0303/p01s02-legn.html.
20. National Center for Education Statistics. (2002). *Student effort and educational progress, Indicator 18*. Accessed August 25, 2006, from http://nces.ed.gov/programs/coe/2002/section3/indicator18.asp.
21. Johnson & Duffett, *Where we are now*, p. 8.
22. The Center for Information and Research on Civic Learning and Engagement. Accessed September 18, 2006, from http://www.civicyouth.org/quick/youth_voting.htm.
23. The Center for Information and Research on Civic Learning and Engagement. Accessed September 18, 2006, from http://www.civicyouth.org/quick/civic_ed.htm.
24. Galston, W. A. (April 2004). "Civic education and political participation." *Political Science Online*. Accessed September 18, 2006, from http://www.apsanet.org/imgtest/CivicEdPoliticalParticipation.pdf.
25. Partnership for 21st Century Skills. (2003). *Learning for the 21st century: A report and mile guide for 21st century skills*. Washington, DC: Author.
26. Resnick, L. B. (1987). *Education and learning to think*. Washington, DC: National Academy Press, p. 7.
27. Quoted in *Education Week*, July 26, 2006, p. 37.
28. Achieve, Inc. (2002). *Staying on course, standards-based reform in America's schools: Progress and prospects*. Washington, DC: Author.
29. National Center for Education Statistics. (2006). *The condition of education, 2006*. Washington, DC: Author, p. 34.
30. National Center for Education Statistics, http://nces.ed.gov/fastfacts/display.asp?id=96.
31. National Center for Education Statistics, http://nces.ed.gov/fastfacts/display.asp?id=96, Indicator 5.

32. National Center for Education Statistics, http://nces.ed.gov/fastfacts/display. asp?id=96, Indicator 8.

33. Federal Interagency Forum on Child and Family Statistics, http://www.child-stats.gov/americaschildren/pop.asp.

34. Esch, C. E., Chang-Ross, C. M., Guha, R., Humphrey, D. C., Shields, P. M., Tiffany-Morales, J. D., et al. (2005). *The status of the teaching profession 2005.* Santa Cruz, CA: The Center for the Future of Teaching and Learning, pp. vii–xii.

35. Farkas, S., Johnson, J., & Duffett, A. (2003). *Rolling up their sleeves: Superintendents and principals talk about what's needed to fix public schools.* New York: Public Agenda, p. 29.

36. Johnson & Duffett, *Where we are now*, p. 17.

37. Porter, A. C., Garet, M. S., Desimore, L., Yoon, K. S., & Birman, B. F. (2000). *Does professional development change teaching practice? Results from a three-year study* (Document 2000-04). Washington, DC: U.S. Department of Education, Planning and Evaluation Service.

38. Johnson & Duffett, *Where we are now*, pp. 16–17.

39. National Center for Education Statistics. (2005). *Digest of education statistics, 2005.* Washington, DC: Author, Table 139. Accessed August 23, 2006, from http://nces.ed.gov/programs/digest/d05/tables/dt05_139.asp.

40. Knudsen, E. I., Heckman, J. J., Cameron, J. L., & Shonkhoff, J. P. (2006). "Economic, neurological, and behavioral perspectives on building America's future workforce." *Proceedings of the National Academy of Sciences Online*, June 26, 2006. See also Dickens, W. T., Sawhill, I. V., & Tebbs, J. (2006). *The effects of investing in early education on economic growth* (Policy Brief #153). Washington, DC: The Brookings Institution.

41. Cuban, L. & Usdan, M. (Eds.). (2003). *Powerful reforms with shallow roots: Improving America's urban schools.* New York: Teachers College Press, p. 165.

42. National Endowment for the Arts. (2004). *Reading at risk: A survey of literary reading in America* (Research Division Report No. 46). Washington, DC: Author, p. ix.

43. Center on Education Policy, *Do you know . . . The* latest *good news about American education?*, p. 32.

44. Johnson & Duffett, *Where we are now*, p. 9.

45. U.S. Department of Education, National Center for Education Statistics. (2005). *Revenues and Expenditures for public elementary and secondary education: School year 2002–2003* (NCES 2005-353), Current Expenditures per Student. Accessed September 18, 2006, from http://nces.ed.gov/pubs2005/2005353.pdf.

46. Success for All Foundation, http://www.successforall.net/faqs/index.htm.

47. National Council of Teachers of Mathematics. (2000). *Principles and standards for school mathematics*. Reston, VA: Author.

48. New York State Education Department; Elementary, Middle Secondary, and Continuing Education; Curriculum, Instruction, and Technology Team, http://www.emsc.nysed.gov/ciai/mst/tech.html.

49. "Some states left behind" (editorial). (November 28, 2005). *Los Angeles Times*.

50. Linn, R. (2003). "Accountability: Responsibility and reasonable expectations" (2003 presidential address). *Educational Researcher, 32*(7), 3–13.

51. David, J. L., & Cuban, L. (2006). *Cutting through the hype: A taxpayer's guide to school reforms*. Morris, IL: Education Week Press, p. 19.

52. Achieve, Inc. (February 22, 2006). *States make progress closing high school "expectations gap" but more needs to be done* (press release). Washington, DC: Author.

53. Finnigan, K., Adelman, N., Anderson, L., Cotton, L., Donnelly, M. B., & Price, T. (2004). *Evaluation of the public charter schools program*. Washington, DC: U.S. Department of Education, Office of the Under Secretary, p. ix.

54. Cuban & Usdan, *Powerful reforms with shallow roots*.

55. Zucker, A. A., Shields, P. M., Adelman, N. E., Corcoran, T. B., & Goertz, M. (1998). *A report on the evaluation of the National Science Foundation's Statewide Systemic Initiatives (SSI) Program* (NSF 98-147). Arlington, VA: National Science Foundation.

56. Borja, R. R. (March 2, 2007). "E-rate program, at 10, is lauded for helping wire schools." *Education Week*, p. 11. See also http://www.sl.universalservice.org/funding/previous.asp.

57. Kleiner, A., Lewis, L., & Greene, B. (2003). *Internet access in U.S. public schools and classrooms: 1994–2002* (E.D. Tabs No. 2004-011). Washington, DC: National Center for Education Statistics.

58. American Institutes for Research. (2002). *Implementing the Technology Literacy Challenge Fund educational technology state grants program*. Washington, DC: Author.

59. Gewertz, C. (July 26, 2006). "Pennsylvania high school project stresses rigor, support." *Education Week*, p. 23.

CHAPTER 3

1. Manzo, K. K. (January 24, 2007). "Teachers say testing deters use of current events." *Education Week*, p. 12.

2. Whitehurst, G. (2003). Remarks at the Mathematics Education Summit, Washington, DC. Accessed August 18, 2003, from http://www.ed.gov/inits/mathscience/whitehurst.html.

3. Ragosta, M., Holland, P. W., & Jamison, D. T. (1982). *Computer-assisted instruction and compensatory education: The ETS/LAUSD study. The final report.* Washington, DC: U.S. Department of Education.

4. See U.S. Department of Education's What Works Clearinghouse, http://www.whatworks.ed.gov/.

5. National Commission on Excellence in Education. (1983). *A nation at risk.* Washington, DC: U.S. Department of Education. Accessed January 2007, from http://www.ed.gov/pubs/NatAtRisk/index.html. See also Murnane, R. J., & Levy, F. (1996). *Teaching the new basic skills.* New York: Free Press.

6. Silvernail, D. L., & Lane, D. M. M. (2004). *The impact of Maine's one-to-one laptop program on middle school teachers and students* (Report #1). Gorham, ME: Maine Education Policy Research Institute, University of Southern Maine Office, p. 17.

7. Jeroski, S. (July 2003). *Wireless writing project: Research report. Phase II.* Vancouver, BC: Horizon Research & Evaluation. Accessed November 8, 2005, from http://www.prn.bc.ca/FSJ_WWP_Report03.pdf.

8. Goldberg, A., Russell, M., & Cook, A. (2003). "The effect of computers on student writing: a meta-analysis of studies from 1992 to 2002." *Journal of Technology, Learning, and Assessment, 2*(1), 1–47.

9. Russell, M., & Abrams, L. (2004). "Instructional uses of computers for writing." *Teachers College Record, 106,* 1332–1357.

10. Kulik, J. A. (2003). *Effects of using instructional technology in elementary and secondary schools: What controlled evaluation studies say.* Arlington, VA: SRI International.

11. Burrill, G., Allison, J., Breaux, G., Kastberg, S., Leatham, K., & Sanchez, W. (2002). *Handheld graphing technology in secondary mathematics: Research findings and implications for classroom practice.* Dallas: Texas Instruments. See also Ellington, A. J. (2003). "A meta-analysis of the effects of calculators on students' achievement and attitude levels in pre-college mathematics classes." *Journal for Research in Mathematics Education, 34,* 433–463.

12. See, for example: Tinker, R. (Ed.). (1996). *Microcomputer-based labs: Educational research and standards* (Vol. 156). Berlin: Springer-Verlag.

13. Hudson, S. B., McMahon, K. C., & Overstreet, C. M. (2002). *The 2000 national survey of science and mathematics education: Compendium of tables*. Chapel Hill, NC: Horizon Research.

14. Davis, M. R. (June 20, 2007). "Digital tools push math, science to new levels." *Education Week*, pp. 12, 14.

15. Bayraktar, S. (2001). "A meta-analysis of the effectiveness of computer-assisted instruction in science education." *Journal of Research on Technology in Education, 34,* 173–188.

16. See Molecular Workbench (http://workbench.concord.org/), Molecular Logic (http://molo.concord.org/), and Molecular Literacy (http://molit.concord.org/) for lessons and activities that model the interactions of atoms and molecules.

17. See The Geometer's Sketchpad Resource Center, http://www.dynamicgeometry.com/javasketchpad/gallery/index.php.

18. See MIT: Research in Learning, Assessing, and Tutoring Effectively, http://relate.mit.edu/progress.html.

19. See National Optical Astronomy Observatories News, http://www.noao.edu/outreach/press/pr00/pr0001.html.

20. See The GLOBE Program, www.globe.gov.

21. There is excellent evidence, for example, that the use of technology developed by the SimCalc project increases middle school students' understanding of ratio and proportion, which is a key mathematics concept (http://math.sri.com).

22. Viadero, D. (February 28, 2007). "Lessons learned on 'scaling up' of projects." *Education Week*, p. 16.

23. Paley, A. R. (April 5, 2007). "Software's benefits on tests in doubt: Study says tools don't raise scores." *Washington Post*.

24. Dynarski, M., Agodini, R., Heaviside, S., Novak, T., Carey, N., Campuzano, L., et al. (2007). *Effectiveness of reading and mathematics software products: Findings from the first student cohort* (Report to Congress). Washington, DC: U.S. Department of Education.

25. Ragosta et al., *Computer-assisted instruction and compensatory education*.

26. Kulik, J. A., *Effects of using instructional technology in elementary and secondary schools*, p. v.

27. Dynarski, et al. *Effectiveness of reading and mathematics software products*, p. 71.

28. Helfland, D. (January 30, 2006). "A formula for failure in L.A. schools." *Los Angeles Times*. Accessed June 10, 2007, from http://www.latimes.com/news/education/la-me-dropout30jan30,1,2605555.story.

29. What Works Clearinghouse. (2004). *Intervention report: Cognitive Tutor*. Accessed April 20, 2007, from http://www.whatworks.ed.gov/PDF/Intervention/WWC-CT%20120204%20v10.html.

30. Waxman, H. C., Lin, M.-F., & Michko, G. M. (2003). *A meta-analysis of the effectiveness of teaching and learning with technology on student outcomes*. Naperville, IL: Learning Point Associates.

31. Zucker, A. A., & Kozma, R. E., with Yarnall, L., & Marder, C. (2003). *The Virtual High School: Teaching generation V*. New York: Teachers College Press.

32. Ascione, L. (November 22, 2006). "Music education moves online." *eSchool News online*.

33. Ross, A. (September 4, 2006). "Learning the score: Why Brahms belongs in the classroom." *The New Yorker*, p. 83.

34. Greenway, R., & Vanourek, G. (2006). "The virtual revolution." *Education Next*, 6(2). Accessed September 27, 2006, from http://www.hoover.org/publications/ednext/3210506.html.

35. Borja, R. R. (April 4, 2007). "Students opting for AP courses online." *Education Week*, pp. 1, 16, 18.

36. Watson, J. F., & Ryan, J. (2006). *Keeping pace with K–12 online learning: A review of state-level policy and practice*. Vienna, VA: North American Council for Online Learning.

37. Borja, R. (September 20, 2006). "States given guidance on online teaching, e-school costs." *Education Week*, p. 8. See also Watson & Ryan, *Keeping pace with K–12 online learning*.

38. Picciano, A. G., & Seaman, J. (2007). *K–12 online learning: A survey of U.S. school district administrators*. Needham, MA: The Sloan Consortium (Sloan-C).

39. Yamashiro, K., & Zucker, A. A. (November 1999). *Assessing the quality of Virtual High School courses: Final report of an expert panel review*. Menlo Park, CA: SRI International, p. 19.

40. Yamashiro & Zucker, *Assessing the quality of Virtual High School courses*, p. vii.

41. Cavanaugh, C., Gillan, K. J., Kromrey, J., Hess, M., & Blomeyer, R. (2004). *The effects of distance learning on K–12 student outcomes: A meta-analysis*. Naperville, IL: Learning Point Associates, p. 4.

42. Rockman ET AL. (2006). *Research findings from the West Virginia Virtual School Spanish program* (Research Brief). San Francisco: Author.

43. Zucker et al. *The Virtual High School*.

44. Southern Regional Education Board. (2006). *Report on state virtual schools*. Atlanta, GA: Author. Accessed September 29, 2006, from http://www.sreb. org/programs/EdTech/SVS/State_Virtual_School_Report_06.pdf.

45. Zucker et al., *The Virtual High School*, chapter 6.

46. Michigan Virtual School (press release). Accessed September 29, 2006, from http://www.mivhs.org/upload_2/MIOnlineRequirment42106.pdf.

47. Murnane, R. J., & Levy, F. (1996). *Teaching the new basic skills*. New York: Free Press, p. xvii.

48. Zhao, Y., Pugh, K., Sheldon, S., & Byers, J. L. (2002). "Conditions for classroom technology innovations." *Teachers College Record, 104,* 482–515.

CHAPTER 4

1. Fine, L. (December 12, 2001). "Pen pal effort with Muslim children overseas takes off." *Education Week*, pp. 24–25.

2. Furger, R. (2001). "Laptops for all." *Edutopia online*. Accessed December 20, 2005, from www.glef.org.

3. See, for example, Warschauer, M. (2006). *Laptops and literacy: Learning in the wireless classroom*. New York: Teachers College Press.

4. Rose, D. H., & Meyer, A. (2002). *Teaching every student in the digital age: Universal design for learning*. Alexandria, VA: Association for Supervision and Curriculum Development, p. 35.

5. "Governor Rendell awards $20 million for 'Classrooms for the future'" (press release). Accessed September 20, 2006, from http://www.state.pa.us/papower/cwp/view.asp?Q=456361&A=11.

6. "More news from NECC: Market data retrieval's K–12 technology review highlights, current trends, and future projections." Accessed June 28, 2006, from http://www.mmischools.com/Articles/PrintArticle.aspx?ArticleID=10209.

7. Rockman, S. (October 15, 2004). *A study in learning*. Available online at www.techlearning.com.

8. MDR. (2006). *America's digital schools, 2006*. Accessed August 1, 2007, from http://ads2006.net/ads2006/pdf/ADS2006KF.pdf.

9. See Consortium for School Networking, http://www.k12one2one.org/index.cfm for a list of dozens of laptop programs.

10. Zucker, A. A., & McGhee, R. (2005). *A study of one-to-one computer use in mathematics and science instruction at the secondary level in Henrico County Public Schools*. Menlo Park, CA: SRI International. Available at http://www.ubiqcomputing.org/FinalReport.pdf.

11. Apple Computer. "iBook unleashes student exploration" (Profiles in success: Indianapolis Public Schools). Accessed December 5, 2005, from http://www.apple.com/education/profiles/indianapolis_ibooks/.

12. Silvernail, D. L., & Lane, D. M. M. (2004). *The impact of Maine's one-to-one laptop program on middle school teachers and students* (Report #1). Gorham: University of Southern Maine Office, Maine Education Policy Research Institute, p. 15.

13. Zucker & McGhee, *A study of one-to-one computer use in mathematics and science instruction*.

14. See, for example, webquest.org/, where the database is searchable by subject, grade level, title, etc.

15. Bebell, D. (2005). *Technology promoting student excellence: An investigation of the first year of 1:1 computing in New Hampshire middle schools*. Chestnut Hill, MA: Boston College Technology and Assessment Study Collaborative, p. 10.

16. Jeroski, S. (July 2003). *Wireless writing project: Research report. Phase II*. Vancouver, BC: Horizon Research & Evaluation, Inc. Accessed November 8, 2005, from http://www.prn.bc.ca/FSJ_WWP_Report03.pdf.

17. Zucker & McGhee, *A study of one-to-one computer use in mathematics and science instruction*.

18. Urban-Lurain, M., & Zhao, Y. (2004). *Freedom to learn evaluation report: 2003 implementation*. East Lansing: Michigan State University Center for Teaching and Technology, p. 94.

19. Online posting by Becky Turner, Brooklin, Maine. Accessed June 28, 2006, from http://1to1stories.org/?cat=44.

20. Silvernail & Lane, *The impact of Maine's one-to-one laptop program*.

21. Davis, D., Garas, N., Hopstock, P., Kellum, A., & Stephenson, T. (2005). *Henrico County Public Schools iBook survey report*. Arlington, VA: Development Associates, Inc.

22. Silvernail & Lane, *The impact of Maine's one-to-one laptop program*, p. 17.

23. Jeroski, *Wireless writing project*.

24. Goldberg, A., Russell, M., & Cook, A. (2003). "The effect of computers on student writing: A meta-analysis of studies from 1992 to 2002." *Journal of Technology, Learning, and Assessment, 2*(1), 1–47.

25. Rockman, S. (2003). "Learning from laptops." *Threshold, 1*(1), 24–28.

26. Rockman, S. (2004.) "What does the latest research on mobile computing tell us about teachers, students, and testing?" Accessed December 20, 2005, from http://www.techlearning.com/showArticle.jhtml?articleID=49901145.
27. Penuel, W. (2005). *Research: What it says about 1 to 1 learning*. Apple Computer.
28. Russell, M., & Abrams, L. (2004). "Instructional uses of computers for writing." *Teachers College Record, 106,* 1332–1357.
29. Davis, et al. *Henrico County Public Schools iBook survey report*.
30. Staudt, C. (2005). *Changing how we teach and learn with handheld computers*. Thousand Oaks, CA: Corwin Press.
31. *Scientific American*, February 2004.
32. See One Laptop per Child, http://laptop.org/.
33. Software & Information Industry Association. (2005). *Survey results: State adoption of electronic instructional materials*. Accessed December 16, 2005, from http://www.siia.net/govt/docs/pub/SIIAadoptionSurveyResults.pdf.
34. See, for example: Bonifaz, A., & Zucker, A. A. (2004). *Lessons learned about providing laptops to all students*. Newton, MA: EDC and NEIRTEC. Available at http://www.neirtec.org/laptop.
35. Accessed May 5, 2006, from http://trench2.blogspot.com/.
36. Bleimes, A. (November 15, 2006). "Blogging now begins young." *USA Today*.
37. Borja, R. (July 12, 2006). "N.J. seeks a worldview through online projects." *Education Week*, p. 16.
38. Warschauer, *Laptops and literacy*, p. 47.
39. Cisco Systems, Inc. "High number of CCNA certifications earned in the school district of Philadelphia," from http://www.cisco.com/web/learning/netacad/success_stories/Philadelphia.html.
40. Cisco Systems, Inc. "News @ Cisco," from http://newsroom.cisco.com/Newsroom/flash/evp/Flash7/main.html?videoXML=../xml/high/9F688BCA0DA067AAC04F6CC1E1DC077C_video.xml&defaultTopic=null&defaultSubTopic=null.
41. Wikipedia. "Video game," from http://en.wikipedia.org/wiki/Video_game#Sales.
42. Statistical abstract of the United States, 2006, table 1116. Accessed September 15, 2006, from http://www.census.gov/compendia/statab/information_communications/infocomm.pdf.
43. *NY Times* News Service. (July 23, 2006). "Serious video games want to change world." Accessed September 15, 2006, from http://www.taipeitimes.com/News/bizfocus/archives/2006/07/23/2003320072.

44. *NY Times* News Service, "Serious video games want to change world."
45. Borja, R. (December 6, 2006). "Video games trickle from rec rooms to classrooms." *Education Week*, p. 10.
46. See, for example, the February 2007 special issue of the *Journal of Science Education and Technology*, p. 1.

CHAPTER 5

1. Bartleby.com, The Columbia World of Quotations, http://www.bartleby.com/66/42/24442.html. The President was James Garfield.
2. National Center for Education Statistics, Fast Facts. Accessed May 23, 2007, from http://nces.ed.gov/fastfacts/display.asp?id=64.
3. Harris, W. J., & Smith, L. (2004). *Laptop use by seventh-grade students with disabilities: Perceptions of special education teachers* (Maine Learning Technology Initiative Research Report #2). Orono: Maine Education Policy Research Institute.
4. Harris & Smith, *Laptop use by seventh-grade students with disabilities.*
5. Silvernail, D. L., & Lane, D. M. M. (2004). *The impact of Maine's one-to-one laptop program on middle school teachers and students* (Report #1). Gorham: University of Southern Maine, Maine Education Policy Research Institute, p. 24.
6. The Maine Learning Technology Initiative: Maine Learns, http://www.maine-learns.org/story_detail?story_id=162.
7. McDavid, L. (1999). "Virtual High School breaks the sound barrier: Listening and learning from the true pioneers." *@Concord* (newsletter for the Concord Consortium). Available at http://www.concord.org/publications/newsletter/1999spring/insert-vhs/soundbarr.html.
8. Tom Snyder Productions, Thinking Reader, http://tomsnyder.com/products/product.asp?SKU=THITHI.
9. Kurzweil Educational Systems, http://www.kurzweiledu.com/.
10. The University of Memphis, Institute for Intelligent Systems, http://fedex.memphis.edu/iis/projects/istart.shtml.
11. For example, see WestEd, Using Technology to Support Diverse Learners, http://www.wested.org/cs/tdl/print/docs/tdl/home.htm.
12. Harris & Smith, *Laptop use by seventh-grade students with disabilities.*
13. For example, see BookPALS Storyline Online, http://www.storylineonline.net/.

14. For example, see SparkTop.org, http://www.sparktop.org.
15. AccessIT: The National Center on Accessible Information Technology in Education, http://www.washington.edu/accessit/index.php.
16. Consortium for School Networking. "Using technology to raise the achievement of ALL students," http://www.accessibletech4all.org/index.cfm.
17. NIMAS at CAST, http://nimas.cast.org/index.html.
18. Borja, R. R. (December 6, 2006). "Houghton Mifflin's sale to software maker reflects trend." *Education Week*, p. 7.
19. Public Law 105-394.
20. Alper, S., & Raharinirina, S. (2006). "Assistive technology for individuals with disabilities: A review and synthesis of the literature." *Journal of Special Education Technology, 21*(2), 47–64.
21. Bausch, M. E., & Hasselbring, T. E. (2005). "Using AT: Is it working?" *Threshold* (Winter), 7. Accessed January 31, 2007, from http://www.ciconline.org/threshold.
22. "Forum: The future of assistive technology." (2005). *Threshold* (Winter) 10. Accessed January 31, 2007, from http://www.ciconline.org/threshold.
23. Warschauer, M. (2006). *Laptops and literacy: Learning in the wireless classroom.* New York: Teachers College Press, p. 57.
24. See, for example, ED.gov, OSEP Ideas That Work, http://www.osepideasthatwork.org/toolkit/InstPract_never_to_late.asp.
25. Manzo, K. K. (July 11, 2007). "Teachers seek out software to help students' reading." *Education Week*, p. 26.
26. Loh, E. (2005). *Building reading proficiency in high school students.* Accessed March 5, 2007, from http://www.autoskill.com/pdf/HS_metastudy2005.pdf.
27. AutoSkill International, Inc. (2006). *California learning center: Innovative strategies for reading intervention.* Accessed March 5, 2007, from http://www.autoskill.com/pdf/LosArcosCS.pdf.
28. Renzulli, J. (2002). *Giftedness and high school dropouts: Personal, family, and school-related factors.* Storrs, CT: National Research Center on the Gifted and Talented.
29. See Stanford University EPGY Online High School, http://epgy.stanford.edu/ohs/.
30. Stanford Report. (April 14, 2006). "Stanford to offer first online high school for gifted students." Accessed December 20, 2006, from http://news-service.stanford.edu/news/2006/april19/ohs-041906.html.

31. See http://www.arvs.org/ as well as: AT&T. (2006). *Distance learning: Technology advancements help to close gaps for No Child Left Behind.* Accessed September 22, 2006, from http://www.corp.att.com/edu/docs/MR_distance_learning.pdf.

32. University of California College Prep Online, http://www.uccp.org/.

33. North Central Regional Educational Laboratory, http://www.ncrel.org/sdrs/areas/issues/methods/technlgy/te9rau.htm.

34. See, for example, www.pdictionary.com, www.mylanguageexchange.com, and www.englishbaby.com.

35. ¡Tradúcelo Ahora! Translate Now, http://www.traduceloahora.org/.

36. See, for example, Teachers of English to Speakers of Other Languages (www.tesol.org) and the National Clearinghouse for English Language Acquisition and Language Instruction Educational Programs (www.ncela.gwu.edu).

37. See, for example, http://www.phoenix.k12.or.us/TechStandards_ELL.

38. See MERLOT World Languages Portal, http://worldlanguages.merlot.org/.

39. Meskill, C. (2005). "The language of learning: Using assistive technologies to support English language learners." *Threshold* (Winter) 24. Accessed January 31, 2007, from http://www.ciconline.org/threshold.

40. Zehr, M. A., & Manzo, K. K. (April 12, 2006). "Technology becomes substitute for English teacher." *Education Week*, p. 22.

41. VOA News, http://www.voanews.com/specialenglish/about_special_english.cfm.

42. Cited at www.evalutech.sreb.org. Another review can be found at http://www.serve.org/seir-tec/publications/NewsWire/Vol7.1.pdf.

43. Khadaroo, S. T. (August 2, 2007). " 'Listening' computer revs up reading skills." *The Christian Science Monitor*. Accessed August 7, 2007, from http://www.csmonitor.com/2007/0802/p13s01-legn.htm.

44. Oates, R., & Blubaugh, D. (2006). *Assessment goes online.* Washington, DC: Consortium for School Networking.

45. Zehr, M. A. (February 7, 2007). "Pilot program could help English-learners." *Education Week*, pp. 15–16.

46. EdSource Online, http://www.edsource.org/pub_abs_el07.cfm.

47. North Central Regional Educational Laboratory, http://www.ncrel.org/engauge/resource/stories/elpaso.htm.

48. North Central Regional Educational Laboratory, http://www.ncrel.org/sdrs/areas/issues/methods/technlgy/te9san.htm.

49. microObservatory Guest Observer Portal, http://mo-www.harvard.edu/microobs/guestobserverportal/.

50. Bugscope, http://bugscope.beckman.uiuc.edu.
51. A good introduction to UDL is: Rose, D. H., & Meyer, A. (2002). *Teaching every student in the Digital Age: Universal design for learning.* Alexandria, VA: Association for Supervision and Curriculum Development.
52. Rose & Meyer, *Teaching every student in the Digital Age*, p. 166.
53. Interview conducted June 4, 2007.

CHAPTER 6

1. American Educational Research Association. (2004). *Teachers matter: Evidence from value-added assessments.* Washington, DC: Author. Research Points series, 2:2, AERA.
2. Guarino, C. M., Santibanez, L., & Daley, G. A. (2006). "Teacher recruitment and retention: A review of the recent empirical literature." *Review of Educational Research, 76,* 173–208.
3. Honawar, V. (June 20, 2007). "Schools have no handle on $7 billion cost of teacher turnover, study finds." *Education Week*, p. 26.
4. U.S. Department of Education, National Center for Education Statistics. (2005). *The condition of education, 2005,* NCES 2005-094. Washington, DC: U.S. Government Printing Office.
5. See http://www.teachinflorida.com/.
6. Quoted in Lemberg, J. (July 28, 2002). "Program helps teachers share lesson plans." *The Boston Globe.* Accessed April 25, 2007, from http://ase.tufts.edu/education/projects/projectVPglobeArticle.asp.
7. Majors, S. (December 15, 2006). "Simulator training on the rise." *WashingtonPost.com* (Associated Press). Accessed January 17, 2007.
8. Institute for Creative Technologies, http://www.ict.usc.edu/.
9. Guarino et al., "Teacher recruitment and retention."
10. e-Mentoring for student success. Accessed March 28, 2007, from http://www.emss.nsta.org/results.aspx#Research.
11. Jaffe, R., Moir, E., Swanson, E., & Wheeler, G. (2006). "EMentoring for student success." In C. Dede (Ed.). *Online professional development for teachers: Emerging models and methods.* Cambridge, MA. Harvard Education Press.
12. Jaffe et al., "EMentoring for Student Success."
13. National Education Association. (2004). *Gains and gaps in education technology: An NEA survey of educational technologies in U.S. schools.* Washington, DC: Author.

14. CDW-G. (2006). *Teachers talk tech 2006: Fulfilling technology's promise of improved student performance.* Accessed July 21, 2006, from http://newsroom.cdwg.com/features/TeachersTalkTech2006Results.pdf.
15. Warschauer, M. (2006). *Laptops and literacy: Learning in the wireless classroom.* New York: Teachers College Press, p. 87.
16. Warschauer, *Laptops and literacy*, p. 75.
17. Warschauer, *Laptops and literacy*, p. 69.
18. Adelman, N., Donnelly, M. B., Dove, T., Tiffany-Morales, J., Wayne, A., & Zucker, A. A. (2002). *The integrated studies of educational technology: Professional development and teachers' uses of technology.* Washington, DC: U.S. Department of Education.
19. Hupert, N., & Heinze, J. (2006). "Results in the Palm of their hands: Using handheld computers for data-driven decision making in the classroom." In M. van't Hooft & K. Swan, *Ubiquitous computing in education: Invisible technology, visible impact.* Mahwah, NJ: Lawrence Erlbaum Associates.
20. Olson, L. (May 2, 2007). "Instant read on reading, in palms of their hands." *Education Week*, p. 26.
21. Zucker, A. A. & McGhee, R. (2005). *A study of one-to-one computer use in mathematics and science instruction at the secondary level in Henrico County Public Schools.* Menlo Park, CA: SRI International. Available online at http://www.ubiqcomputing.org/FinalReport.pdf.
22. NEA, *Gains and gaps in education technology*, p. 11.
23. National Education Association. (2006). *Professional community and professional development* (NEA Research Brief). Washington, DC: Author.
24. Quoted in Emerick, S., Hirsch, E., & Berry, B. (2005). *Teacher working conditions as catalysts for student learning* (Infobrief). Washington, DC: Association for Supervision and Curriculum Development, p. 4.
25. Haines, L., & Boone, R. "Teamwork needs technology." In D. Edyburn, K. Higgins, & R. Boone (Eds.). (2005). *Handbook of special education technology research and practice.* Whitefish Bay, WI: Knowledge by Design, pp. 455–480.
26. Teacher Leaders Network, www.teacherleaders.org.
27. Wells, J., Lewis, L., & Greene, B. (2006). *Internet access in U.S. public schools and classrooms: 1994–2005* (Highlights) (FRSS No. 2007-020). Washington, DC: National Center for Education Statistics, p. 50.
28. See http://www.ride.ri.gov/instruction/curriculum/.
29. See http://nces.ed.gov/timss/video.asp.

30. National Center for Education Statistics. (2003). *Highlights from the TIMSS 1999 video study of eighth-grade mathematics teaching* (NCES report 2003-011). Washington, DC: Author.

31. See Annenberg Media, Learner.org, http://learner.org.

32. Doubler, S. J., & Paget, K. F. (2006). "Science learning and teaching: A case of online professional learning." In Dede, *Online professional development for teachers.*

33. Ross, P. E. (August 2006). "The expert mind." *Scientific American.*

34. Emerick et al. *Teacher working conditions as catalysts for student learning* (Infobrief).

35. Quoted in Oppenheimer, T. (2003). *The flickering mind: The false promise of technology in the classroom and how learning can be saved.* New York: Random House, pp. 405–406.

CHAPTER 7

1. Unpublished data from Carasso, A., Steuerle, C. E., & Reynolds, G. (2007.) *Kids' share 2007: How children fare in the federal budget.* Washington, DC: The Urban Institute.

2. Carasso et al., *Kids' share 2007*, p. 3.

3. Rideout, V., Roberts, D. F., & Foehr, U. G. (2005). *Generation M: Media in the lives of 8–18-year-olds.* Menlo Park, CA: Kaiser Family Foundation.

4. Iyengar, S., & Bauerlein, M. (April 18, 2007). "It's not just the schools" (Commentary). *Education Week*, pp. 30, 40.

5. Rideout et al. *Generation M.*

6. Rideout et al. *Generation M.*

7. Stansbury, M. (July 12, 2007). "Groups push for media-literacy education." *eSchoolNews online.* Available online at http://www.eschoolnews.com/news/showStory.cfm?ArticleID=7252.

8. Ash, K. (February 14, 2007). "Maine students to get help from SAT-preparation course." *Education Week*, p. 20.

9. Buckleitner, W. (2006). *College test prep takes a test: A review of ten online SAT test preparation services.* Yonkers, NY: Consumer Reports Webwatch, p. 4.

10. See Kentucky Department of Education, Individual Learning Plan, http://www.education.ky.gov/KDE/Instructional+Resources/Individual+Learning+Plan/default.htm.

11. Borja, R. R. (January 24, 2007). "Kentucky debuts online college and career tool for students." *Education Week*, p. 10.

12. Rodriguez, N. C. (November 12, 2006). "Students' life plans go online." *The Courier-Journal*. Accessed December 13, 2006, from www.courier-journal.com.

13. Quoted in Nguyen, D. (December 1, 2005). "Links to learning: Web sites with voluminous school data help parents make informed choices." *Sacramento Bee*. Accessed December 5, 2005, from the Internet.

14. Nguyen, "Links to learning."

15. Parent and community engagement, The Education Trust, http://www2.edtrust.org/EdTrust/Parents+and+Community.

16. Murray, C. (October 26, 2005). "Student's homework site nets him $1.25M." *eSchoolNews online*. Accessed December 29, 2005, from http://www.eschoolnews.com/news/showStoryts.cfm?ArticleID=5924.

17. Information downloaded from the Fresno website, November 30, 2005. http://www.fresno.k12.ca.us/.

18. Crane, J. P. (February 23, 2006). "At home, sick in bed? That does not compute." *The Boston Globe*. Accessed February 27, 2006, from http://www.boston.com/news/local/massachusetts/articles/2006/02/23/at_home_sick_in_bed_that_does_not_compute/.

19. Crane, "At home, sick in bed?"

20. DePasquale, R. (December 1, 2005). "Faster is better when schools spread the word." *The Boston Globe*. Accessed December 5, 2005, from http://www.boston.com/news/local/massachusetts/articles/2005/12/01/faster_is_better_when_schools_spread_word/.

21. Dillon, S. (November 20, 2006). "Schools slow in closing gaps between races." *The New York Times*.

22. McGreevy, P. (September 21, 2006). "High-tech plan targets crime near two L.A. schools." *Los Angeles Times*.

23. See http://www.parents.ips.k12.in.us/.

24. National Network of Partnership Schools at Johns Hopkins University, http://www.csos.jhu.edu/p2000/.

25. Richard W. Riley awards: Community learning centers for the 21st century, http://www.richardrileyaward.org/en/Index.asp.

26. America's Promise: The Alliance for Youth. (2007). *Every child, every promise: Turning failure into action*. Washington, DC: Author.

27. See Helping America's youth, http://www.helpingamericasyouth.gov/whatishay.cfm.

28. See MENTOR: Expanding the world of quality mentoring, http://www.mentoring.org/.

29. See Digital Learning Commons: Meet the DLC tutors, http://www.learning-commons.org/educators/courses/studentmentors/mentors.php.

30. DeBell, M., & Chapman, C. (2006). *Computer and Internet use by students in 2003*. Washington, DC: U.S. Department of Education, National Center for Education Statistics.

31. Wikipedia. "Antonia Stone," from http://en.wikipedia.org/wiki/Antonia_Stone.

32. See Afterschool Alliance, http://www.afterschoolalliance.org/21stcclc.cfm.

33. See Museum of Science, Boston: Computer Clubhouse, http://www.mos.org/educators/student_resources/computer_clubhouse.

34. See Computer Clubhouse, http://www.computerclubhouse.org/about1.htm.

CHAPTER 8

1. Hoff, D. (May 4, 2006). "Delving into data." *Education Week*, p. 20.

2. Data Quality Campaign. (2005). *Measuring what matters: Creating a longitudinal data system to improve student achievement*, p. 2. Accessed January 17, 2007, from http://www.dataqualitycampaign.org/files/Publications-Measuring_What_Matters.pdf.

3. eSchool News online. (August 18, 2005). "State: Online testing helped raise scores." Accessed August 22, 2005, from http://www.eschoolnews.com/news/showstory.cfm?ArticleID=5826.

4. Hoff, D. J. (November 30, 2005). "States to get more help with education data collection." *Education Week*, p. 22.

5. Hoff, "Delving into data," p. 22.

6. See Write to Learn: Learning through written expression, www.writetolearn.net.

7. Reliability and validity of the KAT™ engine. (2006). Accessed December 22, 2006, from http://www.pearsonkt.com/papers/PKT_Research_VR.01.03-2.pdf.

8. Franzke, M., & Streeter, L. A. (2006). "Building student summarization, writing and reading comprehension skills with guided practice and automated feedback: Highlights from research at the University of Colorado (A white paper from Pearson Knowledge Technologies). Accessed December 22, 2006, from http://www.pearsonkt.com/papers/SummaryStreetWhitePaper-FINAL-1.pdf.

9. Bennett, R.E., Persky, H., Weiss, A.R., & Jenkins, F. (2007). *Problem solving in technology-rich environments: A report from the NAEP Technology-Based*

Assessment Project (NCES 2007–466). Washington, DC: U.S. Department of Education, National Center for Education Statistics.

10. Swanson, C. B. (May 4, 2006). "Tracking U.S. trends." *Education Week*, p. 52.

11. Olson, L. (November 30, 2005). "State test programs mushroom as NCLB mandate kicks in." *Education Week*, p. 10.

12. EdSource, Inc. (June 2006). *Similar students, different results: Why do some schools do better?* Mountain View, CA: Author. Accessed June 18, 2007, from http://www.edsource.org/pdf/simstusumm06.pdf.

13. EdSource, Inc., *Similar students, different results*, p. 10.

14. Robelen, E. W. (November 15, 2006). "Detailed dropout studies guide policy in city schools." *Education Week*, pp. 8–9.

15. See, for example, Newsome, M. (March 14, 2007). "Is a top school forcing out low-performing students?" *Time*. Accessed June 18, 2007, from http://www.time.com/time/nation/article/0,8599,1599099,00.html.

16. Cavanagh, S. (November 14, 2006). "Technology helps teachers home in on student needs." *Education Week*, p. 10.

17. The TI-Navigator™ is one such system.

18. Penuel, W. R., Roschelle, J., & Abrahamson, L. (n.d.). *Research on classroom networks for whole-class activities*. Menlo Park, CA: SRI International.

19. Boudett, K. P., City, E. A., & Murnane, R. J. (Eds.). (2005). *Data wise: A step-by-step guide to using assessment results to improve teaching and learning*. Cambridge, MA: Harvard Education Press.

20. Quoted in Borja, R. R. (May 4, 2006). "Aware of all students." *Education Week*, p. 32.

21. Boudett et al., *Data wise*, p. 18.

22. Hale, E., & Rollins, K. (2006). "Leading the way to increased student learning." *Principal Leadership*, 6(10), p. 8.

23. Hale & Rollins, "Leading the way to increased student learning," p. 8.

24. Waldman, L. (October 9, 2006). "Teaching strategy yields results." *Hartford Courant*.

25. Quoted in Borja, R. R. (May 4, 2006). "Finding the funding." *Education Week*, p. 34.

26. Data Quality Campaign. (2005). *Data quality campaign launched at Data Summit* (Press release), p. 3. Accessed January 17, 2007, from http://www.teach-now.org/DQCrelease.pdf.

27. See www.dataqualitycampaign.org for information about the availability of these data elements.

CHAPTER 9

1. Zucker, A. A. (1982). "Support of educational technology by the U.S. Department of Education: 1971–1980." *Journal of Educational Technology Systems, 10,* 303–320. For a full account of the development of LOGO, see Blaschke, C., Hunter, B., & Zucker, A. (1987). *Support for educational technology R&D: The federal role* (NTIS Report PB88-194626). Falls Church, VA: Education Turnkey Systems

2. KIPP: Knowledge is Power Program, http://www.kipp.org/.

3. Hudson, S. B., McMahon, K. C., & Overstreet, C. M. (2002). *The 2000 national survey of science and mathematics education: Compendium of tables.* Chapel Hill, NC: Horizon Research.

4. North American Council for Online Learning, http://www.nacol.org/about/.

5. For more information, see chapter 3; and see also Zucker, A. A., & Kozma, R. E., with Yarnall, L., & Marder, C. (2003). *The Virtual High School: Teaching generation V.* New York: Teachers College Press.

6. Zucker et al. *The Virtual High School*, p. 134.

7. Stockholm Challenge, http://www.stockholmchallenge.se/index.html.

8. Zucker et al. *The Virtual High School.*

9. SRI Technology: Personal Computing/Computer Mouse, http://www.sri.com/about/timeline/mouse.html.

10. National Assessment of Educational Progress. (2000). NAEP Science Scores. Accessed December 1, 2006, from http://nces.ed.gov/nationsreportcard/science/results/teachcomputer.asp.

11. Nielson, D. L. (2004). *A heritage of innovation: SRI's first half century.* Menlo Park, CA: SRI International.

12. Nielson, *A heritage of innovation*, pp. 1–4.

13. Nielson, *A heritage of innovation*, pp. 1–7.

14. Means, B., & Olson, K. (1995). *Technology and education reform.* Washington, DC: U.S. Department of Education (ERIC publication ED397559). Available online at http://www.eric.ed.gov/ERICWebPortal/Home.portal.

15. Puma, M. E., Chaplin, D., Olson, K., & Pandjiris, A. (2002). *The integrated studies of educational technology: A formative evaluation of the E-Rate program.* Accessed January 10, 2007, from http://www.urban.org/url.cfm?ID=410579.

16. Wells, J., Lewis, L., & Greene, B. (2006). *Internet access in U.S. public schools and classrooms: 1994–2005* (Highlights) (FRSS No. 2007-020). Washington, DC: National Center for Education Statistics.

17. Adelman, N., Donnelly, M. B., Dove, T., Tiffany-Morales, J., Wayne, A., & Zucker, A. A. (2002). *The integrated studies of educational technology: Professional development and teachers' uses of technology*. Washington, DC: U.S. Department of Education.
18. EdTech Home, http://edtech.mathematica-mpr.com/.
19. One good book is: Carlson, C. R., & Wilmot, W. W. (2006). *Innovation: The five disciplines for creating what customers want*. New York: Crown Business.
20. The Denver School of Science and Technology. Accessed August 6, 2007, from http://scienceandtech.org/about-tech.html.
21. NSF statistics in brief, Table 1, Federal R&D.
22. Richtel, M. (August 22, 2005). "Once a booming market, educational software for the PC takes a nosedive." *The New York Times*.]
23. Tinker, R. (Spring 2006). "Perspective: Where are the educational innovations?" *@Concord* (newsletter for the Concord Consortium), *10*, pp. 1, 2.
24. 42 USC §1862
25. Richtel, "Once a booming market, educational software for the PC takes a nosedive."
26. Glennan, T. K., & Melmed, A. (1996). *Fostering the use of educational technology: Elements of a national strategy*. Santa Monica, CA: RAND Corporation.

CHAPTER 10

1. Healy, J. (1998). *Failure to connect*. New York: Simon & Schuster, p. 245.
2. Stansbury, M. (August 1, 2007). "Public wants more tech in classrooms." *eSchool News online*. Accessed August 6, 2007, from http://www.eschoolnews.com/news/showStory.cfm?ArticleID=7268.
3. Warschauer, M. (2006). *Laptops and literacy: Learning in the wireless classroom*. New York: Teachers College Press, p. 148.
4. Warschauer, *Laptops and literacy*, p. 103.
5. Phua, C. (April 5, 2007). "Students click on learning." *Sacramento Bee*. Accessed May 24, 2007, from www.sacbee.com/education/v-print/story/148620.html.
6. National Center for Education Statistics, Fast facts. Accessed May 23, 2007, from http://nces.ed.gov/fastfacts/display.asp?id=66.
7. See Taking TCO to the classroom, http://www.classroomtco.org/, and CoSN Value of investment, http://www.edtechvoi.org/.
8. Devaney, L. (June 21, 2007). "San Diego rolls out laptops with Linux." *eSchoolNews online*. Accessed July 17, 2007, from http://www.eschoolnews.com/news/PFshowstory.cfm?ArticleID=7178.

9. See http://www.doe.state.in.us/INaccess/ and, for a list of open source software, http://www.doe.state.in.us/INaccess/pdf/opensource_programs. pdf.

10. Kauffman, C. (July 25, 2007). "Dallastown school district looks to go paperless." *The York Dispatch.* Accessed July 27, 2007, from http://www.yorkdispatch.com/local/ci_6460121.

11. Bromley, A. E. "Elementary school classrooms get low rating on high-quality instruction." Accessed May 16, 2007, from http://www.virginia.edu/uvatoday/newsRelease.php?id=1780. See also Pianta, R. C., Belsky, J., Houts, R., & Morrison, F. (2007). *Opportunities to learn in America's elementary classrooms* (supporting online material). Accessed April 19, 2007, from www.sciencemag. org/cgi/content/full/315/5820/1795/DC1.

12. Adelman, N., Donnelly, M. B., Dove, T., Tiffany-Morales, J., Wayne, A., & Zucker, A. A. (2002). *The integrated studies of educational technology: Professional development and teachers' uses of technology.* Washington, DC: U.S. Department of Education.

13. New Commission on the Skills of the American Workforce. (2006). *Tough choices or tough times* (Executive Summary), p. 8. Accessed May 19, 2007, from http://www.skillscommission.org/executive.htm.

14. National High School Alliance. (2005). *A call to action: Transforming high school for all youth.* Washington, DC: Author.

15. Murnane, R. J., & Levy, F. (1996). *Teaching the new basic skills: Principles for educating children to thrive in a changing economy.* New York: Free Press.

16. Information Work Productivity Council. (2003). *The information work productivity primer: 2003 research compendium.* Accessed May 20, 2007, from http://www.ipch.ch/downloads/iwpc-productivity-primer-2003.pdf.

17. Lohr, S. (February 2, 2004). "New economy: Researchers seem confident that technology has made American workers more efficient. Now some think they even know why." *The New York Times.*

18. Lemke C., & Martin C. (2004, March). *One-to-one computing in Indiana: A state profile* (Preliminary Report). Accessed January 10, 2006, from http:// www.metiri.com/Solutions/Research.htm.

19. Quoted in Consortium for School Networking. (2005). *Learning spaces 2010.* Washington, DC: Author.

20. Pianta et al. *Opportunities to learn in America's elementary classrooms* (supporting online material).

21. Jackson, L. (March 2007). "Meaningful learning with laptops at Lausanne." *Anytime Anywhere Learning Foundation Newsletter, 2,* p. 3.

22. Fadel, L. (July 27, 2006). "Students don't know much beyond Google." *Dallas Fort Worth Star-Telegram.*

23. Thacker, P. D. (November 15, 2006). "Are college students techno idiots?" *Inside Higher Education.* Accessed November 21, 2006, from http://www.inside-highered.com/news/2006/11/15/infolit.

24. See, for example, Masalski, W. J., & Elliott, P. C. (Eds.). (2005). *Technology-supported mathematics learning environments: Sixty-seventh yearbook.* Reston, VA: National Council of Teachers of Mathematics.

About the Author

Dr. Andrew Zucker is a senior research scientist at the Concord Consortium. He has been a teacher of mathematics, science, and computers, a school computer center director, and, for seven years, a budget and policy analyst at the U.S. Department of Education. Zucker has worked in independent nonprofit organizations for 20 years as an education researcher, developer, strategic planner, and evaluator. He was associate director of the Center for Education Policy at SRI International (the former Stanford Research Institute) before returning to the Boston area in 2003.

Zucker's work at nonprofits has included codirecting a six-year study of systemic education reform in 25 states and Puerto Rico; directing an evaluation of one of the first sets of national education standards; codirecting a five-year evaluation of one of the first online high schools, The Virtual High School; codirecting a project that developed award-winning instructional videotapes for middle school mathematics; and managing a consortium of institutions that were studying 1:1 laptop programs for students (ubiqcomputing.org).

Zucker has published dozens of articles, reports, and book chapters and was lead author of *The Virtual High School: Teaching Generation V* (2003), the first book focused on online high schools. He also has testified before congressional committees, two state legislatures, and the

National Education Goals Panel. He has been a member of the National Council of Teachers of Mathematics for 30 years and served for three years on the editorial panel of the *Journal for Research in Mathematics Education*. Zucker is also a member of the American Educational Research Association, the Consortium for School Networking, and the International Society for Technology in Education.

Zucker graduated from Harvard College in 1967, received a master's in education from Stanford in 1970, and an EdD from the Harvard Graduate School of Education in 1978. He was an Institute for Educational Leadership Education Policy Fellow in 1978–79. He and his wife, Elizabeth F. Zucker, live in Cambridge, Massachusetts.

Index